THE INDEPENDENCE OF THE INTERNATIONAL CRIMINAL COURT

Series Supranational Criminal Law: Capita Selecta, Volume 25

Recently published in the series:

9. *International Criminal Law from a Swedish Perspective,* Iain Cameron, Malin Thunberg Schunke, Karin Pale Bartes, Christoffer Wong and Petter Asp
10. *The Implementation of the European Arrest Warrant in the European Union: Law, Policy and Practice*, Massimo Fichera
11. *The Principle of Mutual Recognition in Cooperation in Criminal Matters: A Study of the Principle in Four Framework Decisions and in the Implementation Legislation in the Nordic Member States*, Annika Suominen
12. *The European Public Prosecutor's Office: Analysis of a Multilevel Criminal Justice System*, Martijn Willem Zwiers
13. *Victimological Approaches to International Crimes: Africa,* Rianne Letschert Roelof Haveman, Anne-Marie de Brouwer and Antony Pemberton (eds.)
14. *The United States and International Criminal Tribunals: An Introduction*, Harry M. Rhea
15. *EU Sanctions: Law and Policy Issues Concerning Restrictive Measures*, Iai Cameron (ed.)
16. *Whose Responsibility? A Study of Transnational Defence Rights and Mutual Recognition of Judicial Decisions within the EU*, Malin Thunberg Schunke
17. *Genocidal Gender and Sexual Violence: The Legacy of the ICTR, Rwanda's Ordinary Courts and* Gacaca *Courts*, Usta Kaitesi
18. *Addressing the Intentional Destruction of the Environment during Warfare under the Rome Statute of the International Criminal Court*, Steven Freeland
19. *Individual Criminal Liability for the International Crime of Aggression*, Gerhard Kemp
20. *Selective Enforcement and International Criminal Law: The International Criminal Court and Africa*, James Nyawo
21. *The Governance of Complementary Global Regimes and the Pursuit of Human Security: The Interaction between the United Nations and the International Criminal Court*, Andrea Marrone
22. *The Rationality of Dictators: Towards a More Effective Implementation of the Responsibility to Protect*, Maartje Weerdesteijn
23. *Extended Confiscation in Criminal Law*, Malin Thunberg Schunke
24. *Convergences and Divergences Between International Human Rights, International Humanitarian and International Criminal Law*, Paul de Hert, Stefaan Smis and Mathias Holvoet (eds.)

# THE INDEPENDENCE OF THE INTERNATIONAL CRIMINAL COURT

## Between a Rock and a Hard Place

Alphonse Muleefu

intersentia
Cambridge – Antwerp – Chicago

Intersentia Ltd
Sheraton House | Castle Park
Cambridge | CB3 0AX | United Kingdom
Tel.: +44 1223 370 170 | Fax: +44 1223 370 169
Email: mail@intersentia.co.uk
www.intersentia.com | www.intersentia.co.uk

*Distribution for the UK and Ireland:*
NBN International
Airport Business Centre, 10 Thornbury Road
Plymouth, PL6 7PP
United Kingdom
Tel.: +44 1752 202 301 | Fax: +44 1752 202 331
Email: orders@nbninternational.com

*Distribution for Europe and all other countries:*
Intersentia Publishing nv
Groenstraat 31
2640 Mortsel
Belgium
Tel.: +32 3 680 15 50 | Fax: +32 3 658 71 21
Email: mail@intersentia.be

*Distribution for the USA and Canada:*
Independent Publishers Group
Order Department
814 North Franklin Street
Chicago, IL 60610
USA
Tel.: +1 800 888 4741 (toll free) | Fax: +1 312 337 5985
Email: orders@ipgbook.com

The Independence of the International Criminal Court. Between a Rock and a Hard Place



ISBN 978-1-78068-857-2
D/2019/7849/63
NUR 828

British Library Cataloguing in Publication Data. A catalogue record for this book is available from the British Library.

*'In assessing the ICC's independence and legitimacy, Alphonse Muleefu is scrupulously even-handed in weighing the claims of the Court's supporters and critics. The book's dialogical approach enables a deep understanding of how the ICC views its role in addressing mass crimes and why the Court's critics - especially in Africa – are so concerned about its impact across the continent. This book is nuanced, thorough and essential reading for anyone trying to fathom where the ICC finds itself 17 years into its existence.'*

Dr Phil Clark, SOAS University of London

*'"The Independence of the International Criminal Court: Between A Rock and A Hard Place" provides a tremendously vivid and fascinating study of politics in action. By analysing the public speeches and written texts that mark critical moments in the court's history, the book offers a desperately needed analysis of the place of politics in the life of the law. Alphonse captures beautifully various key discourses and sets them side-by-side forcing us to contend with the difficulties of the ICC's relationship with Africa and their implications for understanding law in an uneven world. He also turns us to the crude realities of that world as seen in the spoken and written word, highlighting how the key challenge of twenty-first century justice analysis is not only what is done and what is said but also how those things are seen. A refreshing account of the complex dynamics of discourse. A must read.'*

Professor Kamari M. Clarke, The University of California, Los Angeles

*'Dr. Alphonse Muleefu has written a book that calls for an in depth dialogue between the critics and supporters of the International Criminal Court. It is definitely worth reading.'*

Professor Dr Rianne M. Letschert, Rector Magnificus, Maastricht University

*'In his much-needed and penetrating study of the International Criminal Court, Alphonse Muleefu provides an alternative perspective on questions of legitimacy and judicial independence that avoids the simplistic approaches advocated by both the most passionate supporters of the court and its most ardent critics.'*

Professor Mark Goodale, University of Lausanne

*I dedicate this book to my dad, Yohani Bushishi, for his endless support and patience towards my quest for knowledge.*

# PREFACE

In 2010, one of my Public International Law professors, while explaining to our LLM class of Public International Law and Human Rights about the current issues, appreciated the fact that the US was actively involved in the Kampala Review Conference of the Rome Statute of the International Criminal Court. In response, I immediately disagreed. I did not believe that it was a good idea for a non-state party to be that influential; not so long ago it had been busy discrediting the Court and discouraging other countries from cooperating. After writing this book, I think my point of view was an uncompromising one, that of 'you are either in it or out'. For those who believe in the Bible, the Savour is against the lukewarm. In the book of Revelation, chapter 3 verse 16, it is stated that: 'So then, because you are lukewarm, and neither cold nor hot, I will vomit you out of My mouth.'[1] I have come to understand that my professor's point of view was one of optimism, believing that the Court's success will depend on its good relationship with all countries including those that are not parties to the Rome Statute, especially the most powerful. He might have seen the US' engagement as an assurance of the Court's future and a sign of its recognition as a global actor (legitimacy). And probably he might have (wrongly) thought that the US involvement in shaping the rules of the Court was a positive indication that in the near future it would consider becoming a state party. Therefore, I admit to having been naive and idealistic, for believing in a utopian sovereign equality of states, and he was perhaps more realistic because the Kampala Review Conference was about the amendment of the Rome Statute, an important step in shaping the Court, something a powerful state could not have ignored. As Barkin notes, '[t]he first way to influence an [international organisation] is through its creation negotiations, state′s capacity to influence the rules to govern (...)'.[2] The Realists, Barkin observes, see no problem in making rules that govern international organisations according to the interests of the powerful because in their view, weaker states are 'always subject to a similar degree to the preferences of the larger, more powerful states'.[3]

1 The Holy Bible: Containing the Old and New Testaments (New King James Version, Thomas Nelson), 853.

2 J. Samuel Barkin, *International Organizations: Theories and Institutions* (2nd ed., Palgrave Macmillan, 2013), 20.

3 ibid, 12.

The brief exchange outlined above can demonstrate how easily two different people can perceive certain things differently. It also demonstrates that a disagreement might remain unresolved for some time with different consequences. In my case, it has been an inspiration behind the question at the heart of this book. After that classroom debate, I developed an interest in considering all diverging views about the International Criminal Court. Since then, I have been collecting and analysing different opposing arguments about its workings and mandate. However, turning this curiosity into a book could not have been possible without big support from different people and institutions. Special thanks go to the Swiss Federal Commission for Scholarships for Foreign Students (FCS), which awarded me the Swiss Government Excellence Scholarship that allowed me to stay for a whole year at the University of Lausanne. I would like to acknowledge Professor Andreas Ziegler, my contact person at the University of Lausanne for his support during the application process, for providing me with a recommendation and an invitation letter, without which I could not have been awarded the scholarship. I would not have been able to contact Professor Ziegler if it were not through Dr. Roberta Arnold, so thank you so much. I am indebted to all people who wrote reference letters and recommendations throughout the process: Professor Rianne Letschert, Dr. Felix Ndahinda and Dr. Etienne Ruvebana, thank you so very much for your kind support.

Sincere gratitude goes to the management of the University of Rwanda, which authorised me to be away for the entire period of writing this book. The same appreciation goes to different staff members of the Swiss Institute of Comparative Law. The study leave and stay at the University of Lausanne could not have been productive without a very supportive team of librarians who worked tirelessly providing me with all reading materials I needed to complete the book. I am sincerely grateful to the ESN Buddy Program, specifically to Jacques Frauche, for welcoming me to the University, and showing me all important facilities at the campus and the city of Lausanne. Special thanks also go to those who offered their time to discuss with me the different aspects of the subject; to mention just a few: Dr. Eefje de Volder, Professor Barbora Hola, Dr. Thijs Bouwknegt, Professor Mark Goodale and different ICC staff members. I greatly benefited from Dr. Roelof Haveman who agreed to edit the whole manuscript. His constructive critical and candid comments strengthened my arguments.

The library life was very lonely, and I couldn't have remained sane if it were not because of different people (friends) outside the university campus. Without mentioning names, I would like to appreciate the Rwandan community in Lausanne and other friends who were always available to go out with me at different restaurants and bars, and sometimes invited me into their homes. Special thanks again go to those friends who travelled long distances at different times just to be with me for some few days in Lausanne. Thank you to Dr. Annemarie Middelburg and Mr. Erik Walschots, Loes Lijnders, and

Andrew Bayingana. Every visit you made left me filled with a lot of energy and good spirit to continue working. Last but absolutely not the least are my friends and relatives back in Rwanda who kept contacting me through different channels of communication; I am thankful that you kept me in your thoughts while I was far away. I am grateful for the fact that you kept reminding me that there is another important thing in life that I haven't accomplished, and I can promise you to make it a priority now.

# CONTENTS

# LIST OF ABBREVIATIONS

| | |
|---|---|
| AI | Amnesty International |
| ASP | Assembly of States Parties |
| AU | African Union |
| CDA | Critical Discourse Analysis |
| CICC | Coalition for the International Criminal Court |
| CLS | Critical Legal Studies |
| ExCom | The Office of the Prosecutor's Executive Committee |
| FIDH | *Fédération Internationale Ligue des Droits de l'Homme* |
| HRW | Human Rights Watch |
| IAT | Implicit Association Test |
| ICC | International Criminal Court |
| ICJ | International Court of Justice |
| ICTR | International Criminal Tribunal for Rwanda |
| ICTY | International Criminal Tribunal for the Former Yugoslavia |
| IEU | Information and Evidence Unit |
| JCCD | Division of Jurisdiction, Complementarity and Cooperation |
| LRA | Lord's Resistance Army |
| NGOs | Non-Governmental Organisations |
| OTP | Office of the Prosecutor |
| RPE | Rules of Procedure and Evidence |
| SAS | Situation Analysis Section |
| SCSL | Special Court for Sierra Leone |
| UN | United Nations |
| UNDP | United Nations Development Programme |
| UNESCO | United Nations Educational, Scientific and Cultural Organisation |
| UNSC | United Nations Security Council |
| UPDF | Uganda People's Defence Force |
| WHO | World Health Organization |

# CHAPTER 1

# GENERAL INTRODUCTION AND SOME POINTS OF DEPARTURE

## 1.1. CONTEXTUAL BACKGROUND

The adoption of the Rome Statute in 1998 was an international milestone that Africa embraced with great enthusiasm. African countries were the first to support the adoption of the Rome Statute and until today, the International Criminal Court (hereafter ICC or 'the Court') is still – to a large extent – dependent on Africa's cooperation in collecting evidence, accessing crime scenes and arresting suspects. Most of the Court's work is still focused on Africa where more than 80 percent of its investigations are taking place. On 2 February 1999, Senegal ratified the Rome Statute becoming the first country to adopt the treaty creating the Court.[4] In January 2004, less than two years after the treaty had entered into force, the Government of Uganda became the first to refer a situation to the ICC's Prosecutor. The Prosecutor was requested to investigate crimes allegedly committed in the conflict between the Lord's Resistance Army (LRA) and the Uganda People's Defence Force (UPDF), in Northern Uganda.[5] At the moment, 33 African countries are parties to the Rome Statute, making Africa the most represented region in the Assembly of States Parties (ASP), a body entrusted with budget, oversight and legislative powers over the Court.

Africa's initial support for international criminal justice was not coincidental. Before the adoption of the Rome Statute, Africa had had its fair share of serious violations of human rights and was already working with the International Criminal Tribunal for Rwanda (ICTR) in prosecuting perpetrators of the 1994 genocide against the Tutsi and other international crimes committed in Rwanda.[6] From 1996, Sierra Leone experienced horrendous crimes and later sought the United Nations support in the creation of the United Nations Special

---

4 Senegal signed the Rome Statute on 18 July 1998 and ratified it on 2 February 1999, becoming the 1st state party to the International Criminal Court (ICC), http://www.iccnow.org/?mod=country&iduct=152.

5 The ICC, Uganda Situation (ICC-02/04) https://www.icc-cpi.int/uganda.

6 The International Criminal Tribunal for Rwanda was created by the United Nations Security Council Resolution 955 (1994) of 8 November 1994.

Court for Sierra Leone (UNSCSL).[7] These and many other waves of violence in different parts of Africa that preceded the adoption of the Rome Statute provided a good reason for Sub-Saharan Africa in particular to support the creation of a permanent international criminal court. However, the enthusiasm for the Court did not last for so long. The ICC Prosecutor's indictment of Omar Hassan Ahmad Al Bashir, the President of the Republic of Sudan (2009/2010), and charges against Kenyan politicians, in particular Uhuru Kenyatta and William Ruto (2011) who later became the President and Deputy President of the Republic of Kenya respectively, damaged the relationship between the Court and the African Union (AU).[8]

Some African leaders and commentators critical of the Court argue that the ICC is an organisation created to manipulate Africa's internal (mainly) political situations. That the Court is a new 'northern' tool to enforce 'slavery, colonialism and imperialism' against the weak and African countries.[9] Beyond rhetoric, the African Union has taken some concrete steps – though with little success – in obstructing the Court. In response to indictments against the Sudanese President, the AU petitioned the United Nations Security Council (UNSC) to use its powers under Article 16 of the Rome Statute, concerning deferral of investigation and prosecution, a request that was never considered.[10] Since 2009, the AU has made a decision encouraging African countries to not arrest/surrender Omar al-Bashir, allowing him to freely travel on the continent despite the two indictments against him – with few countries not cooperating. The AU has threatened the Court with a potential withdrawal of all African member states from the treaty, a move that would hurt the Court's legitimacy.[11]

---

7 The United Nations Special Court for Sierra Leone was created by an Agreement between the United Nations and the Government of Sierra Leone pursuant to Security Council Resolution 1315 (2000) of 14 August 2000 to prosecute those with the greatest responsibility in the territory of Sierra Leone for crimes committed in the conflict of Sierra Leone since 30 November 1996, see for more details about the Special Court at http://www.rscsl.org/.

8 Amnesty International, 'Malabo Protocol: Legal and Institutional Implications of the Merged and Expanded African Court' [22 January 2016, Index number: AFR 01/3063/2016], 9.

9 Mary Kimani, 'Pursuit of Justice or Western Plot? International indictments stir angry debate in Africa' [October 2009] http://www.un.org/africarenewal/magazine/october-2009/pursuit-justice-or-western-plot; Fletcher Miles, '"T.I.A" – this is Africa – so why the ICC?' [29 April 2014] http://works.bepress.com/fletcher_miles/1/.

10 Dapo Akande, 'The African Union's Response to the ICC's Decisions on Bashir's Immunity: Will the ICJ Get Another Immunity Case?' [2012] http://www.ejiltalk.org/the-african-unions-response-to-the-iccs-decisions-on-bashirs-immunity-will-the-icj-get-another-immunity-case/; see also 'AU Decision on the Progress Report of the Commission on the Implementation of the Assembly Decisions on the International Criminal Court (ICC) – Doc. EX.CL/710(XX)' (Assembly/AU/Dec.397(XVIII)).

11 Despite speculation that the decision for African countries to withdraw from ICC was going to be taken, the Kigali AU 27th Ordinary Session ended without mentioning the issue, allegedly due to some few countries (Botswana, Ivory Coast, Nigeria, Senegal, Tunisia and Algeria) which objected to the motion. See e.g. Robert Mbaraga, 'Africa's Push to Withdrawal from

On 27 June 2014, the AU adopted the Malabo Protocol on the Amendment to the Protocol on the African Court of Justice and Human Rights including crimes under the ICC jurisdiction within the mandate of the African Court.[12] As it is expressed in Amnesty International's 2016 report on the Malabo Protocol, 'the Protocol does not foresee a similar relationship with the ICC despite the fact that it is obvious that such a relationship would be necessary and desirable'.[13] In a separate move, the Government of Kenya petitioned the ASP and achieved an amendment of Rules 68, 100 and 134 of the Court's Rules of Procedure and Evidence (RPE).[14]

On 27 November 2015, the International Federation for Human Rights (FIDH, French acronym), denounced the pressure the Kenyan Government had exerted on the ASP to amend the Rome Statute as a way of undermining the Court's independence, and called

> on all States to continue to support ICC action all over the world and to give it all necessary resources to achieve its mandate, especially where crimes within its jurisdiction are currently being committed and where States are unable or unwilling to prosecute those responsible.[15]

On 22 September 2016, Human Rights Watch (HRW) together with 24 other NGOs issued a press release requesting the AU to stop the 'consideration of a call for mass withdrawal of its members from the ICC',[16] and Kenneth Roth, the Executive Director of HRW, argued that 'if the current attack on [the ICC] succeeds, the Court's future may be in doubt'.[17]

---

ICC blocked, Countries Divided' [The East African, 23 July 2016] http://www.theeastafrican.co.ke/news/Africa-s-push-to-withdraw-from-ICC-blocked--countries-divided/2558-3307472-15hdbkmz/index.html.

12 The Amendment was adopted by the AU Assembly in its 23rd Session held in Malabo, Equatorial Guinea on 27 June 2014.

13 Amnesty International, 'Malabo Protocol: Legal and Institutional Implications of the Merged and Expanded African Court' [2016], 22.

14 Assembly of States Parties (Fourteenth Session), 'List of supplementary items requested for inclusion in the agenda of the fourteenth session of the Assembly: Addendum' (ICC-ASP/14/35/Add.2) of 6 November 2015; see also Nevins Biko, 'Kenya's "victory" at Assembly of States Parties meeting' [The Hague Trials/Kenya, 28 November 2013] https://allafrica.com/stories/201311281686.html.

15 FIDH, 'The Independence of the International Criminal Court must be enhanced' [27 November 2015] https://www.fidh.org/en/issues/international-justice/international-criminal-court-icc/the-independence-of-the-international-criminal-court-must-be-enhanced.

16 Human Rights Watch (HRW), 'UN/African Union: Reject ICC Withdrawal/ Security Council Meeting With AU' [22 September 2016] https://www.hrw.org/news/2016/09/22/un/african-union-reject-icc-withdrawal.

17 Kenneth Roth, 'Africa Attacks the International Criminal Court' (The New York Review of Books, 6 February, June 2014 Issue).

However, it appears that the African Union and/or its member states critical of the Court still lack power (and/or the will) to materialise their threats. The proposal for a massive withdrawal has since failed; Côte d'Ivoire proceeded to become a state party in 2013; Mali referred a situation to the ICC Prosecutor in July 2012; and the Government of Uganda transferred Dominic Ongwen after his surrender in January 2015. Therefore, notwithstanding their criticisms, the Court continues to enjoy some considerable support and cooperation from African countries, and the situation is likely to remain unchanged for quite some time, at least until the completion of ongoing cases from the continent.

Different studies have been conducted on this 'love-hate' relationship between the ICC and African Union,[18] but little is known on whether it is undermining the necessary legitimacy and independence of the Court. This book focuses on narratives concerning the 'institutional independence' of the Court that go beyond the independence of judges (judicial independence). It focuses, in particular, on the Office of the Prosecutor, one of the important organs of the Court.[19] The purpose here is to understand the different competing narratives claiming that the Court's independence and legitimacy are under threat. It also focuses on the choice of the language used in each narrative. Those who criticise the Court – for pursuing 'northern' interests – claim that the Court has surrendered its independence to 'imperialists and neo-colonialists', whereas supporters of the international criminal justice project are concerned that the Court's independence is under onslaught from 'despotic' African leaders. As Robertson notes, '[i]n liberal political and legal culture, if you can successfully describe your opponents as having wilfully abandoned law's constraints, you will have damaged them'.[20]

Protecting the 'institutional independence' of the International Criminal Court is a very important aspect if the Court is to achieve its expected global

18 Susanne D. Mueller, 'Kenya and the International Criminal Court (ICC): politics, the election and the law' (2014) 8:1, 25–42 Journal of Eastern African Studies; Henrietta J.A.N. Mensa-Bonsu, 'The ICC, International Criminal Justice and International Politics' (2015) XL:2, 33–53 Africa Development; Amnesty International, 'Malabo Protocol: Legal and Institutional Implications of the Merged and Expanded African Court' [2016]; Obiora Chinedu Okafor and Uchechukwu Ngwaba, 'The International Criminal Court as a 'Transitional Justice' Mechanism in Africa: Some Critical Reflections' (2015) 9, 90–108 International Journal of Transitional Justice.

19 See the meaning of 'the Court' in the case of The *Prosecutor v. Uhuru Muigai Kenyatta*, Trial Chamber V(B), 'Decision on Prosecution's applications for a finding of non-compliance pursuant to Article 87(7) and for an adjournment of the provisional trial date' (n°. ICC-01/09-02/11 of 31 March 2014) §§26–27; The *Prosecutor v. Uhuru Muigai Kenyatta*, Trial Chamber V(B), 'Second decision on Prosecution's application for a finding of non-compliance under Article 87(7) of the Statute' (n°. ICC-01/09-02/11 of 19 September 2016).

20 Michael Robertson, *Stanley Fish on Philosophy, Politics and Law: How Fish Works* (Cambridge University Press, 2014), 182.

legitimacy and public confidence.[21] The institutional independence is the backbone of its legitimacy as it was envisaged when the drafters of the Rome Statute in the Preamble declared their determination 'to establish an *independent permanent* [Court ...] with jurisdiction over the most serious crimes of concern to the international community as a whole'.[22] Paradoxically, it is this same independence that is a subject of debate from both sides – those who criticise the Court and those who support it. Therefore, there is a need to investigate these accusations and counter-accusations; to understand whether indeed this continued hostile relationship between the AU and the ICC is undermining the Court's independence, subsequently affecting its legitimacy to handle current and future situations/cases. This book attempts to answer the following questions: What are the issues of disagreement between these two opposing interlocutors? If these two opposing sides were to be put together for a dialogue, how could they respond to each other? How do their narratives invoke, reflect and/or impact the Court's independence and legitimacy? In the process of answering these questions other aspects such as the contradictions and exaggerations in each side's narrative, and the common grounds (shared views) will be identified. The intended goal is to see if there is a possibility of bridging the gaps between the two narratives.

There is a lot that can be studied and written on the AU-ICC relationship, but not everything can be covered in this book. The focus is on 'Institutional Independence', specifically analysing the different competing narratives (speeches and texts) about the Court. Balancing different interests including politics is at the heart of the prosecutorial discretion; as Heller notes, 'international prosecutors are never able to prosecute more than a small fraction of the suspects who have committed an international crime'[23] and neither are they capable of investigating all situations where international crimes are suspected to have been committed. Therefore, there is always a need to decide which situation to consider and which suspect in a situation to prosecute. Even if the ICC Prosecutor's decisions might not be based on political considerations, it is undeniable that his/her decisions have political ramifications. Dugard argues that unlike other international tribunals and courts that have existed, the ICC Prosecutor is the only one that has powers to select situations for investigation, and this gives the Prosecutor 'a heavy responsibility and one that is to be exercised independently and without

---

21 Jessica Almqvist, 'International Criminal Courts and Tribunals: A Human Rights Appraisal of the Limits to Judicial Independence for International Criminal Justice' (2015) 28, 91–112 Leiden Journal of International Law, 103ff.

22 Preamble of the Rome Statute (second *Determined*), emphasis added.

23 Jon Kevin Heller, 'The Role of the International Prosecutor' in Cesare Romano, Karen Alter and Yuval Shany (eds.), *Oxford Handbook of International Adjudication* (Oxford University Press, 2013).

fear or favour'.[24] This puts enormous pressure on the Office of the Prosecutor to ensure that the exercise of selection is seen to be fair and impartial.

## 1.2. KEY CONCEPTS

It is important to clarify the meaning and usage of some key concepts such as *independence*, *discretion* and *legitimacy*, because they will be repeatedly used. *Independence* is one of those concepts that are often used without giving their definitions, because there is a tendency to assume that people have the same understanding of what it means. And, for those who understand it, it is often assumed that whenever independence of any justice system is mentioned, people are referring to independence of judges – judicial independence. There is an obvious interest in wanting to know whether judges are independent enough to act as 'neutral arbiters of disputes'.[25] *Black's Law Dictionary* defines 'independence' as 'the state or quality of being independent', and being independent is defined as '[n]ot subject to control or influence of another'.[26] *The Dictionary of International and Comparative Law* defines 'independent' as being 'free from the control of an outside power'.[27] If we take these definitions together, two contrasting interests arise: (i) the desire (or the state) of being free, and (ii) an external actor wanting to interfere. Thus, independence becomes necessary where there is an interest of external interference. If there was no desire from the outside to interfere, or want to control, the existence of independence would not mean much.

In criminal justice, external actors (media, NGOs, corporations, states, individuals etc.) might be interested in the process for either of the two following reasons: (i) preventing a certain investigation or prosecution from taking place, or (ii) encouraging an investigation or prosecution that was not supposed to take place.[28] Whereas decisions to prosecute are often subject to

---

24 John Dugard, 'Palestine and the International Criminal Court: Institutional Failure or Bias?' (2013) 11:3, 563–570 Journal of International Criminal Justice.

25 See where Frank B. Cross states that 'an independent judiciary is regarded as if it were the font of justice, the rule of law and individual rights, if not the font of all good things'. Frank B. Cross, 'Thoughts on Goldilocks and Judicial Independence' (2003) 64:195 Ohio State Law Journal, 1; Theodor Meron, 'Judicial Independence and Impartiality in International Criminal Tribunals' (2005) 99:2, 359–369 The American Journal of International Law; Jerg Gutmann and Stefan Voigt, 'The Independence of Prosecutors and Government Accountability' (2017) ILE Working Paper Series, No. 8, 2; Stefan Voigt and Alexander J. Wulf, 'What makes prosecutors independent? Analysing the institutional determinants of prosecutorial independence' (2017) 1-22 Journal of Institutional Economics, 1–2.

26 Bryan A. Garner (Chief Ed.), *Black's Law Dictionary* (9th ed., Thomson Reuters, 2009), 838.

27 James R. Fox, *Dictionary of International and Comparative Law* (3rd ed., Oceana Publications, Inc., 2003), 157.

28 See Voigt and Wulf, 'What makes prosecutors independent? Analysing the institutional determinants of prosecutorial independence' (2017), 6.

some degree of judicial review, decisions not to investigate or prosecute are outside judicial control, and even where the ICC Pre-Trial Chamber can order for a reconsideration, in case of a (state party or UNSC referral) preliminary examination that was terminated before proceeding to an investigation, the last word remains with the Office of the Prosecutor (OTP).[29] The Rome Statute does not provide powers to the Chambers that can compel the OTP to indict someone or consider a certain situation.[30] In the 'Prosecution's Response to the Government of the Union of the Comoros' "Application for Judicial Review"' concerning the situation on Registered Vessels of the Union of the Comoros, the Hellenic Republic and the Kingdom of Cambodia, the Prosecutor reminds that

> the Prosecutor's 'final decision' under rule 108(3) is just that: a final decision. The Statute grants no power to the Pre-Trial Chamber to review such a decision, nor to review the Prosecutor's independent exercise of discretion under article 53(4).[31]

The significance of studying ICC prosecutorial independence can be summarised in the statement of Levi, Hagan and Dezalay:

> Whereas in many courts international legal practices are linked to how international judges build authority, in the case of international criminal courts the key location for these practices lies upstream in the process, in the office of the Prosecutor.[32]

The OTP is an important factor in defining international criminal justice. Kuczyńska notes that the Prosecutor

> takes part in seeking and developing a historical record of events. He [or she] presents the events that form the background of a crime and identifies the parties to a conflict. He [or she] becomes a historian, demographer and forensic scientist.[33]

Probably this explains why the independence of the ICC Prosecutor is believed to have been the most debated and controversial achievement of the Rome Statute.

---

29 Art. 53(3)(a) of the Rome Statute of the International Criminal Court of 17 July 1998 as corrected and amended up to date (A/CONF.183/9) hereafter 'the Rome Statute'.

30 See Arts. 12–17 of the Rome Statute.

31 The ICC Office of the Prosecutor, 'Situation on Registered Vessels of the Union of the Comoros, the Hellenic Republic and the Kingdom of Cambodia: Prosecution's Response to the Government of the Union of the Comoros' "Application for Judicial Review" (ICC-01/13-58) (Lack of Jurisdiction)' of 13 March 2018 (ICC-01/13-61).

32 Ron Levi, John Hagan and Sara Dezalay, 'International Courts in Atypical Political Environments: The Interplay of Prosecutorial Strategy, Evidence, and Court Authority in International Criminal Law' (2016) 79, 289 Law and Contemporary Problems, 292; see also Gutmann and Voigt, 'The Independence of Prosecutors and Government Accountability' (2017).

33 Hanna Kuczyńska, *The Accusation Model Before the International Criminal Court* (Springer, 2015), 23.

Powerful states, especially the United States, were not comfortable with the idea of an independent Prosecutor, giving such enormous powers to someone beyond state control.[34] Posner and Yoo note that 'one should be skeptical of the claim that states would submit disputes to judges over whom they have no influence (…)'.[35] These remarks would also apply to the ICC Prosecutor.

Independence could be institutional and/or personal independence. Institutional independence is about the protection of the office against external influences, and personal independence is the protection of the office holder(s); providing a conducive environment for the Prosecutor and his or her staff to make fair and impartial decisions. For the ICC, the OTP is protected against interference from outside actors and from other organs of the Court.[36] Article 42(1) *in fin* of the Rome Statute states that members of the OTP 'shall not seek or act on instructions from any external source', and paragraph 5 of the same Article prohibits the Prosecutor and Deputy Prosecutor from engaging in activities that might undermine the confidence or independence expected of their office.[37] Personal independence is well enshrined in the guarantee of tenure, a clear process of election (appointment) of the Prosecutor and the Deputy Prosecutor, and the 'full authority over the management and administration of the Office, (…)'.[38] Rule 101.1 of the Staff Rules of the Court states that '[s]taff members of the Court are international civil servants. Their responsibilities as staff members of the Court are not national, but exclusively international'. Rule 101.3(a) of the same Rules stipulates that the interests of the Court 'take precedence over their other interests', and that '[s]taff members shall ensure their independence from any person, entity or authority outside the Court'.[39] Independence of the OTP is further emphasised in almost all other legal instruments and policy papers, such as the Regulations of the Office of the Prosecutor and the Code of Conduct for the Office of the Prosecutor.

---

34 Jan Wouters, Sten Verhoeven and Bruno Demeyere, 'The International Criminal Court's Office of the Prosecutor: Navigating between Independence and Accountability?' (2008) 8, 273–318 International Criminal Law Review, 278; Martha Minow, C. Cora True-Frost and Alex Whiting, 'The Prosecutor Casts a Shadow: Convener, Collaborator, and Law Enforcer' in Martha Minow, C. Cora True-Frost and Alex Whiting (eds.), *The First Global Prosecutor: Promise and Constraints* (University of Michigan, 2015), 20; Alette Smeulers, Maartje Weerdesteijn and Barbora Hola, 'The Selection of Situations by the ICC: An Empirically Based Evaluation of the OTP's Performance' (2015) 15:1–39 International Criminal Law Review, 3.

35 Eric A. Posner and John C. Yoo, 'Judicial Independence in International Tribunals' (2005) 93:1 California Law Review, 14.

36 Art. 42(1) of the Rome Statute.

37 Art. 42§1 *in fin* and §5 of the Rome Statute.

38 Art. 42(2–4) of the Rome Statute.

39 Rules 101.1 and 101.3 of the Staff Rules of the International Criminal Court (as amended, entered into force on 27 July 2015, ICC/AI/2015/004/Cor.1).

The independence accorded to the OTP has been described as both 'considerable' and 'highly constrained'. Considerable because no case can reach judges without the Prosecutor's intervention, and highly constrained because enforcement of the OTP's decisions, especially those concerning arresting suspects and collecting evidence, is dependent on state cooperation.[40] Nonetheless, the OTP has been strong and unequivocal in stating that its '[i]ndependence goes beyond not seeking or acting on instructions: it means that decisions shall not be influenced or altered by the presumed or known wishes of any party, or in connection with efforts to secure cooperation'.[41] It is the enforcement of this stance that has challenges; it is difficult to expect the work of an international Prosecutor to remain totally apolitical. The ICC Prosecutor's statements on the collapse of the Kenyan cases blamed it on the failure of the Kenyan state to cooperate with her office, intimidation of witnesses, political pressure and meddling.[42]

Therefore, prosecutorial independence on paper and in rhetoric alone is not enough. It is important that the Prosecutor's independence be guaranteed in law but the Prosecutor or those working in the OTP ought not to be biased or be constrained to act in a certain way. It could as well be that in practice the Prosecutor might wilfully concede his or her independence to other actors, especially where there are no oversight measures. Prosecutorial independence needs to be backed up by impartiality and objectivity, and the public needs to be convinced that that is the case. Some scholars have even argued that enforcing international criminal justice is mainly about balancing the need to fight impunity with different geo-political interests.[43] Hartmann in her reference to

---

40 Minow, True-Frost, and Whiting, 'The Prosecutor Casts a Shadow: Convener, Collaborator, and Law Enforcer' (2015), 20–21; see also Leslie Vinjamuri, 'The International Criminal Court and the Paradox of Authority' (2016) 79:275 Law and Contemporary Problems, 277; Sophie T. Rosenberg, 'International Criminal Court in Cote d'Ivoire: Impartiality at Stake' (2017) 15:3 Journal of International Criminal Justice, 472.

41 Para. 26 of the ICC OTP Policy Paper on Preliminary Examinations of November 2013 http://www.legal-tools.org/en/doc/acb906/.

42 Statement of the Prosecutor of the International Criminal Court, Fatou Bensouda, on the withdrawal of charges against Mr. Uhuru Muigai Kenyatta (5 December 2014) https://www.icc-cpi.int/Pages/item.aspx?name=otp-statement-05-12-2014-2; see also Statement of the Prosecutor of the International Criminal Court, Fatou Bensouda, regarding Trial Chamber's decision to vacate charges against Messrs William Samoei Ruto and Joshua Arap Sang without prejudice to their prosecution in the future (6 April 2016) https://www.icc-cpi.int/Pages/item.aspx?name=otp-stat-160406.

43 Kenneth A. Rodman, 'Justice as a Dialogue Between Law and Politics: Embedding the International Criminal Court within Conflict Management and Peacebuilding' (2014) 1-33 Journal of International Criminal Justice, 3ff; Mensa-Bonsu, 'The ICC, International Criminal Justice and International Politics' (2015), 38–41; Allen S. Weiner, 'Prudent Politics: The International Criminal Court, International Relations, and Prosecutorial Independence' (2013) 12, 545–562 Washington University Global Studies Law Review.

the International Criminal Tribunal for the Former Yugoslavia notes that 'le TPI pour l'ex-Yougoslavie, sans doute plus que tout autre, a été conçu pour server d'abord la politique et non pas la justice'.[44] Krever similarly notes that '[t]he International Criminal Court does not, and cannot, exist outside politics and its activities reflect that'.[45] This is not to say that being independent is equal to not having biases. As Hammarskjöld noted, requiring independence is not to say that an international civil servant is not supposed to have 'sympathies or antipathies (…)', it simply means that, '[s]he is requested to be fully aware of those human reactions and meticulously check [her]himself so that they are not permitted to influence [her]his actions'.[46] Rosenberg notes that

> prosecutorial impartiality is understood as upholding the equality of individuals under the law by exclusively acting based on the law and evidence, making informed and unbiased decisions while shedding any prejudgment, preferences, interests or ideological learnings.[47]

These observations leave no doubt on how international criminal justice is interwoven with international politics.

The second most important concept of this book is *prosecutorial discretion*. *The Dictionary of International and Comparative Law* defines 'discretion' as the

44 Roughly translated as 'the ICT for the former Yugoslavia, without a doubt more than any other, was conceived to serve politics first, not justice'. Florence Hartmann, *Paix et Châtiment: Les Guerres Secrètes de la Politique et de la Justice Internationales* (Flammarion, 2007), 30.

45 Tor Krever, 'Africa in the Dock: On ICC Bias' [30 October 2016] http://criticallegalthinking.com/2016/10/30/africa-in-the-dock-icc-bias/#fnref-21994-2; see also Paul D. Schmitt, 'France, Africa, and the ICC: The Neocolonialist Critique and the Crisis of the Institutional Legitimacy' in Kamara M. Clarke, Abel S. Knottnerus and Eefje de Volder, *Africa and the ICC: Perceptions of Justice* (Cambridge University Press, 2016), 127–151; David Bosco, *Rough Justice: The International Criminal Court's Battle to Fix the World, One Prosecution at a Time* (Oxford University Press, 2014); Juan Branco, *L'Ordre et le Monde: Critique de la Cour Penale Internationale* (Fayard, 2016).

46 Dag Hammarskjöld, 'The International Civil Servant in Law and in Fact: Lecture Delivered to Congregation at Oxford University, 30 May 1961' 348 http://www.un.org/depts/dhl/dag/docs/internationalcivilservant.pdf.

47 Rosenberg, 'International Criminal Court in Cote d'Ivoire: Impartiality at Stake' (2017), 480; see also James Hamilton, where he notes that 'prosecutorial independence is not an end in itself. Where it exists it is intended to put the prosecutor in a situation where he or she can take the right decision in a case without fear or favour, without being subjected to improper pressure from another source, whether it can be the media, politicians, the police, a victim seeking revenge or even a misguided public opinion'. The presentation delivered at the European Commission for Democracy through Law (VENICE Commission) conference 'The Independence of Judges and Prosecutors: Perspectives and Challenges' (28 February–3 March 2011) paper entitled 'Prosecutorial Independence and Accountability', 2 http://www.venice.coe.int/webforms/documents/default.aspx?pdffile=CDL-UDT(2011)008-e.

'right (...) to act in the way one thinks best or most appropriate'.[48] *Black's Law Dictionary* defines prosecutorial independence as

> [a] prosecutor's power to choose from options available in a criminal case, such as filing charges, prosecuting, not prosecuting, plea bargaining and recommending a sentence to the court.[49]

Similarly, Takemura states that 'prosecutorial discretion is the power held by an agency or official charged with the enforcement of the law to exercise selectivity in the choice of occasions for the law's enforcement'.[50] Discretion is not unique to criminal prosecutions; every public official that takes decisions involving choosing among different alternatives has a margin of appreciation – discretionary powers – to choose the best alternative. As Danner notes, 'prosecutors must be able to exercise their discretion to pursue or decline particular cases in order to maintain a functioning criminal justice system'.[51] However, administrative justice will still require that such discretionary decisions be transparent, reasoned and fair, and failure to respect those principles becomes an abuse of discretion. *Black's Law Dictionary* defines abuse of discretion as '(...) the failure to exercise sound, reasonable, and legal decision-making'.[52]

The Rome Statute gave to the OTP a mandate to investigate and prosecute heinous crimes including genocide, crimes against humanity, war crimes and 'aggression' (which hasn't been tested so far). The Court's intervention can be triggered if the concerned state(s) is/are 'unwilling or unable genuinely to carry out the investigation or prosecution' – the principle of complementarity.[53] However, it is not possible that the ICC Prosecutor will be able to investigate and prosecute all international crimes that are not genuinely being investigated or prosecuted. Therefore, selectivity among different meritorious situations and cases remains inevitable. Varaki has noted that

> the notion of prosecutorial discretion is particularly critical since the prosecutor is empowered by the statute to initiate independently not only prosecutions but also

48 Fox, *Dictionary of International and Comparative Law* (2003), 88.
49 Garner, *Black's Law Dictionary* (2009), 534.
50 Hitomi Takemura, 'Prosecutorial Discretion in International Criminal Justice: Between Fragmentation and Unification' in Larissa Van den Herik and Carsten Stahn (eds.), *The Diversification and Fragmentation of International Criminal Law* (Brill/Nijhoff, 2012), 635.
51 Allison Marston Danner, 'Enhancing the Legitimacy and Accountability of the Prosecutorial Discretion at the International Criminal Court' in Antonio Cassese and others (eds.), *International Criminal Law: Critical Concepts in Law* (Routledge, 2015), 267.
52 Garner, *Black's Law Dictionary* (2009), 11.
53 Art. 17 of the Rome Statute.

investigations. This is a unique feature that differentiates the ICC from the *ad hoc* and hybrid tribunals.[54]

The powers of the Prosecutor include deciding on which situations to investigate, when to start an investigation, and within the selected situations which cases or crimes to prosecute.[55] This is an extensive mandate bestowed to a Prosecutor with limited resources. This limitation is acknowledged in the OTP Policy Paper on Case Selection and Prioritisation, which states that:

> [T]he Office exercises its discretion in determining which cases should be selected and prioritised for investigation and prosecution. (...) It is not the responsibility or role of the Office to investigate and prosecute each and every alleged criminal act within a given situation or every person allegedly responsible for such crimes.[56]

The most interesting aspect of the ICC Prosecutor's use of discretionary powers is the message the selection communicates to the public on behalf of the international community. In exercising prosecutorial discretion, the Prosecutor is mainly distributing two things: (i) condemnation, and (ii) leniency. Whenever the Prosecutor decides to investigate and/or prosecute some alleged crimes, she/he is selectively choosing which crimes to condemn, and whenever she/he decides to ignore certain crimes, she/he is selectively being 'tolerant or merciful' to those alleged criminal conducts and their alleged perpetrators, and all this is done in the name and on behalf of the international community. Therefore, perception of the independence of the Prosecutor is judged basing on both actions and inactions – whether the distribution of condemnation and leniency is being done uniformly without fear or favour.

The Prosecution needs independence to fully exercise its discretion because prosecutorial independence reinforces the exercise of prosecutorial discretion. Accordingly, Takemura notes that 'the most important rationale for prosecutorial discretion is to preserve prosecutorial independence'.[57] Institutional independence is based on the assumption that independence contributes to the legitimacy of institutions, and that legitimacy is derived from the public perception that an institution is independent and impartial, and that this public trust in turn contributes to the support that is required for the institution's decisions

---

54 Maria Varaki, 'Introducing a Fairness-Based Theory of Prosecutorial Legitimacy before the International Criminal Court' (2016) 27:3 The European Journal of International Law, 773.

55 Anni Pues, 'Towards the "Golden Hour"?: A Critical Exploration of the Length of Preliminary Examinations' (2017) 15:3, 435–453 Journal of International Criminal Justice (Special Issue: The International Criminal Court's Policies and Strategies), 436.

56 Para. 5 of the Office of the Prosecutor's Policy Paper on Case Selection and Prioritisation [2016] https://www.icc-cpi.int/itemsDocuments/20160915_OTP-Policy_Case-Selection_Eng.pdf.

57 Takemura, 'Prosecutorial Discretion in International Criminal Justice: Between Fragmentation and Unification' (2012), 636.

to be accepted.[58] This brings me to legitimacy, another important and controversial concept in studying international institutions.[59]

*Legitimacy* is understood as a subjective belief that a certain institution is the trustworthy authority over certain matters, and because of that belief, the actor will support its decisions.[60] Whereas legality of decisions is important, it is crucial to emphasise that legitimacy is different from legality. As Bühlmann and Kunz note, '[p]ublic beliefs about trustworthiness of judicial institutions do not seem to originate from constitutional rules (*de jure* independence) but from actual events and real life experiences (*de facto* independence)'.[61] This is because, as Hurd notes, legitimacy

> is a subjective quality, relational between actor and institution, and defined by the actor's perception of the institution. The actor's perception may come from the substance of the rule or from the procedure or source by which it was constituted.[62]

This is what d'Aspremont and De Brabandere call 'legitimacy of origin' and 'legitimacy of exercise'.[63] The most challenging part of studying legitimacy is that it is neither permanent nor universal. It is not permanent because public opinion keeps changing, and it is not universal because not all actors will consider an institution legitimate at the same time.[64]

---

58 Kenneth W. Abbott and Duncan Snidal, 'Why States Act through Formal International Organizations' (1998) 42, 3–32 Journal of Conflict Resolution, 5–16.

59 As Junne notes, 'for international organizations (…) it is not immediately clear who forms the constituency that would regard international organizations legitimate or illegitimate'. G.C.A. Junne, 'International Organizations in a Period of Globalization: New (Problems of) Legitimacy' in Jean-Marc Coicaud and Veijo Heiskanen (eds.), *The Legitimacy of International Organizations* (United Nations University Press, 2001), 191; Silje Aambø Langvatn and Theresa Squatrito, 'Conceptualising and Measuring the Legitimacy of International Criminal Tribunals' in Nobuo Hayashi and Cecilia M. Bailliet (eds.), *The Legitimacy of International Criminal Tribunals* (Studies on International Courts and Tribunals), (Cambridge University Press, 2017), 41–65.

60 Marc Bühlmann and Ruth Kunz, 'Confidence in the Judiciary: Comparing the Independence and Legitimacy of Judicial Systems' (2011) 34:2 West European Politics, 320; Ian Hurd, 'Legitimacy and Authority in International Politics' (1999) 53:2 International Organization, 381.

61 Bühlmann and Kunz, 'Confidence in the Judiciary: Comparing the Independence and Legitimacy of Judicial Systems' (2011), 317.

62 Hurd, 'Legitimacy and Authority in International Politics' (1999), 381.

63 Jean d'Aspremont and Eric de Brabandere, 'The Duality of the Legitimacy of Global Actors in the International Legal Order' in Matthew Happold (ed.), *International Law in a Multipolar World* (Routledge, 2012); see also Thomas Obel Hansen, 'The International Criminal Court and the Legitimacy of Exercise' in Per Andersen, Cecilie Eriksen and Bjarke Viskum (eds.), *Law and Legitimacy* (DJOEF Publishers, 2015), 1–27.

64 Darryl Robinson, 'Inescapable Dyads: Why the International Criminal Court Cannot Win' (2015) 28:2, 323–347 Leiden Journal of International Law; Linda E. Carter, Mark S. Ellis and Charles C. Jalloh, *The International Criminal Court in an Effective Global Justice System* (Edward Elgar Publishing, 2016), 1.

Whereas the Court is operating in a highly politicised environment, as Hansen argues, there is a strong belief among its supporters that political considerations undermine the administration of justice.[65] On the contrary, in 2003, Danner had foreseen that '[s]ome states and NGOs might urge [the ICC Prosecutor …] to act in particular cases, while other states may express a clear preference for declination'.[66] The underlying dilemma is whether the Court should expect to continue receiving support even when the Prosecutor is interpreting the law in a manner that is clearly against the preferences of other actors including those that provide it with both material and moral support. This is very critical because it means that the legitimacy of the Court depends not only on fidelity to the law but also on how well the Prosecutor is balancing conflicting interests from different actors. Preserving legitimacy is important. As de Hoon notes '[t]he loss of legitimacy of the Court is worrisome. Justice mechanisms, including criminal law trials, function only by the grace of legitimacy. Without it, justice is not recognized as such, nor accepted, and the exercise becomes futile'.[67]

## 1.3. METHODOLOGICAL APPROACH

To provide answers to these 'not so strict legal questions',[68] requires a combination of different disciplines and research methods. Conducting research on a topic concerning the institutional independence and legitimacy of the International Criminal Court requires combining law with international relations, social science and politics among others. Moreno Ocampo, the first ICC Prosecutor, noted that: 'Understanding the Rome Statute's Justice System will require connecting different fields, in particular international relations, global security, and international and criminal law.'[69] In this book, theoretical and normative reasoning are combined. The classic legal research method of collecting and analysing relevant legal instruments, court decisions, policy documents, narratives (texts and speeches) and available literature (doctrine) are combined with a Critical Discourse Analysis (CDA). The reason for this combination is to ensure that

---

65 Hansen, 'The International Criminal Court and the Legitimacy of Exercise' (2015), 5–6.

66 Danner, 'Enhancing the Legitimacy and Accountability of Prosecutorial Discretion at the International Criminal Court' (2003), 534.

67 Marieke de Hoon, 'The Future of the International Criminal Court. On Critique, Legalism and Strengthening the ICC's Legitimacy' (2017) 17, 591–614 International Criminal Law Review, 594.

68 See 'non-legal topics' in Mathias M. Siems, 'Legal Originality' (2008) 28:1, 147–164 Oxford Journal of Legal Studies, 162ff.

69 Luis Moreno Ocampo, 'Prologue: The Prosecutor's Use of Legal Policies' in Minow, True-Frost and Whiting (eds.), *The First Global Prosecutor: Promise and Constraints* (2015), 15.

both theoretical and normative perspectives are given equal attention. It is hoped that combining these different approaches ensures that whatever useful argumentation that would otherwise be left out is captured.

This book is comprised of five chapters including this general introduction (Chapter 1). Chapter 2 is concerned with narratives around the work of the Court. This is done through a CDA of speeches and texts of those who criticise the Court and those who support it. The purpose of this chapter is to create two seemingly competing narratives: a narrative of those who criticise the Court, and that of supporters. In turn, these two narratives provide a basis to do two things: first, to establish an uninterrupted version of each side's understanding of the Court, and, secondly, to create a dialogue, where each narrative responds to the other. After a dialogue, different contradictions, misinformation and exaggerations on both sides are identified, and in the process showing how the independence and legitimacy of the Court are invoked, reflected or interfered with.

The criticisms of the International Criminal Court from Africa revolve around equality of states, power and dominance under the current international legal order.[70] The AU and some African countries perceive (rightly or wrongly) the Court as an organisation that was created to perpetuate an unequal enforcement of international law.[71] This is certainly a very worrying trend, as Nouwen notes the '*de facto* inequality between states increases legal inequality between individuals, which in turn entrenches *de facto* inequality between states'.[72] To fully understand the current Africa-ICC debate requires using an approach that would help to disentangle the underlying language used in both criticising the Court and supporting it. This then contributes to an understanding of whether there is indeed an attempt to interfere with the Court's institutional independence or not. That is why, in addition to a review of the literature, CDA techniques are very useful. CDA helps in understanding the way language is used in social dominance and power structures. Wodak and Meyer define CDA 'as being fundamentally interested in analyzing opaque as well as transparent structural

70 Read e.g. Nico Krisch, 'International Law in Times of Hegemony: Unequal Power and the Shaping of the International Legal Order' (2005) 16:3 The European Journal of International Law; Hans Köchler; 'Justice and Realpolitik: The Predicament of the International Criminal Court' (2017) 16:1 Chinese Journal of International Law; Rowland J.V. Cole, 'Africa's Relationship with the International Criminal Court: More Political than Legal' (2013) 14, 670 Melbourne Journal of International Law; Lee J.M. Seymour, 'Rhetoric, Hypocrisy Management, and Legitimacy' in Kamari M. Clarke, Abel S. Knottnerus and Eefje de Volder (eds.), *Africa and ICC: Perceptions of Justice* (Cambridge University Press, 2016), 107–123.

71 Reus Schuerch, *The International Criminal Court at the Mercy of Powerful States: An Assessment of the Neo-Colonialism Claim by African Stakeholders* (T.M.C. Asser Press, 2017).

72 Sarah Nouwen, 'Legal Equality on Trial: Sovereigns and Individuals Before the International Criminal Court' (2012) 41, 151–181 Netherlands Yearbook of International Law, 153.

relationships of dominance, discrimination, power and control as manifested in language'.[73] And Van Dijk defines CDA as 'a type of discourse analytical research that primarily studies the way social power abuse, dominance, and inequality are enacted, reproduced, and resisted by text and talk in the social and political context'.[74]

On the face of it, there is already a pattern of words that whoever is studying the ICC-Africa relationship debate would find interesting. On one hand, those criticising the ICC are associating it with neo-colonialism, slavery, racism and western dominance among others,[75] and on the other hand, supporters of the ICC in response to critics describe them as a pro-impunity and anti-victims club of dictators who are protecting themselves or their cronies etc., whilst describing the Court as one of the best representations of justice, democracy and rule of law, and calling for its protection.[76] As Van Dijk notes, 'the justification of inequality involves two complementary strategies, namely the positive representation of the own group, and the negative representation of the others'.[77]

This is not going to be the first time discourse analysis is used in understanding a legal phenomenon; as Shuy notes, 'the area of law provides an open opportunity for discourse analysis, especially since law is such a highly verbal field'.[78] The discourses to be analysed are from different interviews and speeches available on

---

73 Ruth Wodak and Michael Meyer, 'Critical discourse analysis: history, agenda, theory, and methodology' in Ruth Wodak and Michael Meyer (eds.), *Methods for Critical Discourse Analysis* (2nd rev. ed., Sage, 2009), 10.

74 Teun A Van Dijk, 'Critical Discourse Analysis' in Deborah Schiffrin, Deborah Tannen and Heidi E. Hamilton (eds.), *The Handbook of Discourse Analysis* (Blackwell Publishers, 2001), 353.

75 'Ethiopian Prime Minister HaileMariam Desalegn urges African countries to withdraw their membership from ICC' [Tigrai Online, 29 December 2014] http://www.tigraionline.com/articles/ethiopia-rejects-icc.html; David Bosco, 'Why is the International Criminal Court picking only on Africa?' [Washington Post, 29 March 2013] https://www.washingtonpost.com/opinions/why-is-the-international-criminal-court-picking-only-on-africa/2013/03/29/cb9bf5da-96f7-11e2-97cd-3d8c1afe4f0f_story.html?utm_term=.1ae3b02d56a6; speaking of the International Criminal Court, 'the lighter skin you are, the less guilty you are', Rwandan Foreign Minister Louise Mushikiwabo stated. D.W. English: Conflict Zone, 'Justice and injustice in Rwanda' [Louise Mushikiwabo interviewed by Tim Sebastian, 28 October 2015] https://www.youtube.com/watch?v=IsBwbaxsXQ0.

76 Statement of the Prosecutor of the International Criminal Court, Fatou Bensouda: 'The ICC is an independent court that must be supported' [24 November 2015] https://www.icc-cpi.int/Pages/item.aspx?name=otp-stat-24-11-2015; Elizabeth Evenson, 'ICC: Challenging Dictators, The Promise of Kampala's International Criminal Court Review Conference' [27 July 2010] https://www.hrw.org/news/2010/07/27/icc-challenging-dictators; FIDH Press Release, 'Termination of Ruto and Sang case at the ICC: Witness tampering means impunity prevails over justice again' [5 April 2016] https://www.fidh.org/en/region/Africa/kenya/termination-of-ruto-and-sang-case-at-the-icc-witness-tampering-means.

77 Teun A. van Dijk, 'Principles of Critical Discourse Analysis' (2016) 4:2, 249–283 Discourse and Society, 263.

78 Roger W. Shuy, 'Discourse Analysis in the Legal Context' in Deborah Schiffrin, Deborah Tannen and Heidi E. Hamilton (eds.), *The Handbook of Discourse Analysis* (Blackwell Publishers, 2001), 437.

YouTube and in different journalistic texts, NGOs' and AU statements. However, it is important to set some limitations on how CDA is used in this book. The purpose is not to analyse every speech of each individual critic or supporter of the ICC akin to what Clarke does in her chapter 'International Justice and the Politics of Sentimentality', where she provides an in-depth analysis of Mr. Kenyatta's speech parallel to Shamiso Mbizvo's presentation,[79] nor does it analyse every statement of the AU criticising the Court. It is rather an attempt to create a single narrative (discourse) for critics, on one side, based on a combination of different excerpts from speeches and texts, and another narrative of supporters, based on a combination of excerpts from those interlocutors' speeches and texts in their support of the Court. This will produce two representative narratives, one for critics and another for supporters. It is hoped that identification of nuances, misinformation and exaggerations within each group's narrative might help to bridge the gap between the two. The focus is on arguments and not on arguers – in other words, there is no description of speakers.

Whereas there is little direct communication between the two sides of the debate, the two created narratives are presented in a dialogical form. The purpose of this approach is to show that even if there is no such direct communication between the arguers, at least there is some kind of listening going on – on both sides – where there is an attempt to respond to one another. It is important to note that the purpose is not to determine the superiority of one narrative over the other, nor to show which narrative is more persuasive than the other; the focus is on showing how the ICC is being squeezed between those two stories, both as it seems carved in stone – which might be in the end affecting its independence and/or legitimacy.

The question one would want to see answered is whether studying the rhetoric of some African leaders and statements made by the African Union criticising the Court and responses from supporters of the ICC, mainly NGOs and international law lawyers, is relevant to an understanding of the Court's institutional independence. The answer is to a certain extent in the affirmative because statements of heads of state, reports of NGOs, academic writings and teachings of highly qualified publicists are useful materials in the development of international law.[80] It is also important because the Court needs these

---

79 Kamari M. Clarke, 'International Justice and the Politics of Sentimentality' in Kamari M. Clarke, Abel S. Knottnerus and Eefje de Volder (eds.), *Africa and ICC: Perceptions of Justice* (Cambridge University Press, 2016), 78–103.

80 See the Separate further opinion of Judge Eboe-Osuji to the 'Reasons for the Decision on excusal from presence at trial under Rule 134quater' (ICC-01/09-01/11-1186-Anx, of 18 October 2013); Rüdiger Wolfrum, 'Sources of International Law' in Oxford Public International Law – Max Planck Encyclopedia of Public International Law (2011); Samantha Besson, 'Theorizing the Sources of International Law' in Samantha Besson and John Tasioulas, *The Philosophy of International Law* (Oxford University Press, 2010).

main drivers of the discussions on both sides. It needs states' cooperation in collecting evidence and arresting suspects, and it also needs NGOs, in particular the Coalition for the International Criminal Court in benefiting from its local expertise and connections, outreach activities and campaigns for the ratification of the Rome Statute. Therefore, it is possible that before the ICC Prosecutor decides to request the Pre-Trial Chamber for an authorisation to conduct a new investigation, he or she might think twice about the ramifications of that decision on either side of the debate. There are even some signs that the Court and the OTP in particular are listening – or at least following – what is happening on the African Continent. The ICC's office of the Registry has a Situation Analysis Unit, and the OTP has an African working team, responsible for conducting weekly analyses of different dynamics and developments on the continent, which then report to their respective superiors.

Chapter 3 is about understanding the decision-making process at the OTP – in the real world sense (in practice). This chapter is based on consultative interviews with some individuals in the OTP in combination with the interpretation of some ICC legal and policy documents. The purpose is to establish the decision-making process from the time a communication is received through preliminary examination to the moment a decision is taken of whether to proceed to investigations or not. There are different units and individuals involved in the decision-making process; so it is important to know how these internal actors interact. It identifies important issues and stages involved in the decision-making and examines measures that are in place to ensure that prosecutorial independence and discretionary powers are not abused. This approach is based on the understanding that whereas it is important to study how concepts are provided for in legal instruments (rules and articles) and how these norms are explained in different theoretical writings, it is equally important to listen to those whose responsibility it is to interpret them. The combination of consultations with desktop review offers some valuable information to triangulate, thus leading to a better understanding of the decision-making process.

Chapter 4 is a combination of major findings, especially confronting Chapter 2 with Chapter 3 to establish the current picture of the Court. It builds on some identified major highlights in the created competing narratives and procedural aspects identified in the decision-making process. This chapter is at the heart of this book, because it focuses on aspects that contribute to the understanding of the Court's current standing on issues of institutional independence and legitimacy. It provides an analysis that is aimed at showing how the arguers (critics and supporters) might be affecting the independence and/or legitimacy of the Court. Most importantly, it provides some suggestions on strengthening the Court's independence and legitimacy. It is suggested that in the absence of a global authority capable of distributing justice equitably to all the citizens of the world, the International Criminal Court should focus on strengthening its national, sub-regional and regional legitimacies. This can be achieved through the use of a well-packaged message through accommodative language and transparency in explaining the mandate of the Court. The Prosecutor needs to understand that the ICC operates in the context of transitional justice whose purpose is to contribute to the post-conflict governance. The interpretation of 'interests of justice' and the 'principle of complementarity' needs to reflect this reality.

Chapter 5 provides some concluding remarks and more emphasis to the main arguments. This structure is believed to be consistent with the classical legal analysis approach of starting with facts and issues, legal provisions and ending with analysis and opinions.

# CHAPTER 2
# COMPETING NARRATIVES ABOUT THE ICC

There is a lot written and said about the International Criminal Court and its work, with equal amounts of praise and criticism. The purpose of this chapter is to present discursively the two dominant, 'seemingly' competing, narratives about the Court's relationship with Africa. The first story is of people who see the Court as one of the best things to have happened to Africa. This narrative depicts the Court as the main (if not the only) solution to Africa's struggle against its widespread culture of impunity. The second story is of those who see the Court as another 'northern' tool created to dominate, control and abuse Africans, for external interests. This narrative suggests cautious collaboration or complete resistance, if there is no change. The major disagreement between these two stories concerns the Court's independence and legitimacy, especially relating to its selection of situations and cases almost exclusively in Africa. Narratives, as Linde argues, can be used to describe an institution, criticise it, reshape it or defend it.[81]

The majority of the supporters of the Court are its officials, NGOs and some international criminal law lawyers, whereas critics are, among others, some African leaders and opinion-makers. However, the main focus here is not so much on arguers but on their arguments. The purpose is to present discursively the two narratives; a narrative of those who criticise the Court and a narrative of its supporters. After a presentation, a mock dialogue is created between the two narratives. This is important because it seems that these two opposing arguers are not interested in a direct discussion. In the dialogical approach, each narrative responds to the other. Through a critical discourse analysis (CDA), contradictions, misinformation and exaggerations are identified on both sides.

In the creation of each side's story, there is a combination of both official statements, those speaking on behalf of institutions (ICC/NGOs or AU/African leaders), and views of others not speaking in official capacities, but whose talks or texts reinforce the position of either side. This combination is

---

81 Charlotte Linde, 'Narrative in Institutions' in Deborah Schiffrin, Deborah Tannen and Heidi E. Hamilton (eds.), *The Handbook of Discourse Analysis* (Blackwell Publishers, 2001), 518–535.

intended to capture some nuances, because in most cases, those not speaking in official capacities are either clarifying or emphasising certain official positions. Admittedly, it is very difficult to conduct a comprehensive CDA of a legal or justice system, akin to this one, without producing a critical legal study. This is because, as Robertson notes, 'the goal of critical legal studies (CLS) is to uncover and undo the ways in which law facilitates the unjust domination of some groups by others in societies'.[82] However, admitting to this fact is not to say that this is necessarily a critical legal study, because as van Dijk notes, CDA 'does not primarily aim to contribute to a specific discipline, paradigm, school or discourse theory. It is primarily interested and motivated by pressing social issues, (….) in which distinctions between theory, description and "application" become less relevant'.[83] Blackledge notes that

> CDA is centrally interested in language and power because it is usually in language that discriminatory practices are enacted, in language that unequal relations of power are constituted and reproduced, and in language that social asymmetries may be challenged and transformed.[84]

## 2.1. THE TWO TALES OF THE COURT

### 2.1.1. PROPONENTS (PRO.)

The narrative of supporters of the Court goes like this: the International Community, 'a global movement striving to build a more just world', has always wanted to establish an international criminal court. This idea came to fruition in 1998 with the adoption of the Rome Statute, after a series of vigorous negotiations that were spearheaded by small and weak countries in collaboration with the global civil society (the Coalition for the International Criminal Court to be specific).[85] The Rome Statute created a criminal justice system assigning responsibilities to different actors.[86] Among those actors is the permanent International Criminal Court, an independent judicial institution whose mandate is to fight against

---

82 Robertson, *Stanley Fish on Philosophy, Politics and Law: How Fish Works* (2014), 327.

83 Van Dijk, 'Principles of Critical Discourse Analysis' (1993), 252.

84 Adrian Blackledge, 'Discourse and Power' in James Paul Gee and Michael Handford (eds.), *The Routledge Handbook of Discourse Analysis* (Routledge, 2012), 616–627, 617.

85 Paul Nantulya, 'What's next for Africa and the International Criminal Court?' [African Center for Strategic Studies, December 2017] http://africacenter.org/spotlight/whats-next-africa-international-criminal-court-icc/; W. Chadwick Austin and Michael Thieme, 'Is the International Criminal Court Anti-African?' (2016) 28:3, 342–350 Peace Review; see also the story of the Coalition for the International Criminal Court at http://www.coalitionfortheicc.org/about/our-story.

86 In addition to the ICC, actors include the Assembly of States Parties (ASP), the United Nations Security Council (UNSC), state parties, NGOs and individuals.

impunity of serious crimes – 'atrocities that deeply shock the conscience of humanity'.[87]

The ICC is 'the centrepiece of the international criminal justice system'[88] that when created 'raised an extraordinary sense of hope for justice and peace for every individual person and for all the peoples of the world'.[89] According to the ICC Prosecutor, Fatou Bensouda, the idea of the Court is based on

> the belief that the power of law has the capacity to redress the balance between criminals, who wield power, and the victims who suffer at their hands. (...) Law is the ultimate weapon, the weak has against the strong.[90]

It is these 'superlative values' that make supporting the ICC a moral obligation, a sort of devotion.[91]

The ICC is a court of last resort that conducts independent and impartial investigations and prosecutions of international crimes, focusing on those who bear the greatest responsibility. Through a strict application of its adopted laws, it focuses on gravity of crimes and alleged perpetrators of those crimes. According to the former President of the ASP, Wenaweser, 'there is no attempt (...) to try to exercise control over the judicial activities of the Court, (...) if the institution is not independent then it is useless'.[92]

African countries took a lead in accepting international criminal justice through ratifications and self-referrals. Those who criticise the Court for focusing on Africa are self-serving politicians who are interested in protecting themselves and their colleagues. Critics are hypocrites, says Ocampo, the former ICC Prosecutor, and he continues to argue that the claim of African bias 'was invented by President Bashir to cover up his genocide'.[93] In support of the ICC, deGuzman notes that '... the ICC's assertion that the African situations were

---

87 Preamble of the Rome Statute.

88 Jean-Baptiste Jeangène Vilmer, 'The African Union and the International Criminal Court: Counteracting the Crisis' (2016) 92: 6 International Affairs, 1319.

89 Speech of the President of the Assembly of States Parties, Mr. Sidiki Kaba, Fifteenth Session of the Assembly of States Parties [16 November 2016] 1, https://asp.icc-cpi.int/iccdocs/asp_docs/ASP15/ASP15-Opening-Statement-PASP-ENG.pdf.

90 '2012 VLS Charney Lecture – Reflections from ICC Prosecutor Fatou Bensouda' [Vanderbilt University, 28 August 2012] https://www.youtube.com/watch?v=CkuDrnlvKVQ) 4:38–6:00.

91 Vilmer, 'The African Union and the International Criminal Court: Counteracting the Crisis' (2016), 1320; Africa Group of Justice and Accountability, 'PANEL VII: Immunity of Heads of State under International Law' [25 October 2016] https://www.youtube.com/watch?v=VxpGnbZcNNI (Christopher Gevers, 45:10–58).

92 NYU: School of Law, 'IILJ: How Best to Assure the Independence of the ICC Prosecutor' [16 November 2011] https://www.youtube.com/watch?v=zdZbZW7ZD6w (Christian Wenaweser, 1:32:51–1:34:00): Ambassador Christian Wenaweser served as the President of the ASP from 2008, for a 3-year period.

93 Al Jazeera, 'Upfront – Arena: Is the ICC biased against African Countries?' [12 March 2016] https://www.youtube.com/watch?v=1XHyJYOYZDk, Moreno Ocampo.

selected based on their gravity (...) is credible. (...) The African situations under investigation all involve large numbers of victims'.[94] Zeid Ra'ad Al Hussein, the United Nations High Commissioner for Human Rights, states that 'to desert the Court, is to desert victims of the most abominable international crimes, to desert all of [those] who worked so hard and for years on its behalf'.[95]

Kofi Annan states that

> the people of Africa, and particularly the victims (...), stand by the ICC. Most of the continent's democratic governments stand by the ICC, [and that he too stands] by the ICC, because the most heinous crimes must not go unpunished.[96]

James Goldston puts it thus:

> some of these criticisms are often made by leaders themselves who are targeted by the Court, or others who fear they will be, they are entirely predictable, self-interested (...) people who are bearing the burden of being held to account of the crimes they perpetrated.[97]

Similarly, Richard Goldstone states that 'the more autocratic leaders are, the more concerned they are, to protect themselves.[98]

A brief examination of proponents' views reveals at least five major claims. First, ICC is a creation of weak countries under the leadership of Africa in collaboration with the civil society. Second, it is some of these same small countries that are at the forefront of fighting impunity through self-referrals. Third, some of the Court's senior officials are Africans, including some judges, the current Prosecutor and some staff. Therefore, there is no good reason to suspect that such a Court can be against Africa. Kenneth Roth summed it up thus:

> The ICC is hardly an institution that looks anti-African. Its largest block of members – 34 of its 122 states – is from Africa, and they were central in negotiating

---

94 Margaret M. deGuzman, 'Africa Question: Is the International Criminal Court (ICC) targeting Africa inappropriately?' [Topic for March 2013–January 2014, http://iccforum.com/africa].

95 Keynote speech by Zeid Ra'ad Al Hussein, United Nations High Commissioner for Human Rights, at the Assembly of States Parties to the Rome Statute of the International Criminal Court [16 November 2016] https://www.ohchr.org/EN/NewsEvents/Pages/DisplayNews.aspx?NewsID=20873.

96 Kofi Annan, 'State Impunity is back in fashion – we need the international court more than ever' [18 November 2016] https://www.theguardian.com/commentisfree/2016/nov/18/state-impunity-international-criminal-court-african.

97 Africa Group for Justice and Accountability, 'Panel I – Africa and the ICC: Misperceptions and Realities' [18 October 2016] https://www.youtube.com/watch?v=tKcr6W_N6lk (James A. Goldston, 36:20–36:40).

98 ibid (Richard Goldstone, 2:30–2:55).

> the Rome treaty that established the court. (…) The ICC's chief prosecutor is an African – Fatou Bensouda of Gambia. (…) Africans serve among the court's judges and the prosecutor's staff.[99]

Fourth, powerful countries cannot control it, because of its independence – institutional and functional. Fifth, critics are either suspects or despots who fear that the Court might indict them, but the rest of Africa is behind the Court.

### 2.1.2. OPPONENTS (OPP.)

Whereas critics continue to pledge their unwavering support to the idea of fighting against impunity, they argue that the International Criminal Court, as it is today, is incapable of delivering that promise.[100] The main reasons are fivefold: targeting heads of state, selectivity (racism and the nature of the crimes), incompetence, partiality of ICC individual staff, and external interferences.[101] Mamdani argues that 'African countries joined ICC, almost unthinkingly, because when you target the Head of State, you are targeting the sovereignty of a country, the ICC targets not only criminals but targets the sovereignty of states'.[102] Whereas it is acceptable that a state party's sitting head of state can be indicted, it remains very controversial for the ICC Prosecutor to issue a warrant of arrest against a serving head of a state that is not a party to the Rome Treaty.[103]

Mushikiwabo stresses that 'when this Court started, and the idea that this international court will serve all of us, it was supported, "who would not support international justice?" [She retorts.] But the practice is that the lighter-skinned

99 Roth, 'Africa attacks the International Criminal Court' (2014).

100 See also the AU decisions criticising the International Criminal Court; it is stated that AU reiterates 'unflinching commitment to combating impunity …'.

101 Para. 2 of the AU Decision (Assembly/AU/Dec.270(XIV)), 'Decision on the Report of the Second Meeting of States Parties to the Rome Statute on the International Criminal Court (ICC)' – Doc. Assembly/AU/8(XIV) as adopted by the Fourteenth Ordinary Session of the Assembly in Addis Ababa, Ethiopia on 2 February 2010.

102 Al Jazeera, 'Upfront – Arena: Is the ICC biased against African Countries?' (Mahmood Mamdani).

103 African Union, Assembly, 'Decision on the Meeting of African States Parties to the Rome Statute of the International Criminal Tribunal (ICC) Doc. Assembly/AU/13(XIII)', 3 July 2009, Assembly/AU/Dec.245 (XIII) Rev. 1 ('3 July 2009 AU Decision'), §10; The Appeals Chamber (*Prosecutor v. Al Bashir*), 'The African Union's Submission in the "Hashemite Kingdom of Jordan's Appeal Against the 'Decision under Article 87(7) of the Rome Statute on the Non Compliance by Jordan with the Request by the Court for the Arrest and Surrender [of] Omar Al-Bashir'"' (ICC-02/05-01/09-370 of 16 July 2018); The Appeals Chamber (*Prosecutor v. Al Bashir*) 'The League of Arab States' Observations on the Hashemite Kingdom of Jordan's appeal against the "Decision under article 87(7) of the Rome Statute on the noncompliance by Jordan with the request by the Court for the arrest and surrender [of] Omar Al-Bashir"' (ICC-02/05-01109 of 16 July 2018).

you are, the less guilty you are'.[104] The same view is encored by Desalegn who argues that 'the process ICC is conducting in Africa has a flaw. The intention was to avoid any kind of impunity and ill governance and crime, but now the process has degenerated into some kind of race hunting'.[105] Accordingly, Taku states that international justice and the human rights system has never favoured Africans. He gives the example of the fact that those countries that created the UN and human rights instruments in pursuit of peace and protection of human rights 'turned their guns on Africa in its just struggle for recognition and a place among civilized nations'. This is one of the reasons for Africans to doubt international institutions. He shows

> [t]he paradox that these crimes against Africa intensified in the year of the adoption of the Universal Declaration of Human Rights in 1948 – and 1949 – the year of the Geneva Conventions – make Africa, more than any other continent, very sensitive to any form of discrimination.[106]

The issues of the nature of crimes are interwoven with peace versus justice, questionable investigations and prosecutorial discretion. Deya suggests for 'sequencing of peace with justice, start with resolving the conflict and then accountability, excluding one person such as a leader, makes the party disintegrates and more likely to become radical'.[107] Ping accuses the ICC of not being sensitive to whether its conduct can exacerbate conflicts in Africa or not.[108] Whiteley, in response to Roth's article in support of the ICC, argues that 'amnesties may be terrible compromises, but when there isn't any mechanism for arrest, wounded local communities are right to uphold them, and to be sceptical of foreign lawyers looking for glory'.[109] For Clarke,

> African submission to the ICC jurisdiction exists within political and 'structural' inequalities in the global arena, meaning that the ICC's involvement in Africa is

---

104 DW English: Conflict Zone, 'Justice and injustice in Rwanda' (2:52–22:13).

105 Euronews (in English), 'African Union accuses ICC of race hunt against Africans' [28 May 2013] https://www.youtube.com/watch?v=2rPfBEKAPvA; see also AFP News Agency, 'African Union opens talks to discuss ICC withdrawal' [11 October 2013] https://www.youtube.com/watch?v=H-Mqgv2ctYs).

106 Chief Charles Achaleke Taku 'Africa Question: Is the International Criminal Court (ICC) targeting Africa inappropriately?' [topic for March 2013–January 2014, http://iccforum.com/africa (paraphrased)].

107 ThinkingAfrica1, 'The clash between ICC and African Union on justice in Africa?' [Donald Deya interviewed, 13 November 2014] https://www.youtube.com/watch?v=Cbag0ps3DBo.

108 Sudan Tribune, 'African Union moves aggressively to shield Bashir from prosecution' [29 July 2010] http://www.sudantribune.com/spip.php?article35786; see also para. 3 of the AU Decision (Assembly/AU/Dec.245(XIII) Rev.1), 'Decision on the meeting of African States Parties to the Rome Statute of the International Criminal Court (ICC) Doc. Assembly/AU/13(XIII)' as adopted by the Thirteenth Ordinary Session of the Assembly in Sirte, Great Socialist People's Libyan Arab Jamahiriya on 3 July 2009 – Reservation entered by Chad.

109 'Compromise with Kony?' a reply by Jack Whiteley to Kenneth Roth [20 March 2014 Issue] http://www.nybooks.com/articles/2014/03/20/compromise-kony/].

> not simply a question of the ICC's targeting of Africa. Nor is it a matter of whether African states themselves participated in referring particular cases. Rather, it has to do with which crimes can be pursued, which agents can be held responsible (...).[110]

Clarke further argues that the kind of crimes under the Rome Statute do not address the root causes of conflicts in Africa, which leads to selective prosecution of Africans excluding their non-African accomplices – ICC crimes were designed in such a way that leaders from the global north should not be held accountable. She notes that

> the responsibility of contemporary violence goes well beyond that of an individual commander and cannot be addressed through a strategy that limits its practice to law alone. In fact, assigning criminal responsibility to a few representative persons – commanders, heads of state, leaders of rebel groups – obscures the link between Africa's resource crises and contemporary violence.[111]

Similarly, Kagame states that 'some leaders from African countries who are being tried by the ICC, whatever they are being tried for, [their crimes] have been committed in partnership with other countries, which the ICC don't try'.[112] Mamdani draws a distinction between political violence and criminal violence, and argues that most of the civil wars in Africa are political violence that needs political solutions; it is only criminal violence that needs criminal justice, but he contends that the current global order is not capable of providing a rule of law that can hold everybody accountable.[113]

The criticism about selective prosecution concerns both cases and situations, and is connected to allegations of external interferences. Arfi refers to the ICC as 'a joker card' for the powerful states to manipulate geo-political affairs in Africa.[114] Kagame states that '(...) international justice needs to be free of political interference, and to uphold the principle of sovereign equality of states,

110 Kamari Maxine Clarke, 'Africa Question: Is the International Criminal Court (ICC) targeting Africa inappropriately?' [Topic for March 2013–January 2014, http://iccforum.com/africa]; see also Kamari Maxine Clarke, 'Why Africa?' in Richard H. Steinberg (ed.), *Contemporary Issues Facing the International Criminal Court* (Brill/Nijhoff, 2016), 326–332, 326.

111 ibid, Clarke, 'Africa Question'.

112 Seen at Faisal Edroos, 'Rwanda's Paul Kagame accuses ICC of bias against Africa' [Al Jazeera, 29 April 2018] https://www.aljazeera.com/news/2018/04/rwanda-kagame-accuses-icc-bias-africa-180429050656022.html.

113 Al Jazeera, 'Upfront – Arena: Is the ICC biased against African Countries?' (Mahmood Mamdani).

114 Mediapart, 'Retour sur nos enquêtes: les secrets de la justice internationale' [4 October 2017] https://www.youtube.com/watch?v=-FIxo3Ps3Ls (14:45–14:50); see also TV5MONDE, 'Invité de la semaine du Journal Afrique: Justin Koné Katinan, le porte parole de Laurent Gbagbo' [1 November 2017] https://www.youtube.com/watch?v=ClzaflNfAY4; TV5MONDE, 'Gbagbo: le livre polémique sur la crise ivoirienne' [16 July 2014] https://www.youtube.com/watch?v=hEGewdYPXiA.

an objective Rwanda believes, the ICC has completely failed to accomplish'.[115] He concedes, however, that it was a weakness to expect the opposite. Kagame argues that it was a weakness on the side of Africa 'to not have seen this coming, and to have expected from the start that this would be done otherwise, that it would give justice, but as we know it, those behind it are looking at Africa not at themselves'.[116] Madonsela criticises the United Nations Security Council, the fact that non-state parties to the ICC Treaty take decisions against other states. He states that 'some of the world leaders are part of the judging but they're not bound by it. It's like saying: "I'll be the judge but me and my children will not be bound by it." It creates a very unhealthy dynamic'.[117] Kagame insists that

> the ICC problem is a serious problem for Africa and for the Africans, (…) talking about [it …], does not mean that wrong things don't happen in Africa, No, but we are saying by this, that wrong things happen in Africa as much as they happen elsewhere. (…) we cannot have a Court that targets Africans, (…) if it is an international Court, it should handle everybody, without fear, without favour.[118]

The anti-ICC rhetoric has also been directed against the conduct of some of its officials and the Prosecution's capacity to conduct sound investigations. On Kenyatta's inauguration, Museveni argued that 'I was one of those that supported the ICC because I abhor the impunity, however the usual opinionated and arrogant actors using their careless and shallow analysis have now distorted the purpose of that institution'.[119] On his own inauguration, acknowledging the presence of Bashir, Museveni repeated the criticisms of the ICC staff stating that, 'we lost interest in the ICC. The ICC is none of our business. It is a useless body. We had supported the ICC initially, thinking they were serious, but it is a bunch of useless people'.[120] The African Union expressed similar concerns 'over the conduct of the ICC Prosecutor, Mr. Moreno Ocampo' for what was described as his 'egregiously unacceptable, rude and condescending statements (…)'.[121]

---

115 Paul Kagame, 'President Kagame speaks out against ICC – Addis Ababa, 26 May 2013' [26 May 2013] https://www.youtube.com/watch?v=aWr5fU58h8c.

116 ibid.

117 Thuli Madonsela, South Africa's former anti-corruption chief, first seen in Karen Allen, 'Is this the end for the International Criminal Court?' [BBC News, 24 October 2016] http://www.bbc.com/news/world-africa-37750978.

118 President Kagame addresses Print and Broadcast Editors – Amahoro Stadium, 'President Paul Kagame addressing the question of Kenya Cases at ICC' [15 June 2013] https://www.youtube.com/watch?v=3e3LQ_3vu9c (1:24:30ff).

119 Kenya Citizen TV, 'Ugandan President Museveni Stirs Fresh ICC Debate' [9 April 2013] https://www.youtube.com/watch?v=3QrL-_X1vGo.

120 NBS TV Uganda, 'US Reacts to Museveni Swear In Comment of "ICC is Useless …"' [13 May 2016] https://www.youtube.com/watch?v=aSrjdgVN8Vw.

121 Para. 9, AU, 'Decision on the Progress Report of the Commission on the Implementation of Decision Assembly/AU/Dec.270 (XIV) on the second ministerial meeting on the Rome

The AU also blames the ICC top officials (Prosecutor, Registrar and President) for listening more to the NGOs than 'to positions of African Member States to the Rome Statute'.[122] Kagame noted that

> it is evident that political bias and flawed methodology are being deployed in the name of international justice, yet, ICC proponents are ostensibly deaf to increasingly vocal criticisms against the Court's bias about Africans. This is not acceptable and Africa must stand up to it and refuse to be intimidated, or bribed into inaction on this matter.[123]

Critics have threatened with a possible mass withdrawal of all African member states if there is no change in the Court's conduct towards Africa, a pronouncement that is still controversial among some states.[124] In an effort to find an African solution to African problems, in June 2014, member states of the African Union adopted a Protocol on Amendments to the Protocol on the Statute of the African Court of Justice and Human Rights giving criminal jurisdiction, some of which is similar to that of the ICC, to the African Court.[125] Kolade states that

> Africa has long suffered western imperialism and this would be a major move to end a modern racial warfare. Selective judgement would affect the perception of the court's integrity and if the court does not widen its tentacles to prosecute non-African cases, it would be seen as a biased imperialist court.[126]

Oryem, referring to a possible decision on withdrawal, stated that 'our argument has always been that there's a need for the whole of Africa to withdraw from the ICC. We hope that [this] matter will come up at the next AU summit and then we'll be able to pronounce ourselves'.[127]

---

Statute of the International Criminal Court (ICC) Doc. Assembly/AU/10(IX)' (adopted by the Fifteenth Ordinary Session of the Assembly of the Union on 27 July 2010 in Kampala, Uganda) Assembly/AU/Dec.296 (XV).

122 Para. 9, AU, 'Assembly/AU/Dec.590 (XXVI): Decision on the International Criminal Court (Doc.EX.CL/952 (XXVIII))'.

123 Paul Kagame, 'President Kagame speaks out against ICC- Addis Ababa, 26 May 2013'.

124 Controversial because not all African countries agree it is the best solution.

125 See the relevant information about the protocol at https://au.int/en/treaties/protocol-amendments-protocol-statute-african-court-justice-and-human-rights.

126 Habeeb Kolade, 'Is the ICC a Western Imperialist Tool Against Africa?' [Swali Africa, 26 December 2016] http://blog.swaliafrica.com/is-the-icc-a-western-imperialist-tool-against-africa/.

127 Okello Oryem, Uganda's junior foreign affairs minister, as quoted in the 'ICC debate: Africa vs "Infamous Caucasian Court"?' [Al Jazeera, 28 October 2016] https://www.aljazeera.com/news/2016/10/icc-debate-africa-infamous-caucasian-court-161028142708060.html.

### 2.1.3. THE NEED FOR DIALOGUE

These two tales (*Pro. vs. Opp.*) are clearly polarising, and even if there is a lot of exaggeration and misinformation on both sides, it is very difficult to dismiss either of them without responding to some of their views/concerns. Schein, in responding to 'why we have so many problems understanding each other (...)', states that 'the answer is that we are all culturally overtrained not only to think in terms of certain consensually validated categories but also to withhold information that would in any way threaten the current "social order"'.[128] The main question of curiosity is of understanding how each side could respond to the other's arguments. If arguers on both sides of this discussion were, for example, brought together in the same room for a dialogue, what could such a dialogue look like? Such an imagined dialogue between these two arguers is the focus of the next section. To quote Eskowich,

> a conversation in which the two parties have different beliefs should never begin with the intention of converting the other party to your own beliefs. Every worthwhile conversation's goal should be to understand the other person's opinions and help them understand your own.[129]

## 2.2. FROM MONOLOGUE TO DIALOGUE

The two tales above are an indication of the fact that the current narratives about the Court are more monologues – one way communications – than dialogues. The *Concise Oxford English Dictionary* defines a dialogue as a 'discussion directed towards exploration of a subject or resolution of a problem'.[130] The main purpose of a dialogue, as Schein notes, 'is to enable *the group* to reach a higher level of consciousness and creativity through the gradual creation of a shared set of meanings and a "common" thinking process'.[131] A dialogue creates trust among adversaries. Cowan and Arsenault note that, 'when people talk to one another they may learn about and learn from their different perspectives and experiences,

128 Edgar H. Schein, 'On Dialogue, Culture, and Organizational Learning' (1993) 22:2 Organizational Dynamics, 28; see also at p. 33 of the same source: 'we do not always perceive what is accurately out there, what we perceive is often based on our needs, our expectations, our projections, and, most of all, our culturally learned assumptions and categories of thought.'

129 Emily Eskowich https://www.goodreads.com/author/quotes/7390567.Emily_Eskowich.

130 Agnus Stevenson and Maurice Waite (ed.), *Concise Oxford English Dictionary* (12th ed., Oxford University Press, 2011), 396 (dialogue).

131 Schein, 'On Dialogue, Culture, and Organizational Learning', 30.

and they are affected by the knowledge (or belief) that their views are being taken into account'.[132]

This section is an imagined dialogue arising out of the different perspectives concerning the Court. It brings together competing views about the Court into the form of a dialogue. The role of the author is of a disinterested moderator. However, like any other moderator of a discussion involving different participants, he has an important role of alternatingly selecting speakers. In the same vein, since most of the speeches and texts are different standalone claims and sound-bites, the moderator's role is to bring them together to formulate a coherent argument. The fact that this dialogue is created out of different monologues means that, in some instances, it lacks some of the basic elements of a normal dialogue such as respect towards the opposing arguers, flexibility of ideas, and the desire to learn from the opposite side.[133] Nevertheless, saying that speakers are not engaged in a direct dialogue is not the same as saying that they are not listening to each other, or that they are not expecting to be listened to. As Wells notes,

> (...) whenever we speak, we necessarily enter into an ongoing dialogue, since we are always repeating or reacting to positions that others have already expressed, and our utterances are also shaped in expectation of the response of the person(s) to whom they are addressed.[134]

Therefore, it is hoped that bringing together these two perspectives will help in identifying some nuances, inconsistencies, hyperbole, half-truths, misunderstandings and irreconcilable positions in this ongoing debate.

Throughout the dialogue, the supporters of the Court are represented by (*Pro.*≈) whereas the critics are represented by (*Opp.*≈). It is difficult to label a certain perspective as a categorical position of '*anti*' or '*pro*' the Court, hence the use of an approximate symbol (≈) to each abbreviation. The dialogue is arranged according to some of the topics where the two narratives diverge. It is important

---

132 Geoffrey Cowan and Amelia Arsenault, 'Moving from Monologue to Dialogue to Collaboration: The Three Layers of Public Diplomacy' (2008) 616:1, 10–30 The ANNALS of the American Academy of Political and Social Science, 12.

133 For more on understanding the difference between a monologue and dialogue, see Margalit Toledano, 'Dialogue with the enemy: Lessons for public relations on dialogue facilitation drawn from the Israeli-Palestinian conflict' in Somerville Hargie, Margalit Toledano and Maureen Taylor, *International Public Relations* (Taylor and Francis, 2016), 27; Catherine O'Connor and Sarah Michaels, 'When Is Dialogue "Dialogic"?' (2007) 50, 275–285 Human Development, 277; Gordon Wells, 'Semiotic Mediation, Dialogue and Knowledge' (2007) 50, 244–274 Human Development, 255; Cowan and Arsenault, 'Moving from Monologue to Dialogue to Collaboration: The Three Layers of Public Diplomacy' (2008), 12–16.

134 ibid (Wells), 255.

to highlight that this dialogue is not concerned with legal arguments; it is more interested in narratives outside the courtroom rather than legal gimmicks.

### 2.2.1. THE ICC IS TARGETING AFRICA

*Opp.≈:* 'From the time of its inception, I said there was a fraud basis on which it was set up and how it was going to be used. I told people that this would be a court to try Africans, not people from across the world. (…) And I don't believe I have been proven wrong.'[135]

*Pro.≈*: 'There has never been an African bias and it will never be … it is actually the African countries coming to the ICC not the other way round.'[136] 'We are in Africa for two reasons; the most crimes under the ICC jurisdiction are in Africa, and African leaders joined ICC first. Again, African leaders requested the Court's intervention through self-referrals. (…) Most crimes are committed in Asia, Arab countries and Africa. ICC is not in Asia and Arab world, but in Africa.'[137] This is because 'Africa has experienced a large number of atrocities and, statistically speaking, the rate of atrocity crimes committed on the continent would make it a natural focus for the court anyway.'[138]

*Opp.≈:* 'Where is a white man convicted by this court? From the moment it started, are you telling me there are no crimes in parts where people have a light skin? We don't believe in that Court. (…) You are not going to convince me that African countries are sitting here with total independence to do what they want? [If you think so], we don't live in the same world. (…) Do you want me to give you cases where countries were trying to adhere to other organisations and they were told; if you don't adhere to the ICC you will not get say to the World Trade Organization. Come-on, you and I know the manipulation of international justice. It is a fact (…).'[139] 'The worst crimes are committed in the Middle East but of course the ICC will never be able to touch it because a certain member of the Security Council will not allow it to touch. It says something about the ICC, not just blaming the Security Council, the ICC promised us the rule of law, and the test of rule of law is that it should apply to everybody, particularly the most powerful. When the rule of law does not apply

135 Edroos, 'Rwanda's Paul Kagame accuses ICC of bias against Africa' (2018).

136 Interview with Fatou Bensouda, ICC Chief Prosecutor (International Bar Association) https://www.ibanet.org/Conferences/141435505.aspx (18:30–23:24).

137 Al Jazeera, 'Upfront – Arena: Is the ICC biased against African Countries?' (Moreno Ocampo).

138 Max du Plessis, Tiyanjana Maluwa and Annie O'Reilly, *Africa and the International Criminal Court* (Chatham House/International Law 2013/01), 2.

139 DW English: Conflict Zone, 'Justice and injustice in Rwanda' (19:04–21:28).

to the most powerful, then it is not rule of law, it is warlordism, it is the rule of the most powerful, Africa was taken for a ride.'[140]

*Pro.≈*: 'The idea that ICC jumps on Africa is wrong. African leaders asked us to help, but now those committing the crimes are prevailing. (…) when you have crimes, you have victims and criminals, the victims are Africans and criminals are Africans.'[141] 'Law is to protect citizens against rulers, not the other way round.'[142] 'Who will stand for the African victims when leaders conduct massive atrocities to stay in power?'[143] 'You believe there are no crimes in Darfur, Congo, Uganda? In these places we identify people who commit crimes, killing thousands of people, raping hundreds of women, so? I will not ignore these crimes. (…) I have a jurisdiction; I have to investigate crimes where no one else is doing it.'[144] 'I think it is neo-colonialism trying to protect those who commit massive atrocities because they are committed in Africa.'[145]

'The African countries have been the backbone of this Court, and their leadership, especially in the early days, was exemplary. In fact, it was often majestic. We knew only an Africa of courage and adherence to principle.'[146] 'Let me repeat this once more – the ICC is a court of last resort that is complementary to national jurisdictions. If every State prosecuted the crimes listed under the Statute, the ICC would have less work.'[147] 'The ICC is not about popularity, prejudices or media information, is about clear standards.'[148] 'The ICC is needed because victims on the continent don't have anywhere else to go. Africa should stop complaining and start fighting impunity, strengthen their systems and provide justice to victims.'[149]

*Opp.≈:* 'Africa has to complain about one thing, and that is the manipulation of international justice by politically powerful countries, [… that is] a reality.'[150] 'Impunity is a big problem not just in Africa, is a big problem on the other continents, and in several other countries, people get away with things,

140 Al Jazeera, 'Upfront – Arena: Is the ICC biased against African Countries?' (Mahmood Mamdani).

141 ibid, Moreno Ocampo.

142 Anonymous source.

143 Moreno Ocampo, as seen in Karen Allen, 'Is this the end for the International Criminal Court?' (2016).

144 Al Jazeera English, 'ICC questioned on policy in Africa' [5 December 2011] https://www.youtube.com/watch?v=fiuMAHes5s8 (Moreno Ocampo, 2:36–03:17).

145 ibid (Moreno Ocampo, 03:48–03:55).

146 Keynote speech by Zeid Ra'ad Al Hussein, United Nations High Commissioner for Human Rights (16 November 2016).

147 Speech of the President of the Assembly of States Parties, Mr. Sidiki Kaba, Fifteenth Session of the Assembly of States Parties (16 November 2016).

148 Waza Africa, 'Ocampo Exclusive: The first ICC prosecutor talks about the Kenyan trials' [6 February 2014] https://www.youtube.com/watch?v=tHBwQwUzgYo (23:40-24:23).

149 Human Rights Watch, 'African Union: Activists Challenge Attacks on ICC' [5 July 2016] https://www.youtube.com/watch?v=4sbgdFp0Pro.

150 DW English: Conflict Zone, 'Justice and injustice in Rwanda' (19:04–19:29).

George Bush and Tony Blair authored an illegal war, based on deliberately falsified information that has caused the death of hundreds of thousands and they still get away with it, that is not to say that the same should happen in Africa. It is just to be realistic to say that the Rome Statute was not built in a day, we will not perfect it in a day (…).'[151] 'The International Criminal Court from its own record of the work that has been done, since the Rome Statute was adopted, shows clearly with no shadow of a doubt, that it is a court created for Africans, and it is used mostly by Europe to manipulate African politics.'[152]

'The ICC did a strategic mistake by focusing solely on Africa, and African leaders, (…) the fact that it has so far a number of cases from Africa, it will be difficult for the ICC to expand to other places.'[153] 'We cannot support an ICC that carries out justice selectively, which has turned into an external political court or tool where external forces manipulate and control Africa.'[154] 'If this court is going to be serving some and not others, then let us not call it International.'[155] '[T]he flames of conflicts in Africa have been fanned to varying degrees by [northern] powers.'[156] 'It is acknowledged that, to date, international justice has not been and may never be equally applied, for the reason that the ICC is less likely to prosecute leaders of powerful states and those that they protect.'[157] 'What does seem clear from the bumps and pitfalls is that [… International Criminal Justice] is not – and can never be – normalized into a global rule of law. Put in other words, it cannot leapfrog over politics. To pretend otherwise is, in the strict sense, messianic thinking.'[158]

*Pro.≈*: 'Some of these criticisms are based on misunderstandings about the extent of the ICC's jurisdiction. (…) The blame for the ICC's failure to investigate serious situations in non-party states therefore lies not with the ICC but with the Security Council.'[159] 'Why bother about ICC selective prosecution, even assuming that it is true? So long as those who perpetrate heinous crimes in Africa are brought to book, it should be good for Africa, a continent still crippled by mass atrocities. Besides, the ICC is not meant or able to take

---

151 ThinkingAfrica1, 'The clash between ICC and African Union on justice in Africa?' (4:50–8:20).

152 DW English: Conflict Zone, 'Justice and injustice in Rwanda' (18:30–19:03).

153 PressTV Videos, 'Africa Today – ICC vs. African justice' [3 November 2013] https://www.youtube.com/watch?v=mkwfsUsSs8w (Phil Clark, 07:30–08:30).

154 Paul Kagame, 'President Kagame speaks out against ICC- Addis Ababa, 26 May 2013'.

155 DW English: Conflict Zone, 'Justice and injustice in Rwanda' (22:39–23:20).

156 Ovo Catherine Imoedemhe, *The Complementarity Regime of the International Criminal Court: National Implementation in Africa* (Springer, 2017), 148.

157 Imoedemhe, *The Complementarity Regime of the International Criminal Court: National Implementation in Africa* (2017), 150.

158 David Luban, 'After the Honeymoon: Reflections on the Current State of International Criminal Justice' (2013) 11, 505–515 Journal of International Criminal Justice, 508.

159 deGuzman, 'Africa Question: Is the International Criminal Court (ICC) targeting Africa inappropriately?' (2014).

over every case in every country.'[160] 'We are not saying that the ICC has been perfect in the way in which it conducts itself.'[161] 'It is far from being universally enforceable, it doesn't have jurisdiction across the world including the most powerful nations like US and others.'[162] 'We do have this problem of lack of territorial jurisdiction, and this must be recognized, we cannot just go to places that have not signed and ratified the Rome Statute.'[163] 'Just because the Council is incapable of not treating the Court as a judicial institution, it has to treat it as a political tool, which it does, it doesn't mean, we should allow the Court to be treated as a political tool. We need to protect the Court.'[164] 'It is absolutely false to say that the ICC is operating only in Africa, the reason people say that is because they have not realised the powers of preliminary examinations, for example in Colombia.'[165] 'This is a beginning; we needed to start somewhere, in 40 years it will change.'[166] 'We have already started moving out of Africa, [reference is ongoing preliminary examinations and investigations].'[167]

*Opp.≈:* 'Africa is not a third-rate territory of second-class peoples. We are not a project, or experiment of outsiders.'[168] 'We are not against international justice, it seems that Africa has become a laboratory to test the new international law.'[169] 'If you use a fraudulent mechanism or institution against somebody who needs to be held accountable, in the end you are not helping people understand whether this person needs to be held accountable. The mere fact is that the system and institution you are using has flaws.'[170] 'The manner in which the Court has been operating in particular its unfair treatment of Africans leaves much to be desired, apart from promoting justice and reconciliation, and

160 Mandiaye Niang, 'Africa and the Legitimacy of the ICC in Question' (2017) 17:4, 615–624 International Criminal Law Review, 619.

161 Human Rights Watch, 'African Union: Activists Challenge Attacks on ICC' (2016), Allan Ngari.

162 Human Rights Watch, 'African Union: Activists Challenge Attacks on ICC' (2016), Netsanet Belay.

163 TV3 Network Limited Ghana, 'Hot Issues with Fatou Bensouda ICC prosecutor -19/3/2016' [22 March 2016] https://www.youtube.com/watch?v=cUNFORWlQU4&feature=youtu.be (21:21–21:36).

164 Africa Group for Justice and Accountability, 'Panel I – Africa and the ICC: Misperceptions and Realities' Bill Pace, 56:57–57:22.

165 NYU: School of Law, 'IILJ: How Best to Assure the Independence of the ICC Prosecutor' ((2011) Hector Olasolo, 1:06:45–1:08:28).

166 Al Jazeera, 'Upfront – Arena: Is the ICC biased against African Countries?'.

167 TV3 Network Limited Ghana, 'Hot Issues with Fatou Bensouda ICC prosecutor -19/3/2016' (16:10–20:20).

168 Uhuru Kenyatta as quoted in Karen Allen, 'Is this the end for the International Criminal Court?' (2016).

169 Imoedemhe, *The Complementarity Regime of the International Criminal Court: National Implementation in Africa* (2017), 131.

170 Paul Kagame, see in Kezio-Musoke David, 'Kagame tells why he is against ICC charging Bashir' [Daily Nation, 3 August 2008] https://www.nation.co.ke/news/africa/1066-446426-7ulr1ez/index.html.

contributing to the advancing of peace and stability in our continent, the Court has transformed itself into a political instrument targeting Africa and Africans. This unfair and unjust treatment is totally unacceptable, and that is why we have been expressing our serious concerns against the ICC.'[171] 'Clearly, if the intensity and frequency of such abuses in Africa are at the very least not all that higher than on some other continents, and are in some respects even lower, then this tendency of the ICC to fly in a kind of geo-stationary orbit over only Africa cannot be explained simply by stating the obvious fact that such abuses do occur all too often in that region. Some other factors must also be at play in the production of such a biased outcome and that factor or those factors must be playing a more important, if not more critical role in circulating the punishing winds of ICC justice only towards African skies.'[172] 'With ICC all the injustices of the past including colonialism, imperialism, keep coming back in different forms. They control you. As long as you are poor and weak, there is always some rope to hang you. (…) ICC is made for Africans and poor countries.'[173]. 'Supporters of the ICC should be able to demonstrate that it is either distinct from, or has transcended, the ideas, institutions and practices of international law's colonial and racist past.'[174] Otherwise, 'you are going to see how African countries are one by one going to get out of this Court, if they were so happy, they would not (…) be getting out of this Court.'[175]

### 2.2.2. IMMUNITY OF HEADS OF STATE

*Opp.≈:* 'We've had to contend with the ICC pursuing weak, politicised cases. This has become a huge distraction from our duty to serve our people and this continent fully. That is not what Kenya signed up for when we joined the ICC.'[176] 'The Court (…) is problematic, (…) when the African Union said; "please allow African heads of state to run their countries and complete their term, then if you have something you can go after them", we were not listened to.'[177]

171 Tedros Adhanom Ghebreyesus as quoted in 'African Union opens talks to discuss ICC withdrawal' [AFP News Agency, 11 October 2013] available at https://www.youtube.com/watch?v=H-Mqgv2ctYs.

172 Obiora Chinedu Okafor and Uchechukwu Ngwaba, 'Between Tunnel Vision and a Sliding Scale: Power, Normativity and Justice in the Praxis of the International Criminal Court' (2017) 31:1, 179–194 Temple International and Comparative Law Journal, 189.

173 Kezio-Musoke, 'Kagame tells why he is against ICC charging Bashir' (2008).

174 Christopher Gevers, 'SA & the ICC: Justice, or "Just Us"?' [The Con, 18 November 2016] http://www.theconmag.co.za/2016/11/18/sa-the-icc-justice-or-just-us/.

175 DW English: Conflict Zone, 'Justice and injustice in Rwanda' (21:30–21:49).

176 Uhuru Kenyatta as quoted in ICC debate: Africa vs 'Infamous Caucasian Court'? (2016).

177 DW English: Conflict Zone, 'Justice and injustice in Rwanda´ (22:39–23:20).

*Pro.≈*: 'For us we don't care, the fact that we are investigating a president or vice president, Mr. Bashir is a president, Gaddafi was the leader of Libya, we really don't care, we don't think this way, we are criminal prosecutors; we look for the evidence, we try to follow the evidence, we try to prosecute the most responsible, that is the policy.'[178] 'Judicial processes should not be influenced by political circumstances, ICC follows evidence.'[179] 'African states knew (or should have known) what they were getting into when they signed the Rome Statute. An independent international court does undermine classical notions of sovereignty.'[180] 'In the past, the heads of state were able to commit crimes, and nothing happened to them, eventually they go to golden exile. Now, Mr. Gbagbo, a former head of a state is facing justice. This is a new time we are living in, no more crimes, no more atrocities, justice for people.'[181] 'To avoid prosecution, ruthless national leaders too often threaten, corrupt, or compromise judges and prosecutors at home, but those in The Hague should be beyond the reach of such obstructionism.'[182] 'I think this is very important for Côte d'Ivoire, the International Criminal Court is helping Côte d'Ivoire to identify whether Mr. Gbagbo was responsible for the crimes or not, to identify what happened there, establishing the role to help them live together, that is what the International Criminal Court is doing.'[183]

'The ICC is a powerful new tool to control violence in the world, to deter crimes, to promote national proceedings, but it can only be successful, if we never yield to political considerations. We are a new tool, a judicial tool, not a tool in the hands of politicians, who think they can use us when it is convenient or drop us when it is not (…).'[184] 'This immunity is going to incentivise these leaders to stay in power; it is a pervasive incentive to cling on power when you have committed these crimes.'[185] 'I believe that the ICC made a fundamental error not arresting and putting in prison Kenyatta and Ruto, and other Kenyan leaders who voluntarily handed themselves over. (…) People charged with crimes at the level of the jurisdiction of the ICC shouldn't be allowed to roam around free, (…) it may well be that Kenyatta and Ruto wouldn't be President

---

178 Waza Africa, 'Ocampo Exclusive: The first ICC prosecutor talks about the Kenyan trials' ((2014) 19:45–20:25).

179 Mariana Goetz on 'Inside Story – Is Africa snubbing the ICC?' (Al Jazeera English, 6 September 2013) available at https://www.youtube.com/watch?v=DfrA98MzoJM.

180 Editor's Choice (Kurt Mills, 'The International Criminal Court's Africa Problem' [Issue 6, 1 December 2017]; see also Kurt Mills and Alan Bloomfield, 'The African Resistance to the International Criminal Court: Halting the advance of anti-Impunity norm' (2018) 44:1 Review of International Studies, 101–127.

181 Al Jazeera English, 'ICC questioned on policy in Africa' ((2011), Moreno Ocampo).

182 Roth, 'Africa attacks the International Criminal Court' (2014).

183 Al Jazeera English, 'ICC questioned on policy in Africa' ((2011) Moreno Ocampo, 0:14–0:50).

184 '2012 VLS Charney Lecture – Reflections from ICC Prosecutor Fatou Bensouda' (26:30–28:00).

185 Africa Group of Justice and Accountability, 'PANEL VII: Immunity of Heads of State under International Law' (Max Du Plessis, 40:50–43:50).

and Deputy President today, because by the time they handed over themselves, they were not.'[186]

*Opp.≈:* 'You ignore the fact that 'there is also a duty to the country that elected the president that he should govern.'[187] 'Pathologising African leaders and employing the language of "gangs" or "Big Men" clubs, rely on populist if not racist preconceptions.'[188] 'Is there a crime to stay in office? Under which court? You are calling them criminals, impunity has to be linked to crime, what crime are you accusing all African leaders together?'[189] 'The African Union as a union of African peoples does not condone impunity, President Kenyatta and President Al Bashir, these are serving sitting presidents that enjoy immunity. Presidents should be respected as long as they are serving.'[190] 'This will also allow the leadership of Kenya to ensure that the Country does not slide back into the violence and instability.'[191]

### 2.2.3. THE AFRICAN CRIMINAL CHAMBER

*Opp.≈:* 'Africa don't believe in impunity, let us be serious, that is why we set up this African Court, that many other actors are trying to sabotage. We need to be serious about this (...); justice does not belong in one part of the world. Africa is very capable of dispensing justice; we have to admit we have been very slow to get this court to function properly. But the idea that Africans are criminals and the rest of the world, you all are clean, is just a fantasy.'[192]

*Pro.≈*: 'African solution to African problems. A solution, immunity for an African problem, a problem felt by leaders, African leaders, not a solution dreamt of or progressed by African victims. It is a solution that is pushed hard through AU and its lawyers; it is a solution for elites. (...) This protocol was signed in Malabo, Equatorial Guinea, where the President is Teodoro Obiang, who took power in 1971, 45 years ago and is still a president. (...) Of course, there are some progressive features of this statute, but really, let us not feature too much on those, it is a bit like trying to put lipstick on a pig.'[193]

---

186 Africa Group for Justice and Accountability, 'Panel I – Africa and the ICC: Misperceptions and Realities' (James A. Goldston, 7:26–9:10).

187 Al Jazeera English, 'Kenyan victims concerned as leaders seek ICC immunity' [12 October 2013] https://www.youtube.com/watch?v=UYTXccqEa-I (Amina Chawahir Mohamed Jibril).

188 Gevers, 'SA & the ICC: Justice, or "Just Us"?' (2016).

189 DW English: Conflict Zone, 'Justice and injustice in Rwanda' (23:21–23:48).

190 Africanews, 'AU urges ICC to respect the immunity of sitting African presidents' [29 January 2016] https://www.youtube.com/watch?v=0rKIEYCXszM (Julia Dolly Joiner, 0:20–0:42).

191 SABC Digital News, 'Sitting heads of state should not be tried in the ICC – AU' [12 October 2013] https://www.youtube.com/watch?v=Z3G79RBQotc (Nkosazana Dlamini-Zuma).

192 DW English: Conflict Zone, 'Justice and injustice in Rwanda' (23:50–24:24).

193 Africa Group of Justice and Accountability, 'PANEL VII: Immunity of Heads of State under International Law' (Max Du Plessis, 40:50–43:50).

*Opp.≈:* You seem to forget that 'there were already some activities of accountability of international crimes on the African continent before the coming of the ICC.'[194] On the African continent 'we do get some successes, some forward movement, some progress by working at the international level, with the UN (Security Council), even with the ICC and we also do get some successes by working at the African Union level, or working in the regional economic communities, and all this should be taken into context. For instance people forget that in case of Kenya, early 2008, Kenya was totally going to explode, and it is the African Union that saved Kenya (...).'[195] 'While the ongoing tension between the AU and the ICC has accelerated its establishment, the discussions among African leaders on an African Criminal Court precede this tension.'[196]

### 2.2.4. THE ICC HAS AFRICAN OFFICIALS

*Pro.≈*: 'Phakiso Mochochoko's appointment as the Director of the International Criminal Court's Jurisdiction, Complementarity and Cooperation Division (JCCD) in the Office of the Prosecutor is an achievement for Africa's efforts to combat impunity, but more importantly, it is an opportunity to improve Africa's ailing relations with the ICC and the ability of African governments to work with rather than against the court.'[197] 'The ICC should therefore continue and perhaps increase its efforts to combat such perceptions. Appointing an African prosecutor was an important step in this direction.'[198] 'There is no truth in any kind of anti-Africanism against Africa by the ICC. (...) I would (...) like to tell you about the personnel of the ICC. I am the chief prosecutor of the ICC and the last time I checked, I am African.'[199] 'Any time, I hear this about ICC targeting

---

194 PressTV Videos, 'Africa Today – ICC vs. African justice' ((2013), Phil Clark, 12:10–13:40).

195 ThinkingAfrica1, 'The clash between ICC and African Union on justice in Africa?'

196 Abel S. Knottnerus and Eefje de Volder, 'International Criminal Justice and the Early Formation of an African Criminal Court' in Kamari M. Clarke, Abel S. Knottnerus and Eefje de Volder (eds.), *Africa and the ICC: Perceptions of Justice* (Cambridge University Press, 2016) 394.

197 Ottilia Maunganidze and Antoinette Louw, 'An African Advantage: ICC's New Head of Jurisdiction, Complementarity and Cooperation' [Institute for Security Studies, 9 February 2011] https://issafrica.org/iss-today/an-african-advantage-iccs-new-head-of-jurisdiction-complementarity-and-cooperation.

198 deGuzman, 'Africa Question: Is the International Criminal Court (ICC) targeting Africa inappropriately?' (2014).

199 Fatou Bensouda, ICC Prosecutor, responding to the Question, '... *is there any truth about the anti-Africanism of the ICC?*' on Abu-Bakarr Jalloh, Mohammed Khelef, 'Fatou Bensouda: Critics "don't understand the ICC"' [DW, 11 April 2017] http://www.dw.com/en/fatou-bensouda-critics-dont-understand-the-icc/a-38372198.

Africa, ICC doing double justice (standards); it saddens me, especially as an African woman.'[200]

*Opp.≈:* 'You mean no African can serve the interests of other places other than Africa? (...) is it unheard of?'[201] 'To identify Africans in the court's leadership is a red herring. A black president, attorney general and senior judges in the US has hardly stopped that country and its criminal justice system reproducing systemic racism. (...), institutional biases don't require an overt agenda.'[202] 'Africa seemed the perfect target for the ICC's first cases. The (...) involvement was made easier by a history of Africa being represented as a terrain of barbaric violence, of savages committing atrocities against victims in need of a Western saviour. This humanitarian image fit squarely with the international court's stark moral narrative of inhuman criminals and helpless innocents.'[203] 'Just because the ICC has a few black judges doesn't mean they're not susceptible to manipulation, rather their "blackness" is a tool used to circumvent any criticism.'[204] 'Insisting that Bensouda doesn't have a biased agenda is very different from suggesting that the court, and her office in particular, are subject to political pressures – pressures that militate, if not towards targeting Africa, then certainly against pursuing extra-African crimes in which the world's major powers are implicated.'[205]

## 2.3. OBSERVATIONS ON THE DIALOGUE

Clarke persuasively explains how each side of the dialogue is pursuing a long struggle that started many decades before the creation of the Court. For the critics, it is about pan-Africanism, anti-slavery, anti-colonialism, anti-imperialism and anti-racism. Basically, everything against the northern 'and others' domination of Africa. For the supporters, it is a struggle against impunity of international crimes.[206] I believe that these two struggles are equally important and worth fighting. The difficult question is whether both battles can be won concurrently in the current situation. It is clear that each side

200 'Bensouda- ICC Protecting Africans, Not Targeting Them' [AllAfrica, 3 July 2011] at Global Policy Forum https://www.globalpolicy.org/international-justice/the-international-criminal-court/general-documents-analysis-and-articles-on-the-icc/50411-bensouda-icc-protecting-africans-not-targeting-them.html.

201 DW English: Conflict Zone, 'Justice and injustice in Rwanda' (20:00–20:11).

202 Krever, 'Africa in the Dock: On ICC Bias' (2016).

203 Adam Branch, 'The ICC can't live with Africa, but it can't live without it either' [The Conversation, 14 March 2017] http://theconversation.com/the-icc-cant-live-with-africa-but-it-cant-live-without-it-either-74210.

204 Edroos, 'Rwanda's Paul Kagame accuses ICC of bias against Africa' (2018).

205 Krever, 'Africa in the Dock: On ICC Bias' (2016).

206 Clarke, 'International Justice and the Politics of Sentimentality' (2016) 78–103.

believes in its social power and collective resolve to achieve its goals without compromise, even if it is also clear that some collaboration is inevitable. On the side of the supporters, there is no statement that better carries the belief of collective (social) power and the continuation of an age-old struggle than that of Max Du Plessis regarding the failure to arrest ICC suspects and Ali Bashir in particular. In concluding his statement, he noted that:

> We have got to do that which lawyers in international criminal justice have done for years, and that is to recognize that you have got to be patient, being patient. The law in this context is patiently waiting, to ultimately do its work in respect to these officials. As Adolf Eichmann did, 15 years after he has been hiding, and eventually the prosecutors caught up with him, and as they found him, 15 years later, his first reported words to them were: 'I have been waiting for you.' He knew they would eventually come, and the same is true for President Bashir, he can run, he can hide, he can have his lawyers do whatever they want, but at the end of the day, the law will eventually catch up with him. And then too, he will get a chance to turn around and say: 'I have been waiting for you' because 'we have been waiting for him.'[207]

His [Max Du Plessis] use of '*we*' is what Tallgren, quoting Spiegelberg, refers to as 'part of the "arrogance of power" behind the patronizing usurpation of the right to speak for the "free" people of the world, when they have never been asked'.[208] He knows for sure that he is not speaking on behalf of the whole international community, nor does he believe that all lawyers of international criminal justice agree with him. His insistence that 'the law will eventually catch up with him' is a belief in uncompromising interpretation of laws. This is a form of rhetorical coercion, a strategy of silencing the opponent from contributing an alternative idea by closing the debate.[209] Barnett and Finnemore argue that

> [w]hen bureaucrats do something contrary to your interests or that you do not like, they defend themselves by saying 'Sorry, those are the rules' or 'just doing my job.' 'The rules' and 'the job' are the source of great power in modern society.[210]

---

[207] Africa Group of Justice and Accountability, 'PANEL VII: Immunity of Heads of State under International Law' (Max Du Plessis, 44:12–45:00).

[208] Immi Tallgren, 'The Voice of the International: Who is Speaking?' (2015) 13:1, 135–155 Journal of International Criminal Justice, 135 (see at fn 1), quoting H. Spiegelberg, Doing Phenomenology (Martinus Nijhoff, 1975), 215.

[209] See 'Winning the War of Position through Strategic Rhetorical Balancing' in Jack Holland and Mike Aaronson, 'Dominance through Coercion: Strategic Rhetorical Balancing and the Tactics of Justification in Afghanistan and Libya' (2014) 8:1, 1–20 Journal of Intervention and Statebuilding, 2–6; see also Maria Varaki, 'Revisiting the 'Interests of Justice' Policy Paper' (2017) 15:3, 457–458 Journal of International Criminal Justice; Steven L. Winter, 'The Cognitive Dimension of the Agon between Legal Power and Narrative Meaning' (1989) 87:8 The Michigan Law Review, 2225–2279; Blackledge, 'Discourse and Power' (2012).

[210] Michael N. Barnett and Martha Finnemore, 'The Politics, Power, and Pathologies of International Organizations' (1999) 53:4 International Organization, 708.

The same '*we*' is also used by the critics of the Court, and they too ought to know that not all Africans or African leaders agree with them. The fact that both sides know (or at least are expected to know) that their views are not universally shared should ordinarily have been a reason for them to be modest. This is because the insistence that the ICC should focus on a strict interpretation of laws without considering other factors is unwinnable, just as a massive withdrawal of African member states is unforeseeable.

The purpose of this chapter has been that of teasing out a dialogue and seeing whether it is possible to identify some nuances, hyperbole and shared views on which a normal negotiation can be reached between these two interlocutors. As MacCormick notes,

> [w]hen we think about how to argue over matters of practice, morality as much as law, we do notice that, while on some points we can hold quite conclusively that 'that view is wrong', on many other points there remain open questions where, so far as we can judge in practical terms, both views, or more than one view, is reasonable.[211]

With that in mind, the following are some of the observations on the above dialogue.

### 2.3.1. CONFLICTING INTERESTS

Both the critics and supporters have approached the analysis of the ICC and its work as something that always comes with a set of loyalties, which are at times conflicting. For instance, on the side of the supporters, if your arguments are supporting the Court, it means that you are supporting justice for victims against perpetrators of international crimes. On the other side, if your views are critical of the Court, it means that you are denying justice to the victims and supporting despotic leaders, who kill their own citizens. In the same vein, if you express views that are supportive of the Court, you are supporting imperialism – hegemonic powers – against weak countries especially those in Africa. The main cause of the dilemma is that there is some truth in all these statements because a choice will, in most cases, produce more than one effect. You could be supporting the ICC because it is dealing with some of the existing impunity gaps, regardless of its shortcomings, but doing so is subsequently contributing to its shortcomings, including the possible manipulation of justice by the powerful states. You could be criticising the Court because you genuinely believe that it is not providing the justice people hoped for when it was first

---

[211] Neil MacCormick, *Rhetoric and the Rule of Law: A Theory of Legal Reasoning* (Oxford University Press, 2010), 278.

created, but doing so would be indirectly undermining the only available permanent mechanisms that could punish perpetrators of serious crimes.

Being loyal to a certain cause or group (family, community, nation or organisation) is a good thing in itself. As Ent and Baumeister note 'obedience per se is helpful and perhaps indispensable for effective functioning of human society'.[212]

> Loyalty binds people together. (...) a person who has no loyalty whatsoever to anything or anyone (...) would feel no devotion to any higher cause or principle – like truth or justice. (...) A life like that would be empty, devoid of many of the things that make us fully human.[213]

However, the more strongly one becomes loyal towards something the more likely it is that he or she will move away from reason; he or she loses the capacity to search for truth and starts acting according to his/her emotions (feelings). Sellers argues that whereas the standard of reason is truth and its subject is reality, willing to change if it is discovered that what it believed to be true is false, emotions are feelings that animate the purpose of our lives, and are driven by anger, disgust, happiness, harmony or justice.[214]

There are different reasons as to why people can be loyal to different things at the same time including those that might be having conflicting interests,[215] but as Rorty notes, '[t]he tougher things get, the more ties of loyalty to those near at hand tighten and those to everyone else slacken'.[216] The challenge is that legal institutions ought to consider both reason and emotions (sentiments). Lee notes that law issues 'are inextricably bound up with morality or justice', (...) law reflects to a considerable extent the moral standards of the community in which it operates'.[217] Similarly, Sellers argues that 'law gains legitimacy and effectiveness when it marries reason with emotion, that reason and human emotion are the guiding values of any just legal system (...)'.[218] The intricate

---

212 Michael R. Ent and Roy F. Baumeister, 'Obedience, Self-Control, and the Voice of Culture' (2014) 70:3 The Society for the Psychological Study of Social Issues, 575.

213 For a philosophical talk on loyalty, see https://www.philosophytalk.org/blog/loyalty.

214 Mortimer N.S. Sellers, 'Law, Reason, and Emotion' in Marcelo Campos Galuppo and others (eds.), *Human Rights, Rule of Law and the Contemporary Social Challenges in Complex Societies: Proceedings of the 26th World Congress of the International Association for Philosophy of Law and Social Philosophy in Belo Horizonte, 2013* (Franz Steiner Verlag, 2015), 71–87.

215 Elizabeth Kang, 'Conflicting Loyalties Theory: A Cross-Cultural Test' (1976) 15:2, 201–202 Ethnology; Henk Flap, 'The Conflicting Loyalties Theories' (1997) 47:1 L'Année sociologique, 184; Susan A. Bandes, 'Loyalty to One's Convictions: The Prosecutor and Tunnel Vision' (2006) 49, 475 Howard Law Journal.

216 Richard Rorty, 'Justice as a Larger Loyalty' (1997) 4:2 Ethical Perspectives, 139.

217 Simon Lee, *Law and Morals: Warnock, Gillick and Beyond* (Oxford University Press, 1986), 18 (also quoting Atiyah).

218 Sellers, 'Law, Reason, and Emotion' (2015) 71; see also Rorty, 'Justice as a Larger Loyalty' (1997), 140.

question is whether one can support the ICC and not support imperialism, or if it is possible to criticise the ICC without supporting impunity? It is possible because these loyalties are a bit exaggerated, I argue. For instance, you might not support the idea of completely abandoning the Court, and at the same time strongly believe that it needs to seriously examine its ways of working. As Sellers notes, '[i]t is not enough to say that a law is valid according to the terms of the legal system that promotes it. People must also accept that the legal system itself is legitimate before they will defer to its judgments'.[219] Rawls' view is that 'laws and institutions no matter how efficient and well-arranged must be reformed or abolished if they are unjust'.[220]

The reason I suggest that the above loyalties are exaggerated is that it cannot be true that all victims or suspected perpetrators of international crimes want one thing, that victims necessarily want criminal prosecution and in particular at the ICC, or that all suspected perpetrators are against being tried before the Court. The current reality is at least not conclusive on those positions. The communities of Northern Uganda, the supposed victims of the Lord's Resistance Army (LRA)'s conflict, were the ones who opposed the ICC involvement in preference to a peace process. Uhuru Kenyatta and William Ruto were elected in Kenya when they were already under the ICC indictment. I am not saying that these two cases necessarily prove that victims of crime did not want justice or the ICC, I am simply pointing out that it is much more complicated; it is not black and white. The case of Saif Al-Islam Gaddafi of Libya is another interesting example; lawyers pleaded on his behalf for transfer to the ICC for trial instead of Libya.[221] Another controversial issue is to know who speaks on behalf of the victims; Niezen argues that '*[p]ublics are persuadable.* (...) Even though some publics are adamantine in their beliefs, all are to varying extents subject to influence, if not persuasion'.[222] Without saying that the ICC does not consider the interests of victims or that it is completely free of influence from hegemonic powers, it could be said that supporters of the Court are instrumentalising the abstract notion of 'victims' for purposes of gaining legitimacy through the emotion of compassion, as well as some critics might be instrumentalising imperialism to appeal to feelings of some Africans who are still nursing the bad memories of colonialism.

---

219 ibid, Sellers, 82–83.

220 John Rawls, *A Theory of Justice* (Harvard University Press, 1973), 3.

221 The Appeals Chamber, in the case of *Prosecutor v. Saif Al-Islam Gaddafi*, 'Judgment on the Appeal of Libya against the decision of Pre-Trial Chamber I of 31 May 2013 entitled "Decision on the admissibility of the case against Saif Al-Islam Gaddafi"' (ICC-01/11-01/11 OA4 of 21 May 2014.

222 Ronald Niezen, *Public Justice and the Anthropology of Law* (Cambridge University Press, 2010), 37.

The dialogue will be possible when both sides agree that the issue of discussion is not whether perpetrators of heinous crimes ought to be punished, but about the appropriateness of the current legal system. The conversation has to be moved from the 'ideal' Court that was envisioned in Rome to the 'real one' operating since July 2002.

### 2.3.2. AN '*AD HOMINEM*' ARGUMENT

Whereas critics insist that the Court is a 'neo-imperialist tool' behind the veil of international criminal justice,[223] its supporters have focused on discrediting its opponents describing them as dictators and potential indicts of the Court merely interested in self-preservation. Therefore, it is fair to argue that speakers on both sides are conducting an *ad hominem* argument. An *ad hominem* argument is known as 'an argument that constitutes a personal attack or relates to personal matters instead of addressing the merits of the relevant issue'.[224] This is a well-known strategy in rhetorical arguments.[225] However, this kind of counter-argument can be criticised as a tactical way of avoiding the real issues raised – focusing on arguers instead of their arguments – as if it is always true that a discredited speaker can never make a credible argument. For instance, one participant in a conference organised by the Africa Group for Justice and Accountability, a group composed of senior African experts in international criminal law and human rights law, that came together principally to address the issues concerning the relationship between ICC and Africa, gave a courteous warning to the group members. He stated that:

> I was a bit horrified, and I don't want to say who, when one member of the group, speaking in the capacity as a member of the group, not in his own capacity, describing AU and African initiatives to pull-out of the ICC as a club of dictators trying to protect themselves and their friends. Such messages coming out of the group have the potential to completely inflame the situation, and I think you have to package your message properly.[226]

---

223 See e.g. Imoedemhe, *The Complementarity Regime of the International Criminal Court: National Implementation in Africa* (2017), 124–125.

224 Arron Fellmeth and Maurice Horwitz, (*Argumentum ad hominem*) *Guide to Latin in International Law* (Oxford University Press, 2009).

225 Alan Brinton, 'A rhetorical view of the *ad hominem*' (1985) 63:1 Australasian Journal of Philosophy, 50–63; Lawrence M. Hinman, 'The case for ad hominem arguments' (1982) 60:4 Australasian Journal of Philosophy, 338–345; D.N. Walton, 'Argumentation Schemes and Historical Origins of the Circumstantial Ad Hominem Argument' (2004) 18:3 Argumentation, 359–368.

226 Africa Group for Justice and Accountability, 'CLOSING REMARKS: Africa Group for Justice and Accountability on conclusions and lessons learnt' [25 October 2016] https://www.youtube.com/watch?v=go1mjEutvFg (Participant, 19:55–20:59).

It is perfectly legitimate to question the credibility of your enemies. However, the same self-interested argument labelled against critics can as well be used against supporters, who are mainly the ICC officials, members of NGOs and international criminal law lawyers among others, self-interested in the existing revolving doors – as commonly referred to as 'friends of the Court'. Lohne argues that there is constant flow of experts between the Court, NGOs, international law lawyers and scholars, and vice versa.[227] Therefore, one could argue that those supporting the Court are doing so to protect their interests in working with the Court. Kiyani argues that '[t]he insistence that states' views are self-interested (and thus irrelevant) contradicts an essential element of international law-making, particularly in the global South, where the struggle for decolonisation and self-determination is still seen as incomplete'.[228] Again, *ad hominem* is an easy way to discredit an argument. And in case of the ICC, it obscures the fact that critics are not only those referred to as 'despotic politicians' because the situation of Northern Uganda indicates that it was the local communities and religious leaders who were more opposed to the prosecution of the Lord's Resistance Army (LRA), in favour of peace talks, and not the Government.[229]

### 2.3.3. THE ICC IS NOT PERFECT

The arguers on both sides agree that the International Criminal Court is not perfect. However, they disagree on the way forward. Caution needs to be taken because there is no perfect legal system. No national legal system is perfect, nor is the African continental system nor the American nor the European. Therefore, it would be difficult to expect it from a Court that is a mixture of existing systems. The International Criminal Court is a totally new system. However, it is curious to know whether it is learning lessons and willing to adapt.

Nonetheless, each side of the debate seems to prescribe different solutions. Whereas critics are calling for some fundamental changes or a massive withdrawal,

---

227 Kjersti Lohne, 'Global Civil Society, the ICC, and Legitimacy in International Criminal Justice' in Nobuo Hayashi and Cecilia M. Bailliet (eds.), *The Legitimacy of International Criminal Tribunals* (Cambridge University Press, 2017), 449–472.

228 Asad Kiyani, 'Legitimacy, Legality, and the Possibility of a Pluralist International Criminal Law' in Nobuo Hayashi and Cecilia M. Bailliet (eds.), *The Legitimacy of International Criminal Tribunals* (Cambridge University Press, 2017), 100–101.

229 Ramesh Thakur, 'International Criminal Justice: At the Vortex of Power, Norms and a Shifting Global Order' in Charles Sampford and Ramesh Thakur (eds.), *Institutional Supports for the International Rule of Law* (Routledge, 2015), 35; Anna Macdonald, '"In the interests of justice?" The International Criminal Court, peace talks and the failed quest for war crimes accountability in northern Uganda' (2017) 11:4 Journal of Eastern African Studies, 628–648; Bartłomiej Krzan, 'International Criminal Court Facing the Peace vs. Justice Dilemma' (2016) 2:2 International Comparative Jurisprudence, 85.

supporters see whatever failures of the Court as a learning curve – something inevitable for a young institution – and are hoping that it will progressively self-correct. To use Funk's words 'whatever the Court's present deficiencies (...), the answer is not to give up on it, or, even worse, to seek to chop it down'.[230] Whereas supporters argue that most of the Court's failures – such as focusing on Africa and not intervening in other equally worthy situations – should be blamed on the UNSC, which has politicised the Court, critics see the ICC and the Security Council as aimed at one thing – domination of Africa. Wenaweser, the former President of the Assembly of States Parties, reflecting on a conversation he had with Jean Ping, the former chairman of the African Union, stated that:

> The Court did not target Africa, the UNSC created the jurisdiction, the Court just looked at the evidence, and said here is the law, here is my evidence, here are my conclusions, submitted to the judges, the judges said yes you are right, and that is it, it is a judicial process. (...) But when I say that to Jean Ping, he says, 'I don't care, UNSC or ICC is all the same, it is all you white people'.[231]

It is fair to say that there is some truth on both sides. Follesdal argues that '[i]n exploring the legitimacy of international courts it is necessary to decide about the appropriate unit of analysis. Courts can be seen either in isolation, or as a part of the global basic structure'.[232] The Rome Statute created a justice system and allocated different roles to different actors: the role of the Assembly of States Parties (ASP) is different from that of the United Nations Security Council (UNSC), as it is different from that of the Court, and that of an individual state parties. Therefore, it could be wrong, for example, to blame the ICC, a judicial body, for a certain country (state party)'s refusal/failure to arrest a certain suspect duly indicted. However, taking the Court as part of the whole justice system that was created in Rome, where these different actors were expected to act as pillars on which this justice system stands, it should be reasonable to argue that failures or weaknesses of one pillar in this framework are reflected on the whole. It could be true that most of the shortcomings can be attributed to those other actors, in particular the UNSC, but since the Court is at the forefront of the system, we should not be surprised when it becomes the target of criticism. The Court cannot divorce itself from the whole system.

---

230 T. Markus Funk, *Victims' Rights and Advocacy at the International Criminal Court* (2nd ed., Oxford University Press, 2015), 4.

231 NYU: School of Law, 'IILJ: How Best to Assure the Independence of the ICC Prosecutor' ((2011) Christian Wenaweser, 1:28:50–1:29:30).

232 Andreas Follesdal, 'Kant, Human Rights, and Courts' in Andreas Follesdal and Reidar Maliks, (eds.), *Kantian Theory and Human Rights* (Routledge, 2013), 195.

## 2.3.4. AFRICA'S INFLUENCE IN ROME

This statement is flattering to say the least. It is an exaggeration to describe whatever contribution African countries might have made during the Rome Treaty negotiations as influential. Most African countries were represented by fewer than five delegates, and among those counted as African delegates were, as Roger notes, 'graduate students and faculty members belonging to US or western European law schools'[233] and NGOs acting as technical assistants. This was in contrast to other countries such as the United States, France and Italy which had over 50 delegates each.[234] Nouwen puts it thus:

> Most of the negotiations on the Rome Statute did not take place in the plenary, but in dozens of small monolingual groups, all addressing some small element of the Statute. In these discussions, states occupied *different* positions due to different sizes of delegations, different abilities to negotiate in the dominant language and different invitations to meetings.[235]

She further states that '[a]s a result, many informal consultations were conducted only among Western states'.[236] Therefore, suggesting that it was possible for African participants to effectively attend and influence decisions in different sessions taking place simultaneously in different rooms is hyperbolic. This is not to dispute the role that might have been played by some African countries and notable leaders such as Nelson Mandela. However, making a general statement supporting the idea of establishing a permanent international criminal court is different from being influential on the current nature of international criminal justice. Again, the question here is not about whether international criminal justice is worthwhile, as Niang notes, 'none of [those who criticise the Court] rejects the idea of international criminal justice in principle. They question instead the prosecution's strategy and the political influence which they believe that shapes it'.[237]

233 Damien Rogers, *Law, Politics and the Limits of Prosecuting Mass Atrocity* (Palgrave Macmillan, 2018), 176.

234 United Nations, 'United Nations Diplomatic Conference of Plenipotentiaries on the Establishment of an International Criminal Court' (Rome, 15 June–17 July 1998) Official Records Volume II Summary records of the plenary meetings and of the meetings of the Committee of the Whole (A/CONF.183/13 (Vol.11)) – see the list of delegates circulated under the symbol A/CONF. 183/INF/5 and Corr. 1.

235 Nouwen, 'Legal Equality on Trial: Sovereigns and Individuals before the International Criminal Court' (2013), 12.

236 ibid.

237 Niang, 'Africa and the Legitimacy of the ICC in Question' (2017), 619–620.

### 2.3.5. IMMUNITY OF HEADS OF STATE

Undoubtedly, immunity of sitting heads of state, especially of non-state parties, is still a much contested issue on which there is little room for compromise. First, the existing sporadic Court decisions cannot be considered as sufficiently strong evidence to have changed the existing customary law. For instance, in December 2011, the Pre-Trial Chamber I (against Malawi and Chad) determined that customary international law excludes immunity of heads of state if sought by international tribunals/courts.[238] This decision was abandoned in 2014, when the Pre-Trial Chamber II (against the Democratic Republic of Congo) determined that it is the UN Security Council Resolution 1593 (2005) referring the situation of Darfur to the Court that waived Bashir's immunities.[239] In 2017, the Pre-Trial Chamber II (against South Africa), still referring to the same UNSC Resolution 1593 (2005), determined that the said resolution associates Sudan with state parties, thus renouncing all immunities as provided for in the Rome Statute.[240] It is this same reasoning (as in the case of South Africa) that was used against the Hashemite Kingdom of Jordan.[241] However, unlike South Africa, Jordan has decided to appeal the Pre-Trial Chamber II's decision that found it to have failed to comply with the request to cooperate in arresting President Bashir when he was on its territory attending the Arab League meeting. Following the 'Order inviting expressions of interest as *amici curiae* in judicial proceedings'[242] different scholars, the Arab League and the African Union have submitted diverging views. Whereas the scholars differ in many aspects, it is important to highlight that Jordan, the Arab League and African Union unanimously support the existence of President Bashir's immunity.[243] It is also interesting to note

---

238 *Prosecutor v. Omar Al-Bashir*, 'Decision Pursuant to Article 87(7) of the Rome Statute on the Failure by the Republic of Malawi to Comply with the Cooperation Requests Issued by the Court with Respect to the Arrest and Surrender of Omar Hassan Ahmad Al Bashir' (ICC-02/05-01/09) of 12 December 2011; *Prosecutor v. Omar Al-Bashir*, 'Decision pursuant to article 87(7) of the Rome Statute on the refusal of the Republic of Chad to comply with the cooperation request issued by the Court with respect to the arrest and surrender of Omar Hassan Ahmad Al Bashir' (ICC-02/05-01/09) of 13 December 2011.

239 *Prosecutor v. Omar Al-Bashir*, 'Decision on the Cooperation of the Democratic Republic of the Congo Regarding Omar Al Bashir's Arrest and Surrender to the Court' (ICC-02/05-01/09) of 9 April 2014.

240 *Prosecutor v. Omar Al-Bashir*, 'Decision under article 87(7) of the Rome Statute on the non-compliance by South Africa with the request by the Court for the arrest and surrender of Omar Al-Bashir' (ICC-02/05-01/09) of 6 July 2017.

241 *Prosecutor v. Omar Al-Bashir*, 'Decision under article 87(7) of the Rome Statute on the non-compliance by Jordan with the request by the Court for the arrest and surrender or Omar Al-Bashir' (ICC-02/05-01/09) of 11 December 2017.

242 *Prosecutor v. Omar Al-Bashir*, 'Order inviting expressions of interest as amici curiae in judicial proceedings (pursuant to rule 103 of the Rules of Procedure and Evidence)' (No. ICC-02/05-01/09 OA2) of 29 March 2018.

243 *Prosecutor v. Al Bashir*, 'The African Union's Submission in the "Hashemite Kingdom of Jordan's Appeal Against the 'Decision under Article 87(7) of the Rome Statute on the

that whereas the order specifically requested 'the United Nations, the African Union, the European Union, the League of Arab States and the Organization of American States to submit their observations', it is only the African Union and the League of Arab States that have done so. The silence of these other inter-governmental organisations remains difficult to interpret.

Second, arresting a sitting head of state poses some practical and diplomatic challenges. It is difficult to imagine a country that would be willing to champion the practice of arresting a serving head of state. It would need a lot of courage considering the possible diplomatic and political ramifications it would create between the two countries. Köchler notes that 'negating immunity from prosecution even for incumbent heads of state, is a cause of potential conflicts and contradictions between legal obligations also of state parties, as has become evident especially in African diplomacy'.[244] In January 2018, the Assembly of the African Union States resolved to 'place on the agenda of the United Nations General Assembly a request to seek an advisory opinion from the International Court of Justice on the question of immunities of a Head of State and Government and other Senior Officials (...)' under international law.[245] The Ambassador and Permanent Representative of the Republic of Kenya submitted this request on behalf of the African Group to the United Nations Secretary General on 9 July 2018,[246] and it was placed on the agenda under 'F', Promotion of justice and international law as item 89.[247] Whereas the request is yet to be forwarded to the International Court of Justice (ICJ), some reservations have been made regarding subjecting the ICC to the ICJ. The major concern is as to whether this would not endanger the independence of the ICC. Pillai asks whether 'the ICJ [would] in effect function as an appellate court for the ICC, and [whether] would this be advisable?'[248] The possible relationship between

Non Compliance by Jordan with the Request by the Court for the Arrest and Surrender [of] Omar Al-Bashir"" (ICC-02/05-01/09-370 of 16 July 2018); *Prosecutor v. Al Bashir*, 'The League of Arab States' Observations on the Hashemite Kingdom of Jordan's appeal against the "Decision under article 87(7) of the Rome Statute on the noncompliance by Jordan with the request by the Court for the arrest and surrender [of] Omar Al-Bashir"' (ICC-02/05-01109 of 16 July 2018).

244 Köchler, 'Justice and Realpolitik: The Predicament of the International Criminal Court' (2017), 8; see also Kurt Mills and Allan Bloomfield, 'African resistance to the International Criminal Court: Halting the advance of the anti-impunity norm' (2018) 44:1, 105–107 Review of International Studies; Cole, 'Africa's Relationship with the International Criminal Court: More Political than Legal' (2013).

245 African Union, 'Decision on International Criminal Court' Doc. EX.CL/1068(XXXII) (Assembly/AU/Dec.672(XXX)).

246 United Nations General Assembly, 'Request for the inclusion of an item in the provisional agenda of the seventy-third session' A/73/14.

247 United Nations General Assembly, 'Organization of the seventy-third regular session of the General Assembly, adoption of the agenda and allocation of items: First report of the General Committee' (A/73/250) of 19 September 2018.

248 Priya Pillai, 'The African Union, the International Criminal Court, and the International Court of Justice: At the Fault Lines of International Accountability' (2018) 22:10 American

the ICC and ICJ goes beyond the scope of this book; however, it suffices to note that since the ICC jurisdiction is restricted on criminal matters, probably it would be interesting to provide for a neutral court that has jurisdiction over interpreting international law in a broader context considering the fact that the dispute concerns different aspects of state relations.

To reduce the pressure, it remains unanswered whether the ICC Prosecutor is willing to adopt a strategic approach that focuses on other categories of suspects because insisting that providing immunity to sitting heads of state is to incentivise them to remain in power does not explain how indicting them disincentivises them. This is not to say that such a strategy would be easy to justify either. One of the interesting arguments is that the primary responsibility of a head of a state is to protect its citizens, so a head of state that has permitted its own citizens to be killed cannot be called a head of state. This is a valid question of legitimacy, but it is not in the powers of the ICC Prosecutor to decide; doing so would be like giving the Prosecutor the powers to impeach a sitting head of a state that is not a party to the Rome Statute. This is different from the case of countries that have ratified the Rome Treaty because they (through their national processes) voluntarily consented to that loss of immunity. The idea that leaders suspected by the ICC Prosecutor killed their citizens is to confuse the role of the Prosecutor with that of the Chambers. It could be argued that, since the immunity of heads of state is against criminal suspicion, it is against the possibility of initiating a criminal process. Again, since an indictment is not a criminal conviction but a mere suspicion, it would be a violation of the presumption of innocence to conclude that those leaders indicted by the ICC are necessarily criminals before it is proved beyond any reasonable doubt in a court of law.

An alternative argument has been that since most situations where a non-state party sitting head of a state might be indicted are UNSC referrals, it is the Security Council not the Prosecutor that is responsible for removing the immunity. Kiyani argues that this kind of argument is also problematic because 'it rationalises and then imports the skewed imbalances of global politics into global justice mechanisms, leading to further concerns about its legitimacy as an impartial institution that equitably dispenses criminal justice'.[249] Beyond this, whatever was a conversation/discussion would very quickly turn into a confrontation. On one side, the next argument would be that: 'This is how the law is at the moment, take whatever complaint you have to the ASP (for the Rome Statute to be amended) or the UNSC (to refer all worthwhile situations) but don't make it an ICC issue.' Then, on the other side in response it would be

Society of International Law (Insights: https://www.asil.org/insights/volume/22/issue/10/african-union-international-criminal-court-and-international-court).

249 Kiyani, 'Legitimacy, Legality, and the Possibility of a Pluralist International Criminal Law' (2017), 100.

argued that even if this is true, at the moment, 'the law is unfair because it does not treat all the world citizens equally, and it is the ICC that is enforcing it'. At this point, we are deadlocked. My point is that there is no one side of debate that provides satisfying answers; we need to accept nuances.

### 2.3.6. AFRICAN SOLUTIONS TO AFRICAN PROBLEMS

The promise of African leaders to provide 'African solutions to African problems' remains a puzzle. The accelerated creation of a long-overdue International Criminal Chamber in the African justice system has not come to fruition. The June 2014 Malabo Protocol that merged the African Court on Human and Peoples' Rights and the Court of Justice of the African Union, and its inclusion of criminal jurisdiction remains with just 11 signatures and zero ratifications.[250] The Protocol has been praised for covering a number of international/transnational crimes that are important to the continent of Africa but has also been criticised for the inclusion of an immunity clause, lack of political support, limited resources and capacities that are necessary for it to end impunity.[251] It is also important to note that most situations in Africa where countries (including through a regional mechanism) have prosecuted international crimes, such as the case of Habré, have involved some struggles. There is a clear pattern to establish that African countries are willing to act on such crimes when they are under pressure from international powers. This pattern and the absence of a concrete African response could be an opportunity for the Court to engage strategically. For instance, the ICC's intervention could come where the international collective pressure on the countries concerned to undertake their responsibility to prosecute has genuinely failed. But before we get to solutions let us understand first the process of decision-making at the ICC Prosecution, in order to highlight some procedural and practical aspects that have contributed to these disagreements. To use Walton's words '... to understand an argument, it is very often highly important to know something about the context of dialogue in which the argument has occurred'.[252] This is the purpose of the next chapter – describing a process that has generated these disagreements.

---

250 Art. 3 of the Protocol on Amendments to the Protocol on the Statute of the African Court of Justice and Human Rights' as adopted on 27 June 2014.

251 Charles Chernor Jalloh, 'The Nature of Crimes in the African Criminal Court' (2017) 15, 799–826 Journal of International Criminal Justice; Amnesty International, 'Malabo Protocol: Legal and Institutional Implications of the Merged and Expanded African Court'; Matasi W. Martin and Brohmer Jurgen, 'Proposed International Criminal Chamber Section of the African Court of Justice and Human Rights: A Legal Analysis' (2012) 37:1 South African Yearbook of International Law, 248–268.

252 Douglas N. Walton, 'What is Reasoning? What is an Argument' (1990) The Journal of Philosophy, 412.

# CHAPTER 3

# THE ICC PROSECUTOR'S DECISION-MAKING PROCESS

From July 2002 to the time of writing, the Office of the Prosecutor's balance sheet can be summed up as follows: all the 11 situations under investigation are from Africa with the exception of Georgia. Five of these situations are state referrals, four were initiated on the Prosecutor's own initiative (*proprio motu*) and two are United Nations Security Council referrals.[253] All the 26 cases, comprising 42 defendants, are related to investigations from African situations. Of the 42 defendants, 11 are still at large, three are not in ICC custody, 11 defendants have seen their charges either withdrawn, not confirmed, terminated, inadmissible or acquitted, there have been eight convictions of whom more than half were found guilty of obstruction of justice (offences against the administration of justice), four defendants have died, and a further five are still on trial and in ICC custody.[254] The nine situations that are currently under different stages of preliminary examination are diverse; only three are from Africa. The OTP has closed preliminary examinations of situations from Honduras, Registered Vessels of Comoros, Greece, Cambodia, Republic of Korea and Venezuela with a decision not to proceed to an investigation.[255] However, it is noteworthy that there is no single situation from Africa that was put under a preliminary examination that has not proceeded to a full investigation. This picture is partly what upsets some Africans and makes them argue that the Court is meant for Africans and other 'unprotected' weaker states.[256]

It does not require one to look too far away to realise that crimes of similar or higher magnitude are (or have been) committed in other parts of the world. Therefore, the question on everyone's mind should be: how did we end up with this scenario? Is this coincidental or is the system built in such a way that international criminal justice is supposed to look like this? This chapter examines the decision-making process within the OTP. The assumption is that

---

253 ICC, 'Situations under Investigations' https://www.icc-cpi.int/pages/situation.aspx.

254 ICC, 'Cases: 42 Defendants' https://www.icc-cpi.int/Pages/defendants-wip.aspx.

255 Details available at the ICC website (Preliminary Examinations) https://www.icc-cpi.int/pages/pe.aspx.

256 The argument is that powerful states will shield their weaker allies against the reach of international criminal justice.

understanding the decision-making process will contribute to identifying areas of weaknesses and strengths of the system. The intention is to understand the process from the time a communication is received at the OTP, throughout the preliminary examination to the point when a decision is made, of whether to proceed to an investigation or not. Understanding administrative justice is important in determining whether the decision-making process is fair and transparent, or not. This chapter is concerned with the different decisions that are made before the pre-trial phase, and later decisions that are taken during investigations that are not subject to judicial review – under the prosecutorial independence and discretionary powers. However, the chapter does not go into details of investigation and prosecution because it is believed that these two stages are conducted under some form of judicial supervision unlike the preliminary examination process. The choice of decisions before pre-trial phase is based on the fact that not as many criticisms have been directed against the Court judgments.[257]

## 3.1. BEFORE PRE-TRIAL PROCEEDINGS: PRELIMINARY EXAMINATIONS

The ICC procedure can be triggered through either of the following ways:

1. a state party referral to the Office of the Prosecutor (Articles 13(a) and 14 of the Rome Statute – example situations include the Central African Republic I&II; Democratic Republic of Congo, Mali and Uganda);
2. the United Nations Security Council (UNSC) referral to the Office of the Prosecutor under Chapter VII of the United Nations Charter (Article 13(b) – situations of Darfur, Sudan and Libya);
3. Prosecutor's own initiative (*proprio motu*) 'on the basis of information on crimes within the jurisdiction of the Court' (Article 15 – the situation examples includes Kenya and Georgia); and

[257] This analysis is based on consultative interviews with different scholars and some staff at the ICC OTP conducted between 15 January and 15 February 2018, and a review of the literature. I conducted consultative interviews with Mr. Phakiso Mochochoko, Director, JCCD, Dr. Emeric Rogier, Head of Situation Analysis Section in the OTP, Dr. Hans Bevers and Dr. Rod Rastan, Legal Advisors to the OTP and Dr. Abdoul Aziz Mbaye and Mr. Richard Nsanzabaganwa, International Cooperation Advisers of the OTP, and a team from the Situation Analysis Unit in the Registry. To elucidate some of the assumptions on issues about the subject, I have had conversations with Dr. Eefje de Volder, the Co-Founder of Impact Now, an organisation that focuses on issues of human trafficking and conflict-related sexual violence; Dr. Barbora Hola, Associate Professor of Criminology at the Free University of Amsterdam and Dr. Thijs Bouwknegt, Researcher and Lecturer at Netherlands Institute of Holocaust and Genocide Studies at the University of Amsterdam.

4. it could also be as a result of a declaration lodged to the Register by a non-state party accepting the jurisdiction of 'the Court with the respect to the crime in question …'. The Prosecutor may request an authorisation to investigate. (Article 12(3) – e.g. the situation of Ivory Coast.)

The before pre-trial activities start with an examination of the seriousness of information (communication or referral) received to determine whether there is a reasonable basis to proceed to an investigation or not.[258] According to paragraph 4 of the OTP's Policy Paper on Preliminary Examinations:

> The preliminary examination of a situation by the Office may be initiated on the basis of: (a) information sent by individuals or groups, States, intergovernmental or non-governmental organisations; (b) a referral from a State Party or the Security Council; or (c) a declaration accepting the exercise of jurisdiction by the Court pursuant to article 12(3) lodged by a State which is not a Party to the Statute.[259]

Article 14(2) of the Rome Statute requires, 'as far as possible, a referral [… to] specify the relevant circumstances and be accompanied by such supporting documentation as is available to the State referring the situation'. According to the preliminary examination activities reports, most of the assessment work is related to information submitted under Article 15 of the Rome Statute.[260] The OTP, from the entry into force of the Rome Statute (July 2002) until October 2017, has received 12,590 communications. This means, on average, 800 communications per year, which is more than two communications daily including weekends and holidays.[261] However, these communications are wide-ranging from anything such as a 'pension claim dispute' to some serious allegations of heinous crimes, and as a result, most of them are found to be manifestly outside the jurisdiction of the Court. For instance, in the period 2015–2017, the OTP received 1,547 communications (2015: 502, 2016: 477 and 2017: 568) of which 69 percent 'were manifestly outside the Court's jurisdiction', 14 percent concerned a 'situation already under analysis', 8 percent 'were linked to an [ongoing] investigation or prosecution' and just 9 percent 'warranted a further analysis'.[262]

258 Rule 104 of the ICC Rules of Procedure and Evidence (RPE).

259 Para. 4 of the ICC OTP Policy Paper on Preliminary Examinations of November 2013.

260 'Information on crimes' refers to information on crimes within the jurisdiction of the Court pursuant to Art. 15. See Reg. 2 (Use of Terms) of the Regulations of the Office of the Prosecutor (ICC-BD/05-01-09).

261 Para. 18 of the OTP Report on Preliminary Examination Activities 2017 dated 4 December 2017 https://www.icc-cpi.int/itemsDocuments/2017-PE-rep/2017-otp-rep-PE_ENG.pdf.

262 Para. 18 of the OTP Report on Preliminary Examination Activities 2017; para. 18 of the OTP Report on Preliminary Examination Activities 2016 of 14 November 2016 https://www.icc-cpi.int/iccdocs/otp/161114-otp-rep-PE_ENG.pdf; para. 18 of the OTP Report on Preliminary Examination Activities 2015 of 12 November 2015 https://www.icc-cpi.int/iccdocs/otp/otp-pe-rep-2015-eng.pdf.

The Prosecutor will acknowledge receipt of all communications submitted, and after conducting a preliminary examination, if he or she concludes that there is no reasonable basis to proceed to an investigation, informs 'those who provided information'.[263] The process of handling communications is one of the most significant exercises of the OTP because it is at this stage that meritorious situations are determined. Therefore, the manner in which communications are handled shapes the initial image of the Court and the Prosecution. However much this exercise is important as an entry point to the Court, it is also the least controlled stage of the ICC's proceedings. As Stahn notes 'the conduct of preliminary examinations poses delicate issues in relation to the interplay between law and politics. They are less judicialized than later steps of the criminal proceedings'.[264] There is no clear procedure on how to conduct a preliminary examination, no timeframe for which a situation is supposed to remain under preliminary examination, and no obligation on the OTP to reveal information concerning the kinds of communications received, or activities and contacts happening behind the scenes. In circumstances where the Prosecutor has shared information such as the periodic preliminary examination activities reports, it has been done so of his/her own will, furthering transparency. The Prosecutor's decision not to investigate is not subject to judicial review, the decision to investigate is based on a minimum standard of proof – 'reasonable basis' – and all is done in the name of confidentiality and prosecutorial independence.

The details on the process of handling communications can be found in the Regulations of the Office of the Prosecutor, the Policy Paper on Preliminary Examinations, the Policy Paper on Interests of Justice, and the different preliminary examination activities reports. Furthermore, in order to understand the process of decision-making at the OTP one needs to understand its structure and composition. The OTP is comprised of three divisions, two sections (Administration and Legal advisory) and experts units (gender and children), and the Prosecutor can appoint independent expert advisors. The Division of Jurisdiction, Complementarity and Cooperation (JCCD) is responsible 'for the preliminary examination and evaluation of information' submitted to the OTP, and provides advice to the Executive Committee (ExCom) on matters of jurisdiction and cooperation.[265] The Investigation Division is responsible for all preparations and conducting investigations including security and wellbeing of witnesses and victims.[266] The Prosecution Division is responsible for preparation of prosecution and assessing issues related to litigation, and

[263] Art. 15(6) and Rule 49.

[264] Carsten Stahn, 'Damned If You Do, Damned If You Don't: Challenges and Critiques of Preliminary Examinations at the ICC' (2017) 15, 413434 Journal of International Criminal Justice, 416.

[265] Reg. 7 of the Regulations of the Office of the Prosecutor.

[266] ibid, Reg. 8.

developing strategies thereof.[267] None of these divisions and units is allowed to take a decision independently without the Prosecutor's approval. The supreme organ responsible for advising the Prosecutor is the Executive Committee (ExCom). The ExCom is composed of the three heads of divisions and the Prosecutor, and benefits from different expertise available at the OTP. The ExCom is also 'responsible for the development and adoption of the strategies, policies and budget of the Office, provide strategic guidance on all the activities of the Office and coordinate them'.[268] In the corporate sense, one could equate ExCom to a board of directors because every decision before it goes to the OTP – for approval or not – has to be defended before the ExCom. The ExCom can approve the proposal as submitted, recommend for some modifications, request additional information or reject it.[269]

Most of the before pre-trial phase work is conducted at the (JCCD). The JCCD is composed of two sections: the Situation Analysis Section and the Cooperation Advisory Section. The Situation Analysis Section (SAS) is the gatekeeper of all communications. The SAS is a small team of 12 staff, composed of Legal Analysts, Context Analysts and Crime Analysts, whose mandate is to provide 'advice on complex matters of fact and law regarding jurisdiction, admissibility, and the interests of justice, in particular taking into account the interests of victims'.[270] It is responsible for overseeing the preliminary examinations on behalf of the JCCD.

Article 15(2) of the Rome Statute states that

> [t]he Prosecutor shall analyse the seriousness of the information received. For this purpose, he or she may seek additional information from (… any) reliable sources that he or she deems appropriate, and may receive written or oral testimony at the seat of the Court.[271]

Rule 46 of the ICC Rules of Procedure and Evidence provides for the protection of those who provide information to the Prosecutor, and Rule 48 provides that the Prosecution '[i]n determining whether there is a reasonable basis to proceed with an investigation under article 15, paragraph 3, (… to) consider the factors

---

267 ibid, Reg. 9.

268 ibid, Regs 4, 6, 8 and 11(a) of the Regulations of the Office of the Prosecutor.

269 See e.g. Jens Meierhenrich, 'The evolution of the office of the prosecutor at the international criminal court: insights from institutional theory' in Martha Minow, C. Cora True-Frost and Alex Whiting (eds.), *The First Global Prosecutor: Promise and Constraints. Law, Meaning, and Violence* (University of Michigan Press, 2015), 97–127.

270 The number of 12 staff is as of February 2018; see paras. 6 and 7 of Annex II: Resource justification for mandated activities of the Report of the Court on the Basic Size of the Office of the Prosecutor (17 September 2015) as submitted to the Fourteenth Session of the Assembly of States Parties (ICC-ASP/14/21), see also a table on p. 17 of the same Basic Size Document, para. 29.

271 ICC Rome Statute.

set out in article 53, paragraph 1 (a) to (c)'.[272] And, Article 53(1) provides for the Prosecutor to conduct an (a) assessment of 'the reasonable basis to believe that the crime within the jurisdiction of the Court has been committed'; (b) the admissibility criteria as provided for under Article 17 (complementarity principle and gravity of alleged crimes), and finally (c) the interests of justice.[273]

The communications that come to the OTP are processed through different stages of assessment, depending on their veracity. There is no specific format or process of sending information/communications to the OTP. It can be through an email, or a physical document(s) submitted through the post office or directly brought in by an individual, or through any other means. It can be submitted by states, individuals, international organisations or NGOs.

The first phase of processing communications is their labelling into different categories – *the 'proper' initial assessment* – a kind of administrative sorting. The Information and Evidence Unit (IEU) that manages the email and database systems of the OTP is responsible for centralising all communications. Every information submitted is received, registered (labelled) and secured. The moment 'materials are scanned and placed in TRIM', all authorised individuals at the OTP can access it.[274] At this phase, the IEU makes four types of labelling: (i) filters out information that is manifestly outside the jurisdiction of the Court;[275] (ii) communications concerning a situation that is already under preliminary examination; (iii) communications concerning a situation under investigation, and (iv) communications concerning a situation under prosecution.[276] The IEU, upon the approval of the JCCD, produces a monthly report indicating the information received and recommendations made on each communication, and if the Prosecutor agrees, he or she proceeds to inform the sender accordingly. The communication that is manifestly outside the jurisdiction of the Court is also kept because it might be revisited depending on new information and future circumstances.[277] Communications concerning ongoing situations, either at preliminary examination, investigation or prosecution, are forwarded to their respective teams for consideration. If a communication is found not to be manifestly outside the jurisdiction of the Court and it does not concern a situation that is already under consideration, that communication is looked

272 ICC Rules of Procedure and Evidence.

273 ICC Rome Statute.

274 Para. 27 of Annex III: Resource Justification Supporting Activities of the Report of the Court on the Basic Size of the Office of the Prosecutor (17 September 2015) as submitted to the Fourteenth Session of the Assembly of States Parties (ICC-ASP/14/21).

275 Communications that are manifestly outside the jurisdiction of the Court might include those alleging that the conduct happened before the entry into force of the Rome Statute (July 2002), alleging that the conduct is not a crime under the jurisdiction of the Court, or allegations concerning a non-state party that has not accepted the jurisdiction of the Court.

276 Para. 78 of the OTP Policy Paper on Preliminary Examinations.

277 Para. 79 of the OTP Policy Paper on Preliminary Examinations.

into further. It proceeds to the next phase. If they are different communications referring to a similar situation, all those communications are put together.

The second phase is the *subject matter jurisdiction*. The preconditions for the ICC to exercise jurisdiction[278] are set in Article 12 of the Rome Statute. The alleged crimes should be genocide, crimes against humanity, war crimes and 'aggression' – material jurisdiction. The alleged conduct must have happened (or be happening) on the territory of a state party, or on the territory of a non-state party that has accepted the jurisdiction of the Court – temporal jurisdiction. The conduct must have happened since the Rome Statute entered into force (July 2002) and since the state concerned accepted the jurisdiction of the Court, or subjected to the United Nations Security Council referral. Alternatively, the alleged perpetrator(s) must be nationals of the state party – personal jurisdiction.

It is during the second phase that analysists will focus on determining facts and legal issues. This includes establishing facts and context behind the alleged perpetration, crime patterns and potential individual (group) suspects. The purpose is to describe the facts of what is alleged to have really happened. The legal analysis focuses on showing that since this is what is alleged to have happened, it is within the jurisdiction of the Court or not, for the following legal reasons, and describes possible legal issues that might arise at later stages. Even if this is not an investigation per se, the Prosecutor can ask for more information from the sender(s), states, international organisations, United Nations Agencies and NGOs and use any available public information to analyse the situation. If it is determined that what is alleged is indeed within the jurisdiction of the Court, the assessment moves to the next phase.

The third phase is the assessment of the *admissibility* requirements as set out in Article 17 of the Rome Statute. The focus is on establishing whether or not there are ongoing national proceedings concerning the alleged conduct(s), and if the potential suspects have not been tried – the complementarity principle. Unlike *ad hoc* Tribunals (ICTY and ICTR) that operated on a basis of concurrent jurisdiction with supremacy over national courts, the ICC is built on the idea that states retain their sovereign right (primary responsibility) over criminal matters. The ICC intervenes in situations where the states concerned are either unwilling or unable genuinely to conduct the prosecution. In the case of an ongoing proceeding at national level, the ICC is supposed to back off because national courts should take precedence. The complementarity principle therefore requires the OTP to engage with concerned state(s) and monitor whether they are genuinely conducting proceedings. It is only when it is clear that there are no ongoing domestic proceedings, or that proceedings are meant to shield suspects that the ICC Prosecutor can intervene. This embedded monitoring of national

278 Jurisdiction refers to the Court's authority to exercise control over a matter.

proceedings is what is often blamed for the long delays of some situations on preliminary examination.[279]

The second aspect under the admissibility phase is gravity, that is whether the alleged crimes are serious enough to call for the intervention of the ICC. The assessment of the gravity threshold is one of the most controversial aspects of the process, because there is no objective way to measure the elements used. The OTP has indicated that in determining the gravity of a crime, it considers both quantitative and qualitative aspects. The quantitative elements may include the number of victims affected, and qualitative aspects may include the gruesome nature of the perpetration of the crime and the outrage it might have caused to the international community. It is arguable whether these standards of unwillingness and inability of states (complementarity principle) and the seriousness of alleged crimes (gravity) are assessed in a consistent manner throughout all situations.[280]

In the process of assessing the admissibility requirements, complementarity and gravity (scale, nature, manner of the commission of the crime and impact), the OTP continues 'to collect information on the subject-matter jurisdiction, in particular when new or ongoing crimes are alleged to have been committed within the situation'.[281] If the analysis concludes that the communication(s) meets the jurisdiction requirements and the required threshold of gravity, and that the complementarity principle is adhered to, meaning no ongoing national proceedings against potential suspects (those who bear the greatest responsibility), then the preliminary examination proceeds to the fourth and final stage.

The fourth stage of preliminary examination is the assessment of *the interests of justice*. The OTP is required to weigh its decisions against the interests of justice in at least two stages: the first consideration is when the Prosecutor can refrain from proceeding to an investigation if '[t]aking into account the gravity of the crime and the interests of victims, there are nonetheless substantial reasons to believe that an investigation would not serve the interests of justice (Article 53(1)(c))'. The second consideration is when the Prosecutor may refrain from a prosecution when it is established that doing so would be contrary to the interests of justice (Article 53(2)(c)). During the preliminary examination, the focus is on whether 'there are substantial reasons to believe that an investigation would not serve the interests of justice'.

---

279 Para. 2 of Annex II: Resource justification for mandated activities of the Report of the Court on the Basic Size of the Office of the Prosecutor (17 September 2015) as submitted to the Fourteenth Session of the Assembly of States Parties (ICC-ASP/14/21).

280 Thomas O. Hansen, 'Reflections on the ICC Prosecutor's Recent Selection Decisions' (2013) 17, 125–158 Max Planck Yearbook of United Nations Law (Brill); David Bosco, 'Discretion and State Influence at the International Criminal Court: The Prosecutor's Preliminary Examinations' (2017) 11:2, 395–414 American Journal of International Law.

281 Reg. 29(2) of the Regulations of the Office of the Prosecutor; paras. 9 and 82 of the OTP Policy Paper on Preliminary Examinations.

Consideration of the interests of justice comes after all other requirements have been met. The Prosecution has no duty to prove that conducting an investigation will serve the interests of justice because the duty to investigate international crimes is presumed to be in the interests of justice.[282] It is only when doing so is against the interests of justice that the Prosecution may decide not to investigate a situation that would otherwise have deserved an investigation. It is believed that the drafters of the Rome Statute expected that the use of the interests of justice to lead to refraining from conducting an investigation would apply in rare circumstances only, because '[i]f the Prosecutor determines that there is no reasonable basis to proceed and his or her determination is based solely on [… interests of justice] he or she [… is required to] inform the Pre-Trial Chamber'.[283] The OTP believes that whenever conditions of jurisdiction and admissibility are met, for the situation to proceed to an investigation, there is a duty on the Prosecutor to do.[284]

The remaining challenge is that it is unclear what entails the interests of justice. The OTP so far has not stopped from conducting an investigation on the ground that doing so would be against the interests of justice, and the 2007 Policy Paper on the Interests of Justice does not illustrate or list some of the issues that might be considered during the assessment of interests of justice. We at least know, according to the OTP, what is not part of the interests of justice. It has been repeatedly stated in the different policy documents that alternative mechanisms, such as truth commissions, and broader matters of international peace and security are outside the interests of justice considerations. It is believed that matters of peace and security 'falls within the mandate of other institutions'.[285]

The process of preliminary examination as described above (on communications) applies also to the information that comes to the OTP through either state or UNSC referrals. The only difference is that, if the reasonable basis to proceed is established, state and UNSC referrals carry a mandatory obligation to open an investigation without the Prosecutor having to request for an authorisation. The purpose of conducting a preliminary examination in all situations is to assess the veracity of the information received. This is done to ensure that conditions of jurisdiction, admissibility and interests of justice are met. In the case of a state or UNSC referral, if there is a determination that there is no reasonable basis to proceed, the Pre-Trial Chamber may request the Prosecutor to reconsider that decision.

---

282 Para. 71 of the OTP Policy Paper on Preliminary Examinations.

283 Art. 53(1) *in fin*, of the Rome Statute.

284 Para. 4(b) of the OTP Policy Paper on the Interests of Justice.

285 Para. 6(b) of the Policy Paper on the Interests of Justice; see also para. 69 of the OTP Policy Paper on Preliminary Examinations.

The moment a preliminary examination is completed, the JCCD submits its report to the ExCom, which in turn gives recommendations. If the ExCom is satisfied, the report will go to the Prosecutor who takes the final decision. If the report concerns communications submitted under Article 15 of the Rome Statute, and the Prosecutor decides to proceed to an investigation, he or she will request authorisation to investigate. At this point, it is up to the judges to decide whether the Prosecution has discharged its duty of proving that there is a reasonable basis to start an investigation or not. If approved, the investigation will start, and the information will be transferred from the JCCD to the Investigation Division and will be assigned to an integrated team composed of investigators and trial lawyers. The team members will discuss and make a plan for conducting an investigation including what needs to be done for diplomatic and cooperation matters, and all their recommendations will also be defended at the ExCom. Once again the final decision will be taken by the Prosecutor.

## 3.2. DECISION-MAKING DURING INVESTIGATIONS

The moment the Prosecutor concludes that there is a reasonable basis to proceed to an investigation – in the case of a state or UNSC referral – he or she will immediately proceed to open it. However, in case his or her conclusion is based on communications received under Article 15, the Prosecutor will first request an authorisation to investigate (*proprio motu*). The Pre-Trial Chamber will grant the authorisation if it is satisfied that there is indeed a reasonable basis to believe that crimes under the jurisdiction of the Court have been committed, and that potential cases may be admissible. If not satisfied, the request will be refused without affecting a possible reapplication with new facts and materials.[286] Upon approval, the preliminary examination material is handed over to an integrated team, composed of some staff from all the three divisions of the OTP. The number of staff members from each division forming the integrated team changes continuously according to the stage of an investigation. The first phase of an investigation involves studying the preliminary examination material, the context of the situation country/territory, establishing field contacts, security analysis and logistical preparations. It is after members of the integrated team have agreed on the plan of conducting an investigation, including what needs to be done for diplomatic and cooperation matters, that their recommendations will be defended before the ExCom, subject to the Prosecutor's final approval to proceed.[287]

---

286 Art. 15(4)–(5) of the Rome Statute.

287 Para. 10, Annex 1: Extrapolation of the Estimated Demand and para. 43 Annex II: Resource Justification of Mandated Activities, of the Report of the Court on the Basic Size of the Office of the Prosecutor (17 September 2015, ICC-ASP/14/21).

After the approval of the investigation proposed plan, the second phase is the active 'actual' investigation. This is a period for collecting evidence; both documentary and witness statements. The OTP has a duty to contribute to establishing the truth, and as such, investigation goes beyond collecting incriminating evidence to include exculpatory evidence, evidence that exonerates the suspect.[288] This is the longest phase of an investigation process because it involves in-depth analysis and several field missions either to the situation territory and/or other places where evidence may be found.[289]

The third phase of an investigation is a wrap-up. The team prepares case file(s) whilst planning for prosecution. The ICC does not conduct trials *in absentia*, so after gathering enough evidence during the active investigation phase, the Pre-Trial Chamber on the request of the Prosecutor may issue an arrest warrant or a summons to appear if '[t]here are reasonable grounds to believe that the person [sought] has committed a crime within the jurisdiction of the Court (...)'.[290] If there are no prospects of an immediate arrest and surrender, or of voluntary appearance of the suspect, the Prosecution will adopt necessary measures for the protection of witnesses and strategies for maintaining their contacts pending future appearance or arrest of the suspect.[291]

The OTP operates a confidential Case Selection Document (hereafter 'the Document') composed of potential cases across all situations under investigation. Potential cases that are included in the Document are first identified based on conclusions made in the preliminary examination material. The Document is continuously updated and/or reviewed as investigations collect more and more information. The purpose of the Document is to ease the process of case selection and prioritisation because it provides a compilation of all case hypotheses.[292]

All case hypotheses in the Case Selection Document must be based on allegations within the jurisdiction of the Court and admissible – legal criteria.[293] However, the OTP policy is not clear on the level of proof needed at this stage. The Rome Statute provides different levels of evidence needed at each different stage of the proceedings. For the Pre-Trial Chamber to authorise an investigation (*proprio motu*) requires the Prosecutor to prove that 'there is *a reasonable basis* to proceed with an investigation'. To issue a warrant of arrest or a summons to appear, the Prosecutor needs to 'support each charge with sufficient evidence

288 ibid, paras. 11–13, Annex 1; Art. 54(1)(a) of the Rome Statute.
289 ibid, para. 11, Annex 1.
290 Art. 58(1)(a) of the Rome Statute; see the whole of Art. 58 of the Rome Statute for more details on the content of an arrest warrant and the procedure on the summons to appear, and amendments thereof.
291 Paras. 13–21, Annex 1: Extrapolation of the Estimated Demand of the Report of the Court on the Basic Size of the Office of the Prosecutor. An investigation in hibernation is used to refer to those investigations that have been put on hold pending arrest and surrender of suspects.
292 Paras. 10–15 of the 2016 Policy Paper on Case Selection and Prioritisation.
293 ibid, paras. 24–25.

to establish *substantial grounds to believe* that the person committed the crime charged'. Once the suspect is brought (or appears) before the Court for the first time – during the confirmation hearing – the Prosecutor has to prove that '[t]here are *reasonable grounds* to believe that the person has committed a crime within the jurisdiction of the Court'. And, for someone to be convicted of a crime, 'the Court must be convinced of the guilt of the accused *beyond reasonable doubt*'.[294] Therefore, the educated guess is that a case on the Document is based on minimum evidence – reasonable basis – because the initial case hypothesis is based on preliminary examination material. Conversely, based on previous experiences where a number of cases have collapsed due to lack of sufficient evidence and some investigations hibernated before collecting enough evidence, the Office has adopted a policy of collecting enough evidence at an early stage – trial ready at the confirmation of charges stage.[295]

The fact that potential cases falling within the legal criteria would still be too many compared to the capacity of the OTP, selective investigation and prosecution among meritorious cases is unavoidable. The 2016 OTP Policy Paper on Case Selection and Prioritisation has been adopted to guide the process, increase transparency and dissuade some criticisms.[296] During the selection process, the Prosecution considers: (i) gravity – whereas the element of gravity is used throughout the process of investigation, at this time the threshold needed is much stricter; (ii) the degree of responsibility – *de facto* responsibility in the alleged criminal conduct, including 'the deterrent and expressive effects' of each mode of liability preferred; and (iii) charges – crimes representing what many victims suffered and the nature of some crimes.[297] Additionally, the OTP conducts a comparative assessment within and across situations to prioritise them considering representation of parties to the conflict, impact of an investigation, deterrent effect on ongoing crimes, prospects of conviction (quality and quantity of evidence, ability to investigate, and possibility for the suspect to appear before the Court).[298]

The whole process of an investigation involves making different controversial decisions that are of concern to some observers.[299] This is to a

---

294 Arts. 15(3), 58(1)(a), 61(5) and (7) and 66(3) of the Rome Statute respectively (emphasis added).

295 Para. 13, the ICC OTP Strategic Plan/2016-2018 of 16 November 2015, 9 https://www.icc-cpi.int/iccdocs/otp/EN-OTP_Strategic_Plan_2016-2018.pdf.

296 Para. 3 of the 2016 Policy Paper on Case Selection and Prioritisation.

297 ibid, paras. 34–46.

298 ibid, paras. 47–50.

299 William A. Schabas, 'Victor's Justice: Selecting "Situations" at the International Criminal Court' (2010) 43, 535 The John Marshall Law Review; Alana Tiemessen, 'The International Criminal Court and the politics of prosecutions' (2014) 18:4–5, 444–461 The International Journal of Human Rights; Hanna Kuczyńska, 'Selection of Defendants Before the ICC: Between the Principle of Opportunism and Legalism' (2014) 34, 187–224 Polish Yearbook of International Law.

certain extent because the entire process of collecting evidence depends on the OTP's ability to receive cooperation. As already noted, the Prosecutor will need state cooperation in accessing witnesses and crime scenes, and sometimes from non-state actors especially NGOs and international organisations acting as intermediaries.[300] In spite of numerous challenges related to the nature of international criminal investigations and cooperation, there is no situation that has moved to an investigation stage that has not resulted in individual cases (suspects). However, decision-making remains controversial. The Prosecution independently decides within a situation and across situations which conduct(s) and person(s) to prosecute, and which ones to avoid.[301] It is up to the Prosecutor's discretion to decide the number of charges to prefer against a suspect.[302] He or she can decide to investigate both sides in the conflict or just one. In so doing, the Prosecutor bestows on some individuals the title of victimhood while denying it to others. Schabas takes issue with this process of sorting. He argues that in the selection process it 'is often not obvious why [some crimes …] are *more* serious than other cases which are effectively ignored'.[303]

Rod Rastan, Legal Advisor at the Office of the Prosecutor, in his response to Schabas and Lepard's criticisms, argues that '[t]he results of selection will always be unsatisfactory because not every crime will be prosecuted'.[304] Stahn similarly notes that '[t]he number of cases that the ICC has dealt with is limited, and likely to remain highly selective in the future'.[305] Certainly, this is not to say that all criticisms of the selection process are not founded. Robinson in his pessimistic compromise suggests that: 'The interesting conversation is not just to show that some particular choice is flawed, because they all are; it is to discuss

---

300 Elena A Baylis, 'Outsourcing Investigations' (2009) 14 UCLA Journal of International Law and Foreign Affairs (University of Pittsburgh Legal Studies Research Paper No. 2010-20); Caroline Buisman, 'Delegating Investigations: Lessons to be Learned from the Lubanga Judgment' (2013) 11:3 Northwestern Journal of International Human Rights, 29–82; Dermot Groome, 'No Witness, No Case: An Assessment of the Conduct and Quality of ICC Investigations' (2014) 3:1 The Penn State Journal of Law & International Affairs, 1–29.

301 'It is not the responsibility or role of the Office to investigate and prosecute each and every alleged criminal act within a given situation or every person allegedly responsible for such crimes (…).' Para. 5 of the ICC OTP Policy Paper on Case Selection and Prioritisation.

302 *ICC Prosecutor v. Thomas Lubanga Dyilo*, Warrant of Arrest of 10 February 2006 (ICC-01/04-01/06) (3 counts); *ICC Prosecutor v. Dominic Ongwen*, Decision on the Confirmation of Charges of 23 March 2016 (ICC-02/04-01/15) (70 counts).

303 William A. Schabas, 'The Short Arm of International Criminal Law' in William A. Schabas, Yvonne McDermott and Niamh Hayes (eds.), *The Ashgate Research Companion to International Criminal Law: Critical Perspectives* (Ashgate, 2013), 404.

304 Rod Rastan, 'Comment on Victor's Justice & the Visibility of *Ex Ante* Standards' (2010) 43, 569 The John Marshall Law Review, 591.

305 Stahn, 'Damned If You Do, Damned If You Don't: Challenges and Critiques of Preliminary Examinations at the ICC' (2017), 414–415.

how to choose among the flawed options'.[306] The most difficult knot to untie in this whole debate is in the nature of the subject, namely criminal investigations. Like all other criminal investigations, ICC investigations are highly secretive. The secrecy of investigations combined with the fact that the Prosecutor seeks cooperation from external actors, sometimes in closed-door meetings, allows observers to speculate on motives and strengthens the perception of collusion. Critics have reported some suspicious exchanges (phone calls and meetings) between the Prosecutor and officials of some powerful states, on matters of ongoing investigations.[307] Brooks argues that the unresolved criticism about the ICC is that 'powerful states will be happy to support international justice efforts as long as only powerless states are under scrutiny'.[308]

The desire to influence the ICC investigations and prosecutions does not come from state officials alone. Kenneth Roth, the Executive Director of Human Rights Watch, speaks about how he called Moreno Ocampo, the first ICC Prosecutor, to ask him why he had decided to indict just two individuals in the Darfur situation.[309] The fact is that there is nothing wrong with people individually or collectively pursuing their interests because attempting to influence the Prosecution is not illegal per se, and it cannot be concluded that all interferences are necessarily negative. Therefore, it is the Prosecutor who is expected to act independently – regardless of differing pressures – who is expected to rise above those interests, and act in a manner that is transparent and consistent in the eyes of observers – 'the objective duty to act consistent with the appearance of impartiality to a reasonable observer'.[310] This is what makes improving administrative procedural justice very important to the legitimacy of criminal justice systems. Because, it is through a clear and transparent administrative process that observers may assess the objectivity of a mechanism. Otherwise, as the middle ground diminishes, observers are left with few options: to either trust wholeheartedly that everything the OTP is doing is done independently; is fair, objective and impartial, or that the system is riddled with external interferences.

---

306 Robinson, 'Inescapable Dyads: Why the International Criminal Court Cannot Win' (2015), 332 and 347.

307 Bosco, *Rough Justice: The International Criminal Court in a World of Power Politics* (2014), 139ff; Schmitt, 'France, Africa, and the ICC: The Neocolonialist Critique and the Crisis of the Institutional Legitimacy' (2016), 127–151; Branco, *L'Ordre et le Monde: Critique de la Cour Penale Internationale* (2016).

308 Rosa Brooks, 'Friends Don't Let Friends Drive Drunk: The Role of U.S. Allies in Keeping the U.S. Honest' (2017) 48, 923 Georgetown Journal of International Law, 924.

309 UChannel, 'What Next for Darfur: Policy Action or the Status Quo?' [29 November 2007] https://www.youtube.com/watch?v=8dpSKYV4yMQ (Kenneth Roth presentation at the Panel Discussion).

310 Pues, 'Towards the "Golden Hour"?: A Critical Exploration of the Length of Preliminary Examinations' (2017), 447.

## 3.3. THE ICC-OTP POLICIES: *EX POST* JUSTIFICATIONS

In an effort to increase transparency and clarity, the OTP has adopted different policy papers, prosecutorial strategy reports and strategic plans, and produced several reports on some of its preliminary activities.[311] Whereas the OTP is very clear in stating that policy papers are internal documents, which do 'not give rise to legal rights', it is also clear that these documents serve as authoritative sources of reference especially when it comes to issues under the Prosecutor's discretionary powers. Therefore, whenever the Prosecutor adopts a policy paper interpreting the meaning of a certain concept or clarifying his or her mandate – broadly or narrowly – he or she is making law.[312] Certainly, interpretation of laws is unavoidable whether it is done through a policy paper or not, because legal provisions are often vague or incomplete when it comes to their application in reality.[313] MacCormick argues that 'every application of law requires some act of interpretation, since one has to form an understanding of what the text says in order to apply it, and any act of apprehension of meaning can be said to involve interpretation'.[314] However, since some of the documents were adopted during ongoing debates about specific demands – relating to a specific situation under investigation – it has resulted in some positions that are either difficult to apply in other contexts or superfluous in nature.

### 3.3.1. INTERESTS OF JUSTICE

The 2007 OTP Policy Paper on the Interests of Justice is one of those policy papers that were adopted during an ongoing debate on the subject. It was adopted during peace negotiations in the situations of the Northern Uganda 'Juba Talks' and Darfur-Sudan, and some actors were calling for the Prosecutor to consider using his discretionary powers under the 'interests of justice' to stop investigations and prosecutions.[315] During that period, different voices

---

311 ICC OTP Policies and Strategies available at https://www.icc-cpi.int/about/otp/Pages/otp-policies.aspx.

312 Alvarez commenting on ICC Prosecutor states that '[t]he Office of the Prosecutor (OTP) may also prove to be a formidable law-maker'. See José E. Alvarez, *The Impact of International Organizations on International Law* (Brill/Nijhoff, 2017), 305.

313 Bernard S. Jackson, *Law, Fact and Narrative Coherence* (Deborah Charles Publications, 1988), 130; ibid, 286, 301–305.

314 MacCormick, *Rhetoric and the Rule of Law: A Theory of Legal Reasoning* (2005), 121.

315 Macdonald '"In the interests of justice?" The International Criminal Court, peace talks and the failed quest for war crimes accountability in northern Uganda' (2017); Line Engbo Gissel, 'Justice Tides: How and When Levels of ICC Involvement Affect Peace Processes' (2015) 9:3 International Journal of Transitional Justice, 428–448; Kenneth A Rodman, 'Is Peace in the Interests of Justice? The Case for Broad Prosecutorial Discretion at the International Criminal Court' (2009) 22:1 Leiden Journal of International Law, 111–115.

suggested that the adoption of the Policy Paper on the Interests of Justice would contribute to transparency, dispel criticisms and strengthen the legitimacy and credibility of the OTP.[316] However, disagreements about the meaning and usage of the concept that existed at that time continue today.[317] There is an unending debate on what entails being against 'the interests of justice' that would allow the Prosecutor not to investigate a situation or prosecute a case when other legal requirements are fulfilled.[318]

There is an increasing voice arguing that the 'interests of justice' as referred to in Article 53 was meant to be understood in a broader sense than the OTP's current interpretation.[319] The proponents of the OTP's stricter interpretation are mainly members of NGOs.[320] The OTP understands the concept of 'interests of justice' to be applicable in (i) exceptional circumstances – presumption of investigation and prosecution, (ii) in line with the object and purpose of the statute – prevention of international crimes through ending impunity, and (iii) to be different from interests of peace, security and alternative justice mechanisms.[321] There is not much disagreement on the first two aspects (i) and (ii); what is controversial is singling out peace, security and alternative justice mechanisms as factors that are outside the considerations of the interests of justice.

---

316 Darryl Robinson, 'Serving the Interests of Justice: Amnesties, Truth Commissions and the International Criminal Court' (2003) 14:3 European Journal of International Law, 481–505; Philippa Webb, 'The ICC Prosecutor's Discretion Not to Proceed in the "Interests of Justice"' (2005) 305 Criminal Law Quarterly, 305–348; Avril McDonald and Roelof Haveman, 'Prosecutorial Discretion – Some Thoughts on "Objectifying" the Exercise of Prosecutorial Discretion by the Prosecutor of the ICC: Expert consultation process on general issues relevant to the ICC Office of the Prosecutor' (15 April, 2003); Henry Lovat, 'Delineating the interests of justice: prosecutorial discretion and the Rome Statute of the International Criminal Court' (2007) 35:2 Denver Journal of International Law and Policy, 275–286.

317 Varaki, 'Revisiting the 'Interests of Justice' Policy Paper' (2017); Talita de Souza Dias, '"Interests of justice": Defining the scope of Prosecutorial discretion in Article 53(1)(c) and (2)(c) of the Rome Statute of the International Criminal Court' (2017) 30:3 Leiden Journal of International Law 731–751; Linda M. Keller, 'Comparing the "Interests of Justice": What the International Criminal Court Can Learn from New York Law' (2013) 12:1 Washington University Global Studies Law Review, 1–40.

318 Art. 53(1) and (2) of the Rome Statute.

319 Varaki, 'Revisiting the "Interests of Justice" Policy Paper' (2017); Dias, '"Interests of justice": Defining the scope of Prosecutorial discretion in Article 53(1)(c) and (2)(c) of the Rome Statute of the International Criminal Court' (2017); Margaret M. deGuzman, 'Choosing to Prosecute: Expressive Selection at the International Criminal Court' (2012) 33, 265 Michigan Journal of International Law.

320 Amnesty International, 'Open letter to the Chief Prosecutor of the International Criminal Court: Comments on the concept of the interests of justice' (IOR 40/023/2005) of 17 June 2005; Human Rights Watch Policy Paper on 'the Meaning of "the Interests of Justice" in Article 53 of the Rome Statute' of 1 June 2005 https://www.hrw.org/news/2005/06/01/meaning-interests-justice-article-53-rome-statute.

321 The 2007 OTP Policy Paper on the Interests of Justice.

Ordinarily, one could argue that Article 53 is not that very complicated to understand because it provides a known standard of proof – 'substantial reasons'. The Prosecutor stopping an investigation in a situation where doing so would be against the interests of justice is provided for in Article 53(1)(c) which states that: 'Taking into account the gravity of the crime and the interests of victims, there are nonetheless *substantial reasons* to believe that an investigation would not serve the interests of justice.'[322] From this provision, it is clear that the Prosecutor is required to weigh the gravity of the crime and interests of victims against possible 'substantial reasons'. The factors that make up those substantial reasons are not given for obvious reasons; the drafters of the Rome Statute, just like the Prosecutor, could, not have enumerated all possible reasons that could persuade the Prosecutor to stop a worthwhile investigation.[323] The requirement is that those factors need to meet the threshold of being 'substantial reasons' – enough to satisfy the Pre-Trial Chamber as well.[324] The use of substantial evidence is not an unknown standard of proof, it is common in administrative law and other situations that require the balance of probabilities, and it is also used in the ICC where the Prosecutor is required to meet the standard of 'substantial grounds to believe' in order for the Pre-Trial Chamber to confirm charges. For the Prosecutor to stop a prosecution, Article 53(2)(c) states that: 'A prosecution is not in the interests of justice, taking into account all the circumstances, including the gravity of the crime, the interests of victims and the age or infirmity of the alleged perpetrator, and his or her role in the alleged crime.' In this case, the Prosecutor, in addition to considering the gravity of the crime and interests of victims, is also required to consider the age or infirmity of the alleged perpetrator and his or her role in the alleged crime, and again, weigh those conditions against the different possible factors indicating that prosecuting such a case would be against the interests of justice. In both situations (investigation and prosecution), the standard of proof is that those factors should be 'substantial reasons'.

I argue that the Policy Paper should have concentrated on the use of the gravity of the crime, interests of victims and the age and infirmity of the suspect in relation to other possible factors that would persuade the Prosecutor

---

322 Emphasis added.

323 The 2007 OTP Policy Paper on Interests of Justice state that:

> [T]he Statute itself does not try to elaborate on the specific factors or circumstances that should be taken into account in consideration of the interests of justice issue. The approach taken by the Office of the Prosecutor is therefore bound to offer only limited clarification in the abstract: as is the case with many legal problems in jurisdictions throughout the world, the particular approach taken will necessarily have to depend on the facts and circumstances of the case or situation.

324 If the Prosecutor decides not to investigate or prosecute on the basis of 'interests of justice' alone, he or she must inform the Pre-Trial Chamber.

to believe that conducting a certain investigation or prosecution would be against the interests of justice, and avoid mentioning issues of peace, security and alternative justice mechanisms. There is no other explanation as to why these factors (peace, security and other alternative justice mechanisms) were identified for elaboration other than the fact that they were being discussed in ongoing situations. The Prosecutor cannot exhaustively enumerate all the things he or she will not consider in the exercise of his or her discretionary powers. Therefore, selecting some factors becomes suspicious. The 'interests of justice' under Article 53 has lost its broader character and claimed without evidence that punitive justice is always the best alternative to other forms of justice, in cases of atrocious crimes. Thus, as Varaki notes, 'the 2007 policy paper adopted a restrictive approach to the "interests of justice" clause, which does not do justice to its complexity and almost makes it a dead letter'.[325]

### 3.3.2. GEOGRAPHICAL OR REGIONAL BALANCE

The OTP has been criticised for focusing on Africa, as a sign of political manipulations in its decision-making process,[326] a charge it has strenuously denied. I argue that the adoption of a policy statement claiming that 'geographical or regional balancing' is not part of the OTP's considerations is a response to criticisms about its current focus on Africa. All the OTP Preliminary Activities reports (2011–2017) and the 2013 Policy Paper on Preliminary Examinations clearly state that: 'Factors such as geographical or regional balance are not relevant criteria for a determination that a situation warrants investigation under the Rome Statute.'[327] This is to indicate that it is making its decisions based solely on legal criteria and nothing else but the Rome Statute. Schabas, commenting on the OTP's suggestion that its focus on Africa is a result of a legal criteria and the gravity of crimes in particular, states that:

> The 'gravity' language strikes the Observer as little more than obfuscation, a contrived attempt to make the determinations look objective and judicial. The seriousness of the situations in Central Africa is unquestioned. However, there are many serious situations in the territories of the 113 State Parties to the Rome Statute, or elsewhere in the world but involving nationals of State Parties.[328]

---

325 Varaki, 'Revisiting the 'Interests of Justice' Policy Paper' (2017), 456.

326 Kurt Mills, 'Bashir Is Dividing Us: Africa and the International Criminal Court' (2012) 34, 404 Human Rights Quarterly, 411; Schabas, 'Victor's Justice: Selecting Situations at the International Criminal Court' (2010), 545ff; Bosco, 'Discretion and State Influence at the International Criminal Court: The Prosecutor's Preliminary Examinations' (2017).

327 Para. 9 of all Preliminary Examination Activities Reports (2011-2017); see also paras. 11 and 29 of the 2013 OTP Policy Paper on Preliminary Examinations.

328 Schabas, 'Victor's Justice: Selecting Situations at the International Criminal Court' (2010), 549.

If we assume that it is indeed true – that the OTP considers just the legal criteria as set out in the Rome Statute – was it necessary to make a policy statement about something that is obviously expected of the highest lawyer of the Court? What if, in the future, several situations from different regions equally fulfil the legal criteria as established in the Rome Statute, and the Court with its limited resources has to choose from among those potential situations which ones to prioritise, would it not make sense to select a situation from a region that is either not represented or underrepresented, in terms of situations under investigation? It is difficult to exclude completely the fact that geographical or regional representation is an important aspect in judging whether an institution is truly international or not. For example, 'equitable geographical representation' is a very important aspect to consider in the recruitment process of the ICC staff.[329] Even if the example of staff recruitment is extraneous to criminal investigations, it is nonetheless informative of how geographical representation reflects the international character of an institution. Mills note that 'the focus of prosecutions to date has been on Africa and this has affected how many States in Africa perceive the Court'.[330] Bosco shares the same view where he indicates that '[t]he Court's focus on African conflicts, in particular, has provoked tension between the Court and several African leaders (...)'.[331] Kiyani notes that the Court

> has exclusively investigated crimes in Africa so far. In this context, the ICC can be plausibly construed as having not just a jurisdictional problem, but as fetishising certain forms of suffering and perpetration as uniquely African, and projecting external (and often Western-led) interventions as salvation.[332]

Certainly, geographical balancing should not be among the first reasons for the Prosecutor to consider, when deciding on where to conduct an investigation, but ignoring it completely even where there is a clear focus on one region and expect not to face some kind of criticisms is unintelligible.

### 3.3.3. TIPPING THE DOMESTIC BALANCE OF POWER

The ICC OTP prosecutorial strategy has been criticised for affecting domestic politics by conducting one-sided prosecutions. Criticisms of biased prosecutions have been raised in almost all situations but concerns intensified with the situation of Ivory Coast, where it is alleged that all parties involved in the

329 Arts. 44, and 36(8)(ii) of the Rome Statute.
330 Mills, 'Bashir Is Dividing Us: Africa and the International Criminal Court' (2012), 411.
331 Bosco, 'Discretion and State Influence at the International Criminal Court: The Prosecutor's Preliminary Examinations' (2017), 395.
332 Kiyani, 'Legitimacy, Legality, and the Possibility of a Pluralist International Criminal Law' (2017), 101.

post-election violence might have committed international crimes.[333] The danger of focusing on one side of the conflict is that it results in political imbalances making the Court part of domestic politics (politicised) – the prosecuted group considers the Court as a continuation of their persecution while emboldening the unprosecuted group. Rosenberg argues that the Prosecutor to 'avoid tipping the balance of power by shaping prosecutions according to the balance of power'.[334] Obviously, the OTP denies allegations of bias in favour of certain groups. The Prosecution insists that its investigations and prosecutions are guided by evidence and nothing else, and where another side to the conflict is alleged to have been involved in crimes, investigations into those allegations remains a possibility in future but the Office has to start from somewhere – a sequencing approach.[335]

According to the OTP Policy Paper on Case Selection and Prioritisation,

> [t]he principle of impartiality (…) does not mean an 'equivalence of blame' between different persons and groups within a situation, or that the Office must necessarily prosecute all sides, in order to balance-off perceptions of bias (…).[336]

It would be absurd to suggest that prosecutions ought to be guided by a salient desire to balance political interests, as opposed to available evidence – and certainly this is not what is suggested here – it is rather a reflection of a pattern of choices that makes observers question the objectivity of the decision-making processes. As Tiemessen notes, 'the prosecutorial strategy *within* each situation reflects considerable imbalances that reveal the strategic interests of external actors and results in problematic impunity gaps'.[337] The perception is that the Court is not treating like cases alike, and as Perelman notes:

> [w]hen people are heard complaining of having been unjustly treated (…) nobody will suppose that these people were identical with those to whom they compare themselves (…). The fact is, they claim that *certain* elements, regarded as *essential*, and nothing else, ought to have been taken into consideration.[338]

---

333 Schmitt, 'France, Africa, and the ICC: The Neocolonialist Critique and the Crisis of the Institutional Legitimacy' (2016), 127–151; Rosenberg, 'International Criminal Court in Cote d'Ivoire: Impartiality at Stake' (2017); Tiemessen, 'The International Criminal Court and the politics of prosecutions' (2014), 451–456.

334 Rosenberg, ibid, 484.

335 Para. B., of The Office of the Prosecutor Report on Prosecutorial Strategy [14 September 2016], 5 https://www.icc-cpi.int/NR/rdonlyres/D673DD8C-D427-4547-BC69-2D363E07274B/143708/ProsecutorialStrategy20060914_English.pdf; Rosenberg, 'International Criminal Court in Cote d'Ivoire: Impartiality at Stake' (2017), 484ff.

336 Para. 66 of the OTP Policy Paper on Case Selection and Prioritisation.

337 Tiemessen, 'The International Criminal Court and the politics of prosecutions' (2014), 451.

338 Chaïm Perelman, *The Idea of Justice and the Problem of Argument* (Routledge & Kegan Paul, 1977), 81, as in Alphonse Muleefu, *Reparation for victims of collateral damage: A normative and theoretical inquiry* (Wolf Legal Publishers, 2014), 148.

Lately, the OTP seems to have understood the danger of its sequencing approach. The OTP Basic Size Document states the wish to conduct parallel investigations in future where 'both sides have allegedly committed crimes (…) to avoid any perception of partiality'.[339]

The challenge of adopting policies that are *ex post* justifications is that interpretation of general rules is tailored to fit a specific situation under consideration. The danger of interpreting a rule restrictively and focused on a specific situation is that it might be difficult to apply to other situations in future, and that failure could be interpreted as inconsistency, consequently hurting its legitimacy. This is not to say that the Prosecutor should not take positions on matters of (ongoing) public debate, nor respond to critics, because there is a duty on the Office to clarify its mandate and the manner in which it is implementing it. However, the best way to do so could be through the issuance of a press statement rather than adopting a policy paper. The advantage of issuing a specific press statement is that it can be focused, detailed and relevant to that very specific situation, while a policy paper creates an expectation of a general application to all future situations.

339 Para. 3 of Annex II: Resource justification … (ICC-ASP/14/21) of 17 September 2015, 37.

# CHAPTER 4
# BETWEEN INDEPENDENCE AND PRAGMATISM

Chapter 2 provided an illustration of narratives presenting different issues concerning disagreements between the critics and supporters of the Court. Chapter 3 examined the administration of prosecutorial justice focusing on decisions that are within the prosecutorial discretion. This chapter is concerned with raising some issues necessary to consider if there was indeed a desire to have a real dialogue, and examines whether it is possible to resolve the existing disagreements. In other words, is it possible for the Court to create a perception that it is beyond the influence of the powerful states? The reason is simple: perception is very important. As Thakur notes '[t]he sense of justice, fairness and equity is deeply ingrained in human beings (...). One of the most powerful refrains in any society is "That's not fair", leading individuals to resist and disobey and groups to rebel and revolt'.[340]

However, the most critical challenge is that it is very difficult to know who is being referred to whenever people suggest a dialogue between the Court and the AU. It is unclear whether it is a dialogue between the AU and the ICC Prosecutor and/or other ICC officials, or if it is a discussion that is supposed to happen within the Assembly of States Parties (ASP), the legislative body of the Court. Or, to suggest other options, whether it should be a dialogue organised between the AU and the ICC supporters, especially with the Coalition for the ICC, or whether it should be between the AU and the United Nations Security Council (UNSC), or the Security Council with the Court. What about a conversation between the AU and 'northern' powers and possibly powerful individual actors within the global networks capable of influencing the Court? In other words, do we really agree on who represents the Court on all those issues that are raised? Or as Bolton noted, the Court and the Prosecutor are indeed 'simply "out there" in the international system'.[341] As Gevers notes,

---

340 Thakur, 'International Criminal Justice: At the Vortex of Power, Norms and a Shifting Global Order' (2015), 31.

341 John R. Bolton, 'The Risks and Weakness of the International Criminal Court: From America's Perspective' (2001) 64:1 Law and Contemporary Problems, 169.

the legitimacy of the International Criminal Court has moved away from the usual international law state-based consent – as a tactical strategy – to a representation of an imagined international community and abstract victims.[342]

If there is indeed no single actor capable of representing the Court on all matters, is it possible to have a platform capable of bringing together all of the actors concerned into a conversation that would advance the mission of the Court, that of fighting impunity of international crimes, and still provide assurance that the Court will be protected from external interferences? The pessimistic view is that a truthful dialogue is not possible in the near future, before we can deal with current egos on both sides. On one side, African leaders through the AU – especially with the case of Al Bashir – have demonstrated that it is possible to ignore the Court's decisions with little consequences, and on the other side, the OTP has been consistent in its unwillingness to change the current dispassionate interpretation of the Rome Statute. This is an indication that both sides have reasons and powers to stand their ground; African leaders ought to protect their interests the way they see fit and there is nothing unusual about that, while the ICC Prosecution's claim of being under an obligation to strictly enforce the Rome Statute is fine too, and neither side should be coerced to budge an inch. Therefore, for how long will this power struggle go on, and how does it impact the overall mission of ending impunity, which both sides agree is important?

These are difficult questions to which I cannot offer definitive responses. Or maybe, we should simply accept that to a certain extent it might have been expected that the Court was going to be in conflict with some states in cases where it acted in a manner that was contrary to their interests, because in all matters of cooperation sometimes disagreements are inevitable. However, what is unquestionable is the fact that any sustainable relationship needs some genuine desire from both sides to find reason in the other's point of view – something that is missing at the moment. This chapter briefly looks back to highlight the current situation and at the same time forwards to suggest some possible middle ground. Even if it seems that both the supporters and critics of the Court are not interested in talking to each other, it does not mean that there is a complete lack of engagement; some activities have continued to happen with all actors, and the Court seems to be moving on with its work as usual.

342 Africa Group of Justice and Accountability, 'PANEL VII: Immunity of Heads of State under International Law' (Christopher Gevers, 45:10–58); see also Sara Kendall and Sarah Nouwen, 'Representational Practices at the International Criminal Court: The Gap between Juridified and Abstract Victimhood' (2013) 76, 235–262 Law and Contemporary Problems.

## 4.1. WHERE ARE WE?

Whereas the AU's criticisms of the Court started immediately after the indictment of President Omar Al Bashir of Sudan, the blustering rhetoric increased in 2013, after the election of the ICC indicts, Uhuru Kenyatta and William Ruto, as President and Deputy President of the Republic of Kenya respectively. When Charles Jalloh was asked to say one thing that would improve the ICC-Africa relationship, he first retorted 'why don't you drop Kenyan cases?'[343] This was meant to be a joke but it carried some substantial meaning. It would be disingenuous to claim that the collapse of the Kenyan cases was a strategic calculation on the ICC Prosecution's side to reduce pressure. Because, the charges against Kenyatta failed due to lack of enough evidence to proceed to trial[344] and in April 2016, the Trial Chamber V(A) in a majority decision, vacated all charges against Ruto and Sang due to insufficient evidence contrary to the Prosecution's request for the re-characterisation of charges.[345] What could be true though is that this was a blessing in disguise because it is fairly accurate to attribute the current reduction in the anti-ICC rhetoric to the termination of Kenyan cases. The once nervously anticipated massive withdrawal decision that was supposed to be adopted in the Kigali's 27th AU summit of July 2016 failed reportedly due to a lack of consensus.[346] This failure can be partly attributed to Kenya's loss of momentum in pushing through the call due to the collapse of the cases against its leaders – initially it was a Kenyan led call.

In 2017, after the defeat of Yahya Jammeh, the new President of Gambia, Mr. Adama Barrow, reversed his predecessor's decision to withdraw from the Court.[347] In the same period, the High Court of South Africa, after finding that the Government's decision to withdraw from the ICC had

---

343 Africa Group for Justice and Accountability, 'Panel I – Africa and the ICC: Misperceptions and Realities' (Charles C. Jalloh, 1:24:48–1:26:40).

344 Trial Chamber V(B), *The Prosecutor v. Uhuru Muigai Kenyatta* (Decision on the withdrawal of charges against Mr. Kenyatta) ICC-0l/09-02/11 of 13 March 2015.

345 Trial Chamber V(A), *The Prosecutor v. William Samoei Ruto and Joshua Arap Sang* (Decision on Defence Applications for Judgments of Acquittal) ICC-01/09-01/11 of 5 April 2016.

346 Voice of Nigeria, 'Calls For Africa's Withdrawal From ICC Suffers Set Back At AU Summit' [Sahara Reporters, 29 July 2016] http://saharareporters.com/2016/07/29/calls-africas-withdrawal-icc-suffers-set-back-au-summit; HRW Press release, 'UN/African Union: Reject ICC Withdrawal – Security Council Meeting with AU' (2016); Patryk I. Labuda, 'The African Union's Collective Withdrawal from the ICC: Does Bad Law make for Good Politics?' [15 February 2017] https://www.ejiltalk.org/the-african-unions-collective-withdrawal-from-the-icc-does-bad-law-make-for-good-politics/.

347 Elise Keppler, 'Gambia Rejoins ICC: South Africa, Burundi Now Outliers on Exit' [Human Rights Watch, 17 February 2017] https://www.hrw.org/news/2017/02/17/gambia-rejoins-icc; Pap Saine and Lamin Jahateh, 'Gambia announces plans to stay in International Criminal Court' [Reuters, 13 February 2017] https://www.reuters.com/article/us-gambia-justice-icc-idUSKBN15S2HF; Merrit Kennedy, 'Under New Leader, Gambia Cancels Withdrawal

violated the Constitution – for the failure to seek the Parliament's approval – ordered that the notice sent to the UN Secretary General be withdrawn.[348] This averted what was considered as a catastrophe to the Court. To use the words of Plessis and Mettraux: 'From the point of view of the Court, and in particular for the Assembly of States Parties, the [South Africa's] attempted withdrawal was a near-miss disaster.'[349] By the end of 2017, the only African member state that had effectively withdrawn from the Rome Treaty was Burundi. Its decision to withdraw took effect on 27 October 2017, just two days after the ICC Pre-Trial Chamber had authorised the OTP to conduct investigations into crimes against humanity allegedly committed in and outside Burundi since 26 April 2015.[350] Since then, we have continued to witness a number of ICC member states, especially from the West African region, declaring their unwavering support for the Court.[351] Boehme notes that '[w]hile Africa constitutes the most critical region, many African states continue to support the Court and more references expressing loyalty were issued in 2017 than in 2007'.[352]

From 15 June 2012 to 15 June 2021, the OTP has been under a new leadership, Ms. Fatou Bensouda of Gambia. The blustering Mr. Moreno Ocampo of Argentina, the ICC's first Prosecutor, who is often described as having been 'arrogant', 'full of himself', 'boastful', 'a running character' interested in 'showmanship' and more 'amenable to working with the strongest power in the world' than conducting real investigations, has completed his

from International Criminal Court' [NPR, 12 February 2017] https://www.npr.org/sections/thetwo-way/2017/02/14/515219467/under-new-leader-gambia-cancels-withdrawal-from-international-criminal-court.

348 The High Court of South Africa (Gauteng Division, Pretoria), in the matters of *Democratic Alliance and others v. the Minister of International Relations and Cooperation and others* (case n°. 83145/2016) Judgment of 22 February 2017.

349 Max du Plessis and Guénaël Mettraux, 'South Africa's Failed Withdrawal from the Rome Statute: Politics, Law, and Judicial Accountability' (2017) 15:2 Journal of International Justice, 368.

350 ICC Pre-Trial Chamber III, 'The Situation in the Republic of Burundi (Public Redacted Version of "Decision Pursuant to Article 15 of the Rome Statute on the Authorization of an Investigation into the Situation in the Republic of Burundi"', ICC-01/17-X-9-US-Exp, 25 October 2017); Agence France-Presse 'Burundi becomes first nation to leave international criminal court' [The Guardian, 28 October 2017] https://www.theguardian.com/law/2017/oct/28/burundi-becomes-first-nation-to-leave-international-criminal-court.

351 Hlawulani Mkhabela, 'Africa and ICC Going Forward' [L'Afrique en Questions, No. 31, January 2017] https://www.ifri.org/en/publications/editoriaux-de-lifri/lafrique-questions/africa-and-icc-going-forward; ICC Press Release, 'Nigeria and other States renew their support for ICC' [ICC-CPI-20180409-PR1378, 9 April 2018] https://www.icc-cpi.int/Pages/item.aspx?name=pr1378.

352 Franziska Boehme, 'Exit, voice and loyalty: state rhetoric about the International Criminal Court' (2018) 22:3 The International Journal of Human Rights, 421.

nine-year mandate.[353] Mr. Ocampo's staggering ineptitude is something the critics and supporters of the Court can agree on. Kenneth Roth puts it thus:

> [s]ome of the ICC's problems are of its own making. The chief prosecutor for its first nine years, Luis Moreno Ocampo of Argentina, seemed more interested in issuing arrest warrants than undertaking the tough, less glamorous work of conducting rigorous criminal investigations.[354]

Those with kinder comments observe that the ICC's first Prosecutor 'might have avoided examining situations that would be sensitive to the permanent members out of concern that the Council would defer his investigations'.[355] However, the recent revelations, in what is currently referred to as 'Ocampogate', throw some more light onto the shoddy character of the first Prosecutor.[356] The policy document known to have been publicised during his nine-year tenure of office is the controversial 'interests of justice' document but generally little is known about his prosecutorial guidelines and orientation. To the contrary, Bensouda has adopted several policy documents and consistently produces annual reports on preliminary examinations. But still, it remains difficult for Ms. Bensouda to completely distance herself from Ocampo because before becoming the Prosecutor she had served as his deputy.

Besides the two situations, Colombia and Iraq/UK, which have been perpetually under preliminary examination since June 2004 and May 2014 (but previously concluded in 2006) respectively, the Prosecutor has been slowly trying to expand into other regions. In Eastern Europe, from 25 April 2014, Ukraine has been under preliminary investigation, and Georgia has been under investigation since January 2016.[357] On 8 February 2018, the Prosecutor announced that

353 Al Jazeera, 'Upfront – Arena: Is the ICC biased against African Countries?' (Mahmood Mamdani); James Verini, 'The President and the Prosecutor' [The New York Times Magazine, 22 June 2016] https://mobile.nytimes.com/2016/06/26/magazine/international-criminal-court-moreno-ocampo-the-prosecutor-and-the-president.html.

354 Roth, 'Africa attacks the International Criminal Court' (2014).

355 C. Cora True-Frost, 'The International Civil Servant: How the First Prosecutor Engaged the U.N. Security Council' in Martha Minow, C. Cora True-Frost and Alex Whiting (eds.), *The First Global Prosecutor: Promise and Constraints* (University of Michigan Press, 2015) 252.

356 Tjitske Lingsma, 'How Ocampogate harms the International Criminal Court' [30 November 2017, Grojil-blog] https://grojil.org/2017/11/30/how-ocampogate-harms-the-international-criminal-court/; Pierre Hazan, 'ICC scandal: Who is watching the sheriff?' [Justice Info, 18 October 2017] https://www.justiceinfo.net/en/justice-reconciliation/34986-icc-scandal-who-is-watching-the-sheriff.html; Sven Becker and Dietmar Pieper, 'The Ocampo Affair: Current ICC Chief Prosecutor Weighed Down by Predecessor' [17 October 2017] http://www.spiegel.de/international/world/international-criminal-court-scandal-widens-a-1173156.html.

357 The OTP Report on Preliminary Examination Activities 2017 dated 4 December 2017.

she was opening preliminary examinations in the situations of the Philippines and Venezuela.[358] The Prosecutor has also attempted to show an interest in situations involving some of the world's more powerful states. This is going to be the first test of the Court's maturity. Since 16 January 2016, the situation of Palestine involving Israeli soldiers has been under preliminary examination, and on 20 November 2017, the Prosecutor requested an authorisation to conduct investigations into the alleged crimes committed in Afghanistan by, among others, US soldiers and CIA civilians.[359]

The Prosecutor's attempt to expand to into other places has not come without consequences. The announcement of the request for an authorisation to investigate in Afghanistan was met with a stern warning from the US State Department that '(...) an I.C.C. investigation with respect to U.S. personnel would be wholly unwarranted and unjustified'.[360] Bolton, just before becoming the Security Advisor to President Trump, had made an uncompromising statement about the US position towards the Court:

> America's long-term security depends on refusing to recognize an iota of legitimacy in this brazen effort to subordinate democratic nations to the unaccountable melding of executive and judicial authority in the ICC.[361]

Israel's position is also very clear; it does not want the ICC in Palestine. The Israeli Foreign Minister Avigdor Lieberman reportedly said that '[w]e will act in the international arena in order to bring an end to this court'.[362] In November 2016, Russia, because of the Court's investigations in Georgia, decided to withdraw its signature to the Rome Treaty, and the spokesperson of the Ministry of Foreign Affairs, Maria Zakharova, reportedly said that

> Russia stood at the origins of the ICC's founding, voted for its establishment and has always cooperated with the agency. Russia hoped that the ICC will become an

358 See the 'Statement of the Prosecutor of the International Criminal Court, Mrs Fatou Bensouda, on opening Preliminary Examinations into the situations in the Philippines and in Venezuela' [ICC, 8 February 2018] https://www.icc-cpi.int/Pages/item.aspx?name=180208-otp-stat.

359 For all these details, see the OTP Report on Preliminary Examination Activities 2017 dated 4 December 2017.

360 Seen at Rick Gladstone and Marlise Simons, 'Prosecutor's Move in Afghan War Inquiry May Mean Clash with U.S.' [The New York Times, 20 November 2017] https://www.nytimes.com/2017/11/20/world/asia/international-criminal-court-afghanistan-united-states.html.

361 John Bolton, 'The Hague Aims for U.S. Soldiers: A "war crimes" inquiry in Afghanistan shows the danger of the International Criminal Court' [Wall Street Journal, 20 November 2017] https://www.wsj.com/articles/the-hague-tiptoes-toward-u-s-soldiers-1511217136.

362 Thomas Escritt and Anthony Deutsch, 'ICC Opens Investigation into Israeli-Palestinian Conflict' [Reuters, 16 January 2015] https://www.reuters.com/article/us-icc-palestinians-examination-idUSKBN0KP1PR20150116.

> important factor in consolidating the rule of law and stability in international relations. Unfortunately, to our mind, this did not happen. (…)[363]

The Philippines, on 17 March 2018, notified the United Nations Secretary General of its intention to withdraw from the Rome Treaty, following the ICC Prosecutor's announcement that she was conducting preliminary examinations.[364] With this reality in mind, one could correctly argue that, after all, African leaders are not a very strange species when it comes to their dealing with international criminal justice. As Posner and Yoo note, 'one should be skeptical of the claim that states would submit disputes to judges over whom they have no influence'.[365]

Additionally, the Court has obstacles of its own beyond those emanating from state cooperation. The current ongoing situations indicate a seriously slow pace in the conduct of trials, and it is evidently clear that Ms. Bensouda is likely to hand over – to whoever will come after her completing the remaining three years of her tenure – a Court that is still largely African. The Court will have spent close to 20 years focusing on one region, and on this I think Mr. Ocampo was probably correct when he said that we should wait until the Court's maturity reaches 40 years of existence for it to move elsewhere.[366]

The ICC can survive with some few countries including the most powerful opting out of the Rome Treaty. It survived when the US Bush Administration withdrew its signature to the Rome Treaty in 2003 and its subsequent anti-ICC campaign. Therefore, there is no reason to believe that it will not survive this time around. However, what is clear is that the Court believes that it cannot survive without the support of NGOs, in particular the Coalition for the ICC. NGOs are the Court's intermediaries in different ways; providing information and contacts through their local partners; raising awareness about the Court, and conducting lobbying campaigns on behalf of the Court for the ratification of the Statute. Whether it is in Kenya, Nigeria or South Africa, it has been NGOs linked to the Coalition that have petitioned national courts and threatened President Al-Bashir with a possible arrest.[367] In Zambia, when

---

363 Shaun Walker and Owen Bowcott, 'Russia Withdraws Signature from International Criminal Court Statute' [The Guardian, 16 November 2016] https://www.theguardian.com/world/2016/nov/16/russia-withdraws-signature-from-international-criminal-court-statute.

364 'ICC Statement on The Philippines' notice of withdrawal: State participation in Rome Statute system essential to international rule of law' [20 March 2018] https://www.icc-cpi.int/Pages/item.aspx?name=pr1371.

365 Posner and Yoo, 'Judicial Independence in International Tribunals' (2005), 12.

366 Al Jazeera, 'Upfront – Arena: Is the ICC biased against African Countries?' (Moreno Ocampo).

367 'NGOs criticise government over Bashir order' [Capital News, 2 December 2011] https://www.capitalfm.co.ke/news/2011/12/ngos-criticise-government-over-bashir-order/; 'Kenya: Civil Society Welcomes President Bashir's Arrest Warrant' [Hirondelle News Agency,

the Government wanted to conduct an opinion survey on whether it should withdraw from the Court, NGO members of the Coalition came together quickly and mobilised the population around the support of the Court.[368]

However, this entrenched connection of the Court to NGOs has been criticised and it is not helping in reducing the suspicion of neo-colonial bias. The Coalition for the ICC has been accused of being highly centralised, and that its agenda towards the Court is driven by 'international, western-based organisations with a human rights profile'. Lohne goes further in arguing that 'the Coalition functions as a gate-keeper for global civil society access, by having significant influence over who is, or who is not, to pass through the security doors and participate in the ASP meetings'. This selective process, she further notes, excludes other NGOs/Civil society that might have divergent views concerning justice.[369] Barkin notes that:

> Critics of NGO participation in IOs also point out that NGO membership is disproportionately biased toward middle-class, white citizens of Western states. In this sense, NGOs can be criticized as being neo-colonial, as a mechanism for reintroducing rule by the West over the South through non-military means.[370]

To counter the neo-colonial/anti-Africa bias, civil society is sending a team of senior Africans to forge a relationship between the ICC and Africa. The recent creation of the Africa Group for Justice and Accountability, a group of African senior experts in diplomacy, politics, international law and human rights can be seen in that endeavour. The group has the mission of 'enhancing cooperation between Africa and the International Criminal Court' among others.[371] Since its

---

30 November 2011] http://allafrica.com/stories/201112010567.html; 'Sudan's Bashir leaves Nigeria, ICC calls for arrest' [Reuters, 16 July 2013] https://www.reuters.com/article/us-nigeria-sudan-idUSBRE96F0H420130716?feedType=RSS&feedName=topNews; Anne Van der Mei, 'On the Run for International Criminal Justice: Sudanese President Omar al-Bashir Escapes from South Africa' [17 June 2015] https://www.maastrichtuniversity.nl/blog/2015/06/run-international-criminal-justice-sudanese-president-omar-al-bashir-escapes-south.

368 Boniface Cheembe, 'ICC and Africa: The case of Zambia' [The Southern African Centre for the Constructive Resolution of Disputes (SACCORD), 6 June 2017] http://www.coalitionfortheicc.org/news/20170606/icc-and-africa-case-zambia.

369 Kjersti Lohne, *Advocates of Humanity: Human Rights NGOs in International Criminal Justice* (A dissertation submitted in partial fulfilment of the requirements for the degree of philosophia doctor (Ph.D.) – Department of Criminology and Sociology of Law Faculty of Law University of Oslo) – (unpublished version), 107, 122–123.

370 J. Samuel Barkin, *International Organizations: Theories and Institutions* (2nd ed., Palgrave Macmillan, 2013), 16.

371 Mission Statement of the Africa Group for Justice and Accountability http://www.wayamo.com/africa-group-for-justice-and-accountability/; see also the list of members at https://www.scribd.com/document/359932059/The-Africa-Group-for-Justice-and-Accountability-and-its-members-Les-membres-du-Groupe-Africain-pour-la-Justice-et-la-Fin-de-l-Impunite#from_embed.

creation, it has been organising different events throughout the continent explaining different issues of justice and accountability. Whereas its mandate of sensitising African leaders about the ICC is well articulated, what is not clear is the process of channelling whatever that group could consider as legitimate concerns of critics into concrete solutions that would improve the Court's conduct and image. It is also not clear whether these efforts will completely remove the suspicion of neo-colonial bias because, as Barkin states:

> Independent IO decision-making can similarly be criticized as being neo-colonial, because the secretariats of IOs tend to be made up of 'professionals,' people trained in Western techniques for managing their issue-areas. Even if they are acting from the best of intentions, they may focus on what they think they should do rather than what the population at large wants them to do.[372]

The Court's closeness to the NGO network remains problematic because as Voeten notes, 'NGOs advocate particular interpretation of war crimes law and issue press releases demanding convictions or prosecutions. This results in a potential threat to judicial independence that has received little attention'.[373]

Having said that, we should not underestimate the role of NGOs in raising awareness about situations of potential human rights abuse, which in some cases leads to prevention of atrocity crimes, and after such crimes have been committed their role in making sure that individuals suspected of those crimes are held accountable. There is no better example than the *Hissène Habré* case.[374] However, the Court cannot survive on NGOs alone without a strategy that can galvanise a robust support from governments. NGOs, just like the Court, do not have an enforcing capacity; they can expose, name and shame, but without governments willing to enforce the Court decisions, the envisioned end of impunity would remain unpredictable.

## 4.2. WHAT DOES THE ICC DO?

The Preamble of the Rome Statute describes the mandate of the Court as that of punishing perpetrators of international crimes, and as a result, contributing to

---

372 Barkin, *International Organizations: Theories and Institutions* (2013), 16.

373 Erik Voeten, 'International Judicial Independence' in Jeffrey L. Dunoff and Mark A. Pollack (eds.), *Interdisciplinary Perspectives on International Law and International Relations: The State of the Art* (Cambridge University Press, 2013), 423.

374 Reed Brody; 'Bringing a Dictator to Justice: The Case of Hissène Habré' (2015) 13:2, 209–217 Journal of International Criminal Justice; Florian Jeßberger and Julia Geneuss; 'Litigating Universal Jurisdiction' – Introduction (2015) 13:2, 205–208 Journal of International Criminal Justice; Christoph Sperfeldt, 'The trial against Hissène Habré: networked justice and reparations at the Extraordinary African Chambers' (2017) 21:9, 1243–1260 The International Journal of Human Rights.

the prevention of such crimes. There is no requirement to prove the prevention of crimes because it is presumed to come as a consequence of punishing perpetrators.[375] However, the preventive benefits of the Court remain negligible and controversial.[376] The ICC Prosecutor's projection of opening one new situation every year[377] does not support a deterrent narrative. The truth is that the preventive effects resulting from punishments meted out to criminal offenders are equally questionable at domestic level. Therefore, it would be too much to expect preventive effects from an international criminal prosecution without considering policing and other crime-prevention measures. It is unrealistic to assume that criminal prosecutions alone are capable of preventing crimes.

Nonetheless, the Court has made some significant contributions to (ongoing) post-conflict societies and the international community. First, and probably the most significant contribution of the Court that goes even beyond its stated mandate of ending impunity, has been its contribution to the development of international criminal law. In addition to the role of *ad hoc* tribunals and hybrid courts, it would be unusual to find a course on international criminal law that does not mention something about the International Criminal Court especially using its instruments and jurisprudence in defining international crimes, and how such legal instruments have influenced the adoption of international crime legislation in different jurisdictions. Moreover, the Court's jurisprudence has contributed to the clarification of some aspects of international law and international judicial cooperation. For instance, there is probably no other subject of cooperation in international law that has been more frequently debated than the immunity of heads of state. The Court continues to wrestle with different states on their failure to arrest President Al-Bashir,[378] and different scholars, organisations and states have contributed their diverging views.[379]

---

375 Preamble of the Rome Statute (read Affirming and Determined).

376 Hyeran Jo and Beth A. Simmons, 'Can the International Criminal Court Deter Atrocity?' (2016) 70:3, 443–475 International Organization; Benjamin J. Appel, 'In the Shadow of the International Criminal Court: Does the ICC Deter Human Rights Violations?' (2018) 62:1, 3–28. Journal of Conflict Resolution; Edwin Bikundo, 'The International Criminal Court and Africa: Exemplary Justice' (2012) 23:1, 21–41 Law and Critique; Benjamin N Schiff, 'Can the International Criminal Court Contribute to the Responsibility to Protect?' (2016) 30:3, 298–313 International Relations; Daniel Krcmaric, 'Should I Stay or Should I Go? Leaders, Exile, and the Dilemmas of International Justice' (2018) 62:2, 486–498 American Journal of Political Science; Elise Keppler, 'Managing Setbacks for the International Criminal Court in Africa' (2012) 56:1, 1–14 Journal of African Law; Courtney Hillebrecht, 'The Deterrent Effects of the International Criminal Court: Evidence from Libya' (2016) 42:4, 616–643 International Interactions.

377 See the ICC Prosecutor's Basic Size Document.

378 Pre-Trial Chamber II, in *Prosecutor v. Omar Hassan Ahmad Al Bashir*, 'Decision under article 87(7) of the Rome Statute on the non-compliance by Jordan with the request by the Court for the arrest and surrender or Omar Al-Bashir' of 11 December 2017 (ICC-02/05-01/09); Pre-Trial Chamber II, in *Prosecutor v. Omar Hassan Ahmad Al Bashir*, 'Decision under article 87(7) of the Rome Statute on the non-compliance by South Africa with the request by

Second, the Court has established itself as a relevant actor and a standard of reference when it comes to international criminal justice especially in Africa. Whether it is its detractors or supporters, whether it is victims or suspected perpetrators, or even a mere opposition politician who is interested in scoring a campaign point against the government, their rhetoric about human rights violations and/or protection will involve mentioning the ICC. These recurrent utterances referencing the Court in both public and private conversations can be considered as evidence of the Court's relevancy, as an active symbol of justice to victims, and probably a deterrent against the perpetration of international crimes.

However, these two aforementioned contributions are general and to a certain extent abstract in nature. They are general because they impact all states including non-state parties, and are abstract because they are very difficult to measure. It is the actual number of suspected perpetrators indicted and effectively prosecuted before the Court that is often the evidence of its role in fighting impunity.

In the 24 years of the International Criminal Tribunal for the Former Yugoslavia's (ICTY) existence, it indicted 161 persons,[380] the International

the Court for the arrest and surrender of Omar Al-Bashir' of 6 July 2017 (ICC-02/05-01/09); Pre-Trial Chamber I, in *Prosecutor v. Omar Hassan Ahmad Al Bashir*, 'Corrigendum to the Decision Pursuant to Article 87(7) of the Rome Statute on the Failure by the Republic of Malawi to Comply with the Cooperation Requests Issued by the Court with Respect to the Arrest and Surrender of Omar Hassan Ahmad Al Bashir' of 13 December 2011 (ICC-02/05-01/09-139-Corr); Pre-Trial Chamber I, in *Prosecutor v. Omar Hassan Ahmad Al Bashir*, 'Decision pursuant to article 87(7) of the Rome Statute on the refusal of the Republic of Chad to comply with the cooperation requests issued by the Court with respect to the arrest and surrender of Omar Hassan Ahmad Al Bashir' of 13 December 2011 (ICC-02/05-01/09-140-tENG); Pre-Trial Chamber II, in *Prosecutor v. Omar Hassan Ahmad Al Bashir*, 'Decision on the Non-compliance of the Republic of Chad with the Cooperation Requests Issued by the Court Regarding the Arrest and Surrender of Omar Hassan Ahmad Al-Bashir' of 26 March 2013 (ICC-02/05-01/09-151); Pre-Trial Chamber II, in *Prosecutor v. Omar Hassan Ahmad Al Bashir*, 'Decision on the Cooperation of the Democratic Republic of the Congo Regarding Omar Al Bashir's Arrest and Surrender to the Court' of 9 April 2014 (ICC-02/05-01/09-195); Pre-Trial Chamber II, in *Prosecutor v. Omar Hassan Ahmad Al Bashir*, 'Decision on the non-compliance by the Republic of Djibouti with the request to arrest and surrender Omar Al-Bashir to the Court and referring the matter to the United Nations Security Council and the Assembly of the States Parties to the Rome Statute' of 11 July 2016 (ICC-02/05-01/09-266); Pre-Trial Chamber II, in *Prosecutor v. Omar Hassan Ahmad Al Bashir*, 'Decision on the non-compliance by the Republic of Uganda with the request to arrest and surrender Omar Al-Bashir to the Court and referring the matter to the United Nations Security Council and the Assembly of States Parties to the Rome Statute' of 11 July 2016 (ICC-02/05-01/09-267).

379 See the Appeal's Chamber's invitation to international organisations, state parties and professors of International Law to submit their observations on legal matters raised by Jordan concerning the decision of the Pre-Trial Chamber II on its failure to arrest Al Bashir – the Appeals Chamber in the case of in *Prosecutor v. Omar Hassan Ahmad Al Bashir*, 'Order inviting expressions of interest as *amici curiae* in judicial proceedings (pursuant to rule 103 of the Rules of Procedure and Evidence)' of 28 March 2018 (ICC-02/05-01/09 0A2).

380 See Key Figures of Cases at http://www.icty.org/en/cases/key-figures-cases.

Criminal Tribunal for Rwanda (ICTR) indicted 93 individuals (eight of whom are still at large) within a period of 21 years,[381] and the Special Court for Sierra Leone (SCSL) heard 25 cases in a period of 11 years.[382] For the ICC, it has issued arrest warrants (or summons to appear) to 42 persons in its 13 years of existence (since July 2002). This is not a bad record for the ICC given its number of years of existence and the fact that it operates in different situations requiring spending a considerable amount of time conducting contextual analysis for each situation, something that was done once for these other tribunals whose focus was on just one situation. However, when we spread the 42 defendants into eight situations – where investigations have resulted in charges – it gives an average of five persons for each situation. This number is insignificant in affected communities compared to the nature of crimes under the Court's jurisdiction and victims involved in those situations, not forgetting that some of the suspects were accused of crimes against the administration of justice. As Ciampi argues

> [o]ffences against the administration of justice should be prosecuted. But when they amount to most of the Court's case-load for a given situation, one is left to wonder whether this is a proper, or at least acceptable, utilisation of the resources of the Court.[383]

The basic calculations indicate that if the ICC were to indict at least 20 persons in each situation, a number that would still remain relatively small, it would require increasing its current budget at least five times over. This is not likely to happen because of the financing constraints.[384] For instance, the OTP's Basic Size Document sent to the Assembly of States Parties (ASP) in 2015 '(...) to ensure that the Office has the requisite resources to fully meet its mandate under the Rome Statute; and (...) to offer States Parties a reasonably stable basis for budgetary planning (...)', has not been acted upon fully.[385] In the Basic Size Document, the Prosecutor made several requests and one of them was to increase the number of analysts in the Situation Analysis Section (SAS)

---

381 See Key Figures of Cases at http://unictr.unmict.org/en/cases/key-figures-cases.

382 See cases of the Special Court for Sierra Leone at http://www.scsldocs.org/.

383 Annalisa Ciampi, 'Legal Rules, Policy Choices and Political Realities in the Functioning of the Cooperation Regime of the International Criminal Court' in Olympia Bekou and Daley J. Birkett (eds.), *Cooperation and the International Criminal Court: Perspectives from Theory and Practice* (Brill/Nijhoff, 2016), 47.

384 Hans-Peter Kaul, 'The International Criminal Court of the future' in William A. Schabas (ed.), *The Cambridge Companion to International Criminal Law* (Cambridge University Press, 2016) 348; Sara Kendall, 'Commodifying Global Justice: Economies of Accountability at the International Criminal Court' (2015) 13:1 Journal of International Criminal Justice, 121; Stephen Chaudoin, 'How Contestation Moderates the Effects of International Institutions: The International Criminal Court and Kenya' (2016) 78:2 The Journal of Politics, 561.

385 Para.1 of the 'Basic Size Document', 3.

from 12 to 15,[386] but by the time of my visit to the seat of the Court in February 2018, almost three years later, the number of analysts was still at 12. It is these budgetary constraints and other earlier highlighted practical challenges that make the ICC's duty to prosecute, as Varaki notes, an exception rather than a principle.[387] This makes the Court's strategy of focusing on those who bear the greatest responsibility – to maximise its impact – more relevant. Otherwise, the limited resources do not allow the Prosecution to process a significant number of cases. This is at the heart of the Court's selective policy that will always be susceptible to criticism.

The fact is that the Court's contribution to affected communities remains very negligible. If one considers the recurrent insurgencies in Ituri,[388] a place of the Court's first convict, Thomas Lubanga, one wonders whether the lessons of punishing perpetrators are taken seriously. Stone notes that '[t]he ICC is designed as a minimalist Court, acting only in rare situations and then only against a few of the leaders most responsible for atrocities when and if states are willing to support the prosecutor's efforts'.[389] The counter-argument is that the Court is based on the complementarity principle; it is believed that those cases that are left out should be handled through national courts – to reduce the impunity gap. This is a very good theoretical argument but in reality, it is difficult to conclude that those remaining cases are sufficiently handled – maybe further research can provide us with concrete answers. One would simply ask: should this be an ICC problem? The honest answer is probably no, and the Prosecutor is not under an obligation to prove the role of national mechanisms. However, this does not stop the reality from reflecting on the Court's contribution, which is a mere drop in the ocean, a drop that cannot be noticed. The current reality requires the Court to understand its modest role in situations of massive violence and refocus on adopting strategies that would amplify its impact through collaboration with local authorities.

There is an argument to make on whether the Court can make an impact on the global scale where it has failed on the national level. It could be true that

---

386 ibid, para. 29, table at p.17.

387 Varaki, 'Revisiting the 'Interests of Justice' Policy Paper' (2017), 463.

388 Alex Mcbride Wilson, 'Violence Returns to DR Congo's Ituri Province' [Aljazeera, 11 April 2018] https://www.aljazeera.com/indepth/inpictures/violence-returns-dr-congo-ituri-province-180410102912520.html; Fiston Mahamba and Claude Sengenya, 'Politics and oil: the unseen drivers of violence in Congo's Ituri Province' [IRIN, 4 April 2018] https://www.irinnews.org/analysis/2018/04/04/politics-and-oil-unseen-drivers-violence-congo-s-ituri-province; Thijs Van Laer, 'What's Happening in Ituri?' [Guest Blog, Congo Research Group, 5 March 2018] http://congoresearchgroup.org/guest-blog-whats-happening-in-ituri/.

389 Christopher Stone, 'Widening the Impact of the International Criminal Court: The Prosecutor's Preliminary Examinations in the Larger System of International Criminal Justice' in Martha Minow, C. Cora True-Frost and Alex Whiting (eds.), *The First Global Prosecutor: Promise and Constraints* (University of Michigan Press, 2015), 288–289.

even if the limited number of prosecutions cannot make a significant impact on a specific situation community or country, the objective of prosecuting a few persons who are most responsible may be bigger; it might deter potential crimes on a global scale. This claim is very difficult to debate because it concerns proving something that did not happen. As Schabas notes,

> whether the criminals are deterred by a jail with a dozen people in custody and a fewer actually on trial, and perhaps one conviction every decade, is debatable. In any event, performance is impossible to measure because those who are actually deterred cannot readily be identified.[390]

This discussion would be incomplete if our focus restricted itself to the quantitative aspect of the Court's work without saying something about its quality, another critical problem facing the ICC's Prosecution. Some commentators have raised questions about the Court's ability to conduct sound investigations and bring enough evidence before the Chambers,[391] and this is evidenced in the number of acquittals or cases dismissed even before trial. A positive argument could be made that this is a vindication that the Court is fair and impartial. However, it vindicates the judicial organ of the Court and not the Prosecution. Whether someone is acquitted for lack of sufficient evidence or on technical procedural grounds, is a matter of academic debate, but for laypersons it might indicate that the OTP is not diligent in its selection of cases, and in the worst case cause them to think that it is charging innocent people. Ciampi argues that

> [a] wise prosecutorial and judicial strategy ought to result in the selection of cases where not only the suspects can be brought to trial but also the evidence can stand up in court and meet the 'beyond any reasonable doubt' standard of proof.[392]

The work of the Court can also be reflected in what it chooses not to do, an issue we have not thoroughly discussed. In addition to prosecuting international crimes, the OTP is also responsible for distributing international leniency. Prosecutors all over the world (at international and domestic levels) will never have enough resources to investigate and/or prosecute all suspected criminals. Therefore, prosecutors are entrusted with public leniency to distribute – using their discretionary powers – towards some suspected misconduct. The public,

---

390 Schabas, 'The Short Arm of International Criminal Law' (2013), 388.

391 Groome, 'No Witness, No Case: An Assessment of the Conduct and Quality of ICC Investigations' (2014); Kai Ambos, 'Confidential Investigations (Article 54(3)(E) ICC Statute) vs. Disclosure Obligations: The Lubanga Case And National Law' (2009) 12:4, 543–568 New Criminal Law Review: An International and Interdisciplinary Journal.

392 Ciampi, 'Legal Rules, Policy Choices and Political Realities in the Functioning of the Cooperation Regime of the International Criminal Court' (2016), 47.

in return, expects them to be fair and just in that distribution. It is vital for the Prosecutor to be mindful of this. The public ought to know how the ICC Prosecutor and the Rome Treaty justice system distribute not only the punishments but also the international community's leniency.

The impact of the decision of who not to prosecute goes beyond the selection of situations – targeting Africa – to include the selection of cases within specific situations. Whenever a certain group of people complains of being a target of selective prosecution, they are not complaining that the prosecution is targeting innocent people among them; they are saying that persons in other groups who ought to be equally investigated are not being investigated simply because of who they are. When discrimination is perceived to be based on class, race, power, ethnicity, religion, nationality etc., the issue becomes collective. To prove that you are a victim of selective prosecution in an individual criminal case would require you to produce 'evidence establishing unlawful or improper motives and evidence that other similarly suited persons were not prosecuted'.[393] But since the evidence needed to prove motive is often very difficult to obtain this makes the issue of selective prosecution more of a collective discourse than an individual criminal defence. It is because of the Prosecutor's obligation to prosecute and seek punishment for all perpetrators of international crimes (meeting the ICC threshold) that not doing so is considered as being lenient to the suspected individuals. If this leniency is unevenly distributed among different categories of people, or if the distribution is based on wrong reasons such as corruption or race, then there is a problem in the justice system. The issue is not on whether those prosecuted are criminals or not, it is about the selection process. The group of people at whom prosecution is directed, including those who are not intending to commit crimes, have good reasons to complain that they have not been treated fairly in comparison to other groups.

Let me assume that some well-intentioned individuals might not find a problem with prosecuting some criminals – in case the Court is unable to prosecute persons from all groups. In response to this argument, let us examine the issue from two retrospective questions. How many countries would have ratified the Rome Statute, if it was very clear during the negotiations in Rome that the Court was going to prosecute a certain group of people? Second, does the

---

393 Imoedemhe, *The Complementarity Regime of the International Criminal Court: National Implementation in Africa* (2017), 129; see also Sunita Sah, Christopher T. Robertson and Shima B. Baughman, 'Blinding prosecutors to defendants' race: A policy proposal to reduce unconscious bias in the criminal justice system' (2015) 1:2 Behavioral Science & Policy, 69–76; Andrew D. Leipold, 'Objective Tests and Subjective Bias: Some Problems of Discriminatory Intent in the Criminal Law' (1998) 73, 559 Chicago-Kent Law Review; Anne Bowen Poulin, 'Prosecutorial Discretion and Selective Prosecution: Enforcing Protection after United States v. Armstrong' (1997) 34, 1071 American Criminal Law Review.

current workload give some credibility to the impression (wrongly or correctly) that the Court is focusing on Africa? To answer these concerns one needs to go beyond the question of whether the Prosecutor is independent and honest in the selection process or not, because perception, like facts, is important. Probably, the solution could not be in a dialogue between the Court and Africa, and I do not think massive withdrawal is the right thing to do either. I actually doubt whether it will ever happen. The simple exercise the Court is capable of doing on its own initiative is to conduct an audit of both institutional and personnel implicit anti-African (racial) biases and see if there are certain issues to correct about its structure and workings. It would be probably a good thing if the findings were shared for the purposes of transparency. This is not to suggest that the Court is imperialist or racist, but if several people are complaining about a system, certainly it would be wise for whoever is responsible for that institution to conduct a self-evaluation – and see if the alleged biases exist or not – because mere denials can never be enough.

By implicit biases, I refer to 'attitudes or stereotypes that affect our understanding, decision-making, and behavior, without our even realizing it'.[394] We all have biases against certain groups of people. It could be either positive or negative biases. We might perceive certain groups of people as less violent, or more rational than others, we do sometimes associate ourselves with some cause more than others. All our biases and backgrounds, if not constantly checked, (unknowingly) end up influencing our decision-making. As Blasi notes, 'science suggests that there are, indeed, few advocacy situations where stereotypes are not at work'.[395] Falsettio argues that 'a criminal is one who disregards the well-being of other individuals or their society, causing harm in pursuit of *unjustifiable endeavours*. The act they commit must therefore be caught by criminal law'.[396] The aspect of 'unjustifiable endeavours' is important to understanding how implicit biases are formulated during conflicts. If an army is involved in the fighting that the observer associates himself or herself with, he or she is likely to see the damage caused as either accidental or incidental to the cause, and he or she will see whatever damage caused by those he or she does not feel associated with as criminal. The different biases we have about combatants will eventually affect the way we judge their violence. This is unavoidable, but the Prosecutor ought to keep checking that those biases do not affect the Prosecution's conduct. The reason it is difficult to completely eliminate biases is simple: criminal law is linked to morality and morality is linked to our societal values. Considering some

394 Jerry Kang and others, 'Implicit Bias in the Courtroom' (2012) 59, 1124 University of California, Los Angeles, Law Review, 1126.

395 Gary Blasi, 'Advocacy against the Stereotype: Lessons from Cognitive Social Psychology' (2002) 49, 1241 Los Angeles Law Review, 1241.

396 Barbara Falsettio, 'Crossing the Line: Morality, Society, and the Criminal Law' (2009) 5, 182 Cambridge Student Law Review, 183 (emphasis added).

people as pursuing 'unjustifiable endeavours' is not in itself what makes a certain conduct criminal or not, it is what affects the observer's ability to judge objectively certain conducts and actors.[397]

Some implicit biases are subtle and insignificant such as perceiving two colleagues who are late arriving a meeting differently. You might automatically perceive one who is late as due to the fact that he or she is African and see another colleague ('the white') as late probably because she or he was busy. This kind of stereotype can be ignored; it is those major biases such as perceiving a certain group of people as more likely to be criminal than others that needs to be fought. It is those biases that reinforce the existing power imbalances that need to be checked. The attitude will be considered imperialistic, as Cowell notes, when it is 'predicated on the domination of the weaker states and the diminution of their sovereign decision-making capacities'.[398] Kang and others argue that implicit biases 'are not consciously accessible through introspection. If we find out that we have them, we may indeed reject them as inappropriate'.[399]

Implicit biases can be structural and/or personnel based. By 'structural' I refer to what Clarke interrogates when she examines 'the structural inequalities that have made it so that Africa and not the United States, Joseph Kony and not George Bush, crimes against humanity and not pre-emptive intervention form the basis for the court's action'.[400] On 'personnel' implicit biases I refer to individual employee's biases. Let me use one example to explain this. In a chapter entitled 'Rethinking the Tension between Peace and Justice: The International Criminal Prosecutor as a Diplomat' by Robert H. Mnookin, the author makes a hypothetical argument where an ICC prosecution in Afghanistan might be stopped in the interests of justice in case a peace accord is reached that includes an element of immunity for all sides. By 'all sides' he is talking of 'the Taliban and various warlords supporting' the Afghan Government.[401] The author does not (willingly or unwillingly) suspect that NATO soldiers too might have committed some crimes. On the contrary, when you read the ICC Prosecutor's preliminary examination report, it is very clear that different groups including

397 Stephen Jones, *Criminology* (3rd ed., Oxford University Press, 2009) 31–88; Blasi, 'Advocacy against the Stereotype: Lessons from Cognitive Social Psychology' (2002); Falsettio, 'Crossing the Line: Morality, Society, and the Criminal Law' (2009).

398 Frederick Cowell, 'Inherent Imperialism: Understanding the Legal Roots of Anti-imperialist Criticism of the International Criminal Court' (2017) 15:14 Journal of International Criminal Justice, 669; see also Okafor and Ngwaba, 'Between Tunnel Vision and a Sliding Scale: Power, Normativity and Justice in the Praxis of the International Criminal Court' (2017), 179–194.

399 Kang and others, 'Implicit Bias in the Courtroom' (2012), 1132.

400 Kamari Maxine Clarke, 'Is the ICC targeting Africa inappropriately or are there sound reasons and justifications for why all of the situations currently under investigation or prosecution happen to be in Africa?' [ICC Forum, 17 March 2013] http://iccforum.com/africa#Clarke.

401 Robert H. Mnookin, 'Rethinking the Tension between Peace and Justice: The International Criminal Prosecutor as Diplomat' in Martha Minow, C. Cora True-Frost and Alex Whiting (eds.), *The First Global Prosecutor: Promise and Constraints* (University of Michigan Press, 2015), 69–96.

US soldiers and CIA civilians might have committed crimes under the ICC jurisdiction.[402] I agree that this might be an insignificant example because this could be seen as an innocent omission of minor details in a complicated situation, but it says something about how implicit biases may be perpetuated through knowledge production. Implicit biases are about those stereotypes one hypothetically has about certain groups of people. There are different studies indicating that implicit biases can be detected such as using the Implicit Association Test (IAT),[403] and I do not see why the ICC cannot conduct a similar test in order to provide appropriate training to its staff, where necessary.

The idea that the Court is focusing on Africa because the victims are Africans also needs more reasoning to it. Otherwise, to be convincing, one would want to know why the Court prefers African victims to those from other regions. Mensa-Bonsu in reference to the First Prosecutor notes:

> Perhaps because Ocampo was anxious for the court to start work and justify its existence and the huge expense of its operations, he was less than careful in his choice of cases. Perhaps he was playing to the gallery in drawing attention to himself and was in thrall to sensationalism in the choice of cases.[404]

Whatever the case, there should be something more, something that goes beyond that claim of benevolence. It could be that the Prosecutor is implementing the Rome Statute according to the way it was conceived in Rome, when it was expected that state parties would blindly support the Court's decisions and failure to do so would result in the ASP taking tangible sanctions against them, and that the UNSC referrals would be less political. However, since the reality is here now, the Court needs to understand that it is working in a real world that is built on state interests, where power imbalances are at play. Accepting this reality would encourage the Prosecutor to adopt a realistic strategy instead of pretending that there are no 'political interests' at play.

## 4.3. WHAT CAN THE ICC DO? A LOOK AT TRANSITIONAL JUSTICE

It is becoming increasingly difficult to have an honest discussion about what is needed for societies that are experiencing massive violations of human rights

402 The OTP 'Report on Preliminary Examination Activities 2017', 51–61.

403 Christine Jolls and Cass R. Sunstein, 'The Law of Implicit Bias' (2006) 94, 969 California Law Review; Kang and others, 'Implicit Bias in the Courtroom' (2012); Anthony G. Greenwald, Brian A Nosek, and Mahzarin R. Banaji, 'Understanding and using the Implicit Association Test: I. An improved scoring algorithm (2003) 85:2, 197–216 Journal of Personality and Social Psychology.

404 Mensa-Bonsu, 'The ICC, International Criminal Justice and International Politics' (2015), 44.

without some individuals insisting on the involvement of the Court. It is clear that the movement to stop impunity of international crimes is unstoppable, which is good, but it cannot be true that one form of justice is capable of delivering us to that mission. And certainly, a court with a record of three convictions in 15 years is not the system capable of providing such a solution.[405] Therefore, the Prosecutor needs to acknowledge some realities, especially the limitations of the Court and the geo-political environment the Court is working in, to be able to devise ways that strengthens the Court's legitimacy. In this section I offer the suggestion that collaborating with local, national and regional mechanisms is probably what is going to amplify the Court's impact.

Parmentier argues that: 'Any volume on international criminal law would be incomplete without paying closer attention to the broader legal, political, and societal context within which this body of law is originating, as well as operating'.[406] To put it slightly differently, it could be argued that before this understanding becomes a mantra in scholarly works, it should be ingrained first and foremost in practices of every international criminal justice system. It should be understood that no international criminal justice system should claim legitimacy if it is not 'paying closer attention to the broader legal, political, and societal context within which' it is operating.

In countries where the ICC is inclined to intervene (where international crimes have been committed) transitional justice is always an important issue to discuss. And in fact, prosecutions of perpetrators of heinous crimes, whether national or international, are part and parcel of transitional justice. 'Transitional justice' is generally understood as a combination of different measures and mechanisms that are aimed at addressing numerous challenges resulting from massive violations of human rights in a given society. These may include prosecutions, truth findings, memorialisation, reconciliation, reparations and institutional reforms.[407] The strength of transitional justice is that it does not claim to provide the same solutions to all situations. It is aimed at finding responses that are appropriate to specific challenges. Immediately after a conflict or when an abusive regime has been removed from power, a new leadership (sometimes assisted by international actors) is faced with questions of prosecuting perpetrators of crimes, establishing lasting peace, uncovering the truth, providing reparations, reforming abusive institutions, remembering the

---

405 As of 28 June 2018, the ICC had secured the convictions of Mr. Lubanga, Mr. Katanga, and Mr. Al Mahdi (excluding those found guilty of offences against administration of justice).

406 Stephan Parmentier, 'Transitional Justice' in William A. Schabas (ed.), *The Cambridge Companion to International Criminal Law* (Cambridge University Press, 2016), 52.

407 Ruti G. Teitel, 'Transitional Justice Genealogy' (2003) 16, 69–94 Harvard Human Rights Journal, 69; ICTJ, 'What is Transitional Justice?' [2009] https://www.ictj.org/sites/default/files/ICTJ-Global-Transitional-Justice-2009-English.pdf; The Report of the Secretary-General of the United Nations on 'The rule of law and transitional justice in conflict and post-conflict societies' (S/2004/616 of 23 August 2004), 8.

past, eradicating poverty and many others. Clark and Palmer, like many other scholars in this field, have correctly argued that transitional justice 'is an unruly arena', 'under-theorised', with 'mixed roots of origin', encompassing different disciplines which 'is one of its greatest strengths but also poses important theoretical, analytical and empirical challenges'.[408] This could be a true description of transitional justice as a field of study, and probably due to the fact that it is still developing,[409] and maybe given the nature of the subject, a coherent theory is not possible or desirable. This book does not seek to contribute to any particular theory.

However, it is argued that transitional justice is concerned with matters of state governance. The desire to come to terms with the past, the notions of building a peaceful future, efforts of transforming the formally discriminating structures into inclusive systems, are all issues of governance. By 'governance', I refer to Fukuyama's definition, which states that it is 'a government's ability to make and enforce rules, and deliver services, regardless of whether that government is democratic or not'.[410] Most societies in transition are preoccupied with the desire to create a governable society; resolving the root causes of violence and at the same time sending a message that massive violations of human rights should not be tolerated. As Mutua notes,

> (...) in order to move forward to an inclusive and fair society, no major party can be left behind. Those who have been aggrieved must find justice in order to let go of hatreds of the past but equally important is the place of the perpetrators of the abusive past in the future of the society.[411]

These are very complicated issues with few answers, and that is why understanding the broader legal, political and societal context is very important. Transitional justice measures and/or mechanisms will be specific

---

408 Phil Clark and Nicola P. Palmer, 'Challenging Transitional Justice' in Nicola P. Palmer, Phil Clark and Danielle Granville (eds.), *Critical Perspectives in Transitional Justice* (Intersentia, 2012), 1–16; see also Claudio Corradetti, and Jack Volpe Rotondi (eds.), *Theorizing Transitional Justice* (Ashgate, 2015), 2–3; Susanne Buckley-Zistel and others (eds.), Transitional Justice Theories (Routledge, 2014), 1–8.

409 Dustin N. Sharp, 'Emancipating Transitional Justice from the Bonds of the Paradigmatic Transition' (2015) 9, 150–169 International Journal of Transitional Justice; Paul Gready and Simon Robins, 'From Transitional to Transformative Justice: A New Agenda for Practice' (2014) 8, 339–361 The International Journal of Transitional Justice; Jennifer Balint, Julie Evans and Nesam McMillan, 'Rethinking Transitional Justice, Redressing Indigenous Harm: A New Conceptual Approach' (2014) 8, 194–216 The International Journal of Transitional Justice; Wendy Lambourne, 'Transitional Justice and Peacebuilding after Mass Violence' (2009) 3, 28–48 The International Journal of Transitional Justice.

410 Francis Fukuyama, 'What is Governance' (2013) 26:3 Governance: An International Journal of Policy, Administration, and Institutions, 3.

411 Makau Mutua, 'What Is the Future of Transitional Justice?' (2015) 9, 1–9 International Journal of Transitional Justice, 2.

in every situation depending on the nature of the violence; how that violence ended (was it a negotiated settlement or a victory of one party?); the proximity of perpetrators with their victims (if they are living together or not); whether previous abusers are still influential within their constituencies; limitations on resources to respond to challenges, and how to prioritise those different demands through the existing infrastructure and many others. I argue that all these questions are issues of governance because they concern the government's ability to deliver services and law enforcement.

Transitional justice and criminal prosecution in particular is principally the responsibility of state agencies, and this primacy of national authorities over third parties' involvement is recognised in the Rome Statute.[412] Therefore, it should be logical that if the ICC is going to provide that service, its interventions should be aligned with national priorities – to avoid contradictions. This is very important because transitional justice issues are more than legal matters, they concern law, society and politics, and as Whittington, Kelemen and Caldeira note:

> Law is one of the central products of politics and the prize over which many political struggles are waged. (…) Law is the principal instrument by which the government exerts its will on society, and as such it might be thought to lie (at least indirectly) close to the heart of the study of politics.[413]

McEvoy notes that: 'Legal institutions associated with transitional justice can and should operate most effectively if they run in conjunction with properly managed, effective, and accountable local or indigenous processes (…)'.[414] My suggestion is that if every measure responding to post-conflict challenges is adopted with an intention of contributing to 'good' governance (government's ability to deliver), we would achieve a coherent explanation of post-conflict interventions. And as such, we would be able to determine which mechanisms are jeopardising other governance interventions instead of strengthening them, and hence need to be either redesigned, replaced or simply abandoned.

There are two major surmountable policy challenges the Court would need to overcome in order to align itself with the above reasoning. First is the Court's timing – the when to intervene question. Unlike *ad hoc* tribunals and hybrid courts that were created after a conflict, the ICC is a permanent

412 'Emphasizing that the International Criminal Court established under this Statute shall be complementary to national criminal jurisdictions' (Preamble of the Rome Statute).

413 Keith E. Whittington, R. Daniel Kelemen and Gregory A. Caldeira, 'The Study of Law and Politics' in Keith E. Whittington, R. Daniel Kelemen and Gregory A. Caldeira (eds.), *The Oxford Handbook of Law and Politics* (Oxford University Press, 2013), 1 and 3.

414 Kieran McEvoy, 'Beyond Legalism: Towards a Thicker Understanding of Transitional Justice' (2007) 34:4 Journal of Law and Society, 428.

court that sometimes intervenes in ongoing conflicts. For instance, the UNSC Resolution 1970 (2011) that referred the situation of Libya was adopted on 26 February 2011, and it took the OTP just two weeks to complete a preliminary examination.[415] This means that the ICC could have started conducting field investigations, if it ever did, the same day NATO started bombing Libya, on 19 March 2011.[416] The investigation took just three months to issue the three warrants of arrest against President Gaddafi, his son and his chief of military intelligence, accusing them of murder and persecution as crimes against humanity.[417] This kind of early involvement of the Court and issuance of indictments against certain suspected abusers in ongoing conflicts, I argue, feeds into war propaganda and could adversely affect the Court's legitimacy by linking its work to either side of the conflict depending on who is being indicted and who is not.

I am not suggesting that the Court should never intervene in ongoing conflicts; it is the early issuance of warrants of arrest that is counterproductive. The Prosecutor can sequence her interventions with an aim of maximising the impact. Let us be realistic; early issuance of indictments does not contribute to achieving the intended objectives of the Court. It does not necessarily lead to an immediate arrest and surrender of powerful suspects because active participants on the ground are more interested in either winning the war or achieving peace, and it does not stop the commission of crimes. On the contrary, it might harden suspects and incentivises attacks against witnesses in order to destroy evidence.

I would like to suggest sequencing where the Prosecutor can, for instance, conduct a preliminary examination and then stops after collecting some possible evidence (investigations). Other necessary next steps should wait until the conclusion of the conflict. This could put pressure on all belligerents because each side would be fearful of being a potential target of prosecution, subsequently encouraging them to respect the laws of fighting. It would also save the Court from political manipulation and partisan NGOs and media anecdotal reports – the fog of war. Because as Nathanson notes: 'our feelings

415 Paras. 4–8 of the United Nations Security Council Resolution 1970 (2011) adopted by the Security Council at its 6491st meeting, on 26 February 2011 (S/RES/1970 (2011); see also Bosco, 'Discretion and State Influence at the International Criminal Court: The Prosecutor's Preliminary Examinations' (2017), 400.

416 NATO, 'NATO and Libya (Archived)' [9 November 2015] https://www.nato.int/cps/ic/natohq/topics_71652.htm.

417 ICC Pre-Trial Chamber I, 'Situation in the Libyan Arab Jamahiriya: Warrant of Arrest of Abdullah Al-Senussi' (no. ICC-01/11 of 27 June 2011); ICC Pre-Trial Chamber I, 'Situation in the Libyan Arab Jamahiriya: Warrant of Arrest for Muammar Mohammed Abu Minyar Gaddafi' (no. ICC-01/11 of 27 June 2011); ICC Pre-Trial Chamber I, 'Situation in the Libyan Arab Jamahiriya: Warrant of Arrest for Saif Al-Islam Gaddafi' (no. ICC-01/11 of 27 June 2011).

about these things also depend on who the victims and perpetrators are. We have less sympathy for some victims than for others as well as varying positive and negative attitudes towards perpetrators.'[418] To issue warrants of arrest depending on information received through third parties risks introducing those intermediaries' implicit biases into the Court.

This is why I argue for the Prosecutor to issue indictments after the fighting – when all guns are silenced – and after conducting a general contextual analysis considering all collected evidence and proposed national mechanisms. This would give her/him a general picture of the violence and a possibility to determine who really bears the greatest responsibility in the commission of crimes, because as already noted, the Court can only prosecute a limited number of persons. This suggestion can be criticised on the fact that some protracted conflicts can go on and on for years, the issue of victims and witnesses who might die before seeing justice and the disappearance of evidence. This is probably true, but nor does the issuance of warrants of arrest provide a solution, and we have already seen the situation of Colombia that has been under preliminary examination for more than 10 years.

Another problem of the ICC's early involvement in ongoing conflicts is that it is not consistent with the Rome Statute especially the complementarity principle. The early intervention of the Court makes it difficult for other actors on the ground to find a viable national solution. It is possible that national actors might decide that the national judicial sector should be strengthened to handle the cases instead of the ICC, but since by the end of a conflict the Court is already there, it makes it difficult for actors on the ground to think of a national solution. In this case, the Court becomes a *de facto* self-imposed solution, hence becoming another issue to manage in addition to other difficult challenges. In this case, the Court might be accepted even where it was not the best solution to deal with the situation. This is very dangerous for a fragile society in transition because it takes away the opportunity to see things within a broader context considering all the consequences and how to manage them – it undermines institutional development and ownership. As Thakur notes, 'international criminal justice takes away from domestic authorities the options of alternative modes of healing and restitution with a view to reconciliation that puts the traumas of the past firmly in the past'.[419] For the Court to preserve its legitimacy, I argue, it needs to reverse its aloof nature. It should work on improving its relationship with national actors so that they too can trust its interventions. This can be possible if

418 Stephen Nathanson, 'Are Attacks on Civilians Always Wrong?' in Lovell and Primoratz (eds.), *Protecting Civilians during Violent Conflict: Theoretical and Practical Issues for the 21st Century*, (Routledge, 2012), 18; see also Muleefu, *Reparation for victims of collateral damage: A normative and theoretical inquiry* (2014), 26–34.

419 Thakur, 'International Criminal Justice: At the Vortex of Power, Norms and a Shifting Global Order' (2015), 37.

it is perceived as complementary to local mechanisms, contributing to resolving governance challenges as opposed to being imposed on them.

For this to happen, the Court needs to overcome its negative perception about politics and politicians, the second surmountable challenge. The current practical challenges should be indicative of the fact that it is difficult to deliver criminal justice services while ignoring the concerns of national authorities. The Ocampo response to this suggestion would probably go like this: 'For us we don't care, we are criminal prosecutors, we look for the evidence, we try to follow the evidence, we try to prosecute the most responsible, and that is the policy.' And Bensouda would probably say: 'We are not a tool in the hands of politicians, who think they can use us when it is convenient or drop us when it is not.' These arguments are idealistic and misleading. It is fair to argue that a framework that allows a situation where Sudan and Libya are referred and not Myanmar, Yemen and Syria is prone to political manipulation. The state's decision to arrest this suspect and not that other suspect is political. The decision to share certain collected intelligence information about a certain group in a conflict and not about another group is political. Most, if not all, matters of cooperation are political in nature. Therefore, the Prosecutor's refusal to engage with actors on the ground cannot be supported by the fear of politics. The Prosecutor needs to respond truthfully to concerns of political ramifications resulting from the Court's intervention to deal with suspicions of an external 'witch-hunt'. This might not necessarily stop those capable and willing (for whatever reasons) to politicise the Prosecutor's work from doing so. To acknowledge the need to deal with politicians is not the same as asking the Prosecutor to do politics. However, the refusal can instead be seen as a pretext of not wanting to respond to certain pertinent questions. Yet, the distance might not save the Court from being turned on and off, at the will of politicians. For instance, after President Museveni's description of the ICC as 'a useless body' and its staff as 'a bunch of useless people', the United States, not a state party to the Rome Statute, and some other delegates from western countries left the inaugural ceremony in protest. Bruce Wharton, the US-PDAS Bureau of African Affairs, said later in a press conference that their decision was due to the presence of Omar al-Bashir, an ICC indict, and Museveni's disparaging comments about the Court. He went on to clarify that the United States deals with the Court on a case-by-case basis.[420] On 10 September 2018, Bolton, the National Security Advisor to the US President, threatened that US would sanction the ICC and its officials if the Court went ahead to investigate alleged war crimes and crimes against humanity committed in Afghanistan and Palestine.[421]

---

420 NBS TV Uganda, 'US Reacts to Museveni Swear In Comment of "ICC is Useless ..." (https://www.youtube.com/watch?v=aSrjdgVN8Vw).

421 'Bolton Threatens ICC with US Sanctions' [BBC, 11 September 2018] https://www.bbc.com/news/world-us-canada-45474864; 'Bolton: International Criminal Court dead to us'

The ICC Prosecutor might not be conducting political persecutions but this contradictory relationship between the US and the Court is certainly political.

For purposes of argument, let me accept that the Prosecutor might not want to be associated with some local mechanisms because sometimes it is not clear whether they will succeed, and probably it is not even a good idea for the Court to be overtly entangled with politics. However, the Prosecutor needs to accept that local actors (maybe because of misunderstanding) might not see prosecution as the best solution, and in this case, they deserve some explanations as to how the Court's intervention is going to benefit their broader context beyond legal arguments. A situation where thousands of people have been killed and thousands of perpetrators are roaming the streets and villages, is a desperate place that deserves compassion. Even if it is fair to argue that it is the role of the government – not the Court – to resolve political disputes, it should also be understandable when those local actors request that whoever else that is choosing to intervene in their situation should observe the 'do no harm' principle. Doing otherwise is akin to assuming that the work of lawyers is more important than other professions. That it is more important to that of politicians. This is no different from saying that we (prosecutors) will do our job regardless of the consequences and you politicians will pick up the mess afterwards. McEvoy's calling on lawyers to be unassuming states that:

> The combination of the intellectual and technical demands of law, a traditionally elevated social status, the importance of the subject matter, the relatively closed social and professional worlds of lawyers, the peculiarities of legal education and models of professional self-governance, and a range of other factors can contribute to a sense of elitism and arrogance in the legal profession. (…) Such innate tendencies in the law profession, allied to the imperialist tendencies associated with even well-meaning international involvement in transitional contexts, make the case for greater legal humanity in such sites all the more pressing.[422]

The suggestion of considering the broader benefits of the Court's intervention seems to be contrary to the Prosecutor's stated policy on the interests of justice. The Policy Paper on the Interests of Justice and the Policy Paper on Preliminary Examinations state that '(…) the Prosecutor is not required to establish that an investigation or prosecution is in the interests of justice'.[423] This interpretation is true but it is also true that the Rome Statute does not prevent the Prosecutor

[CNN, 10 September 2018] https://edition.cnn.com/videos/world/2018/09/10/bolton-us-protect-citizens-international-criminal-court-sot-vpx.cnn.

422 McEvoy, 'Beyond Legalism: Towards a Thicker Understanding of Transitional Justice' (2007), 425–426.

423 The ICC OTP Policy Paper on the Interests of Justice, (2007), September 2007), 3; see also para. 7 of the ICC OTP Policy Paper on Preliminary Examinations of November 2013.

from doing it. I also agree that circumstances that might lead the Prosecutor to stopping an investigation or prosecution that meets the requirements of jurisdiction and admissibility will be exceptional. Nonetheless, the Prosecutor is required to conduct an assessment of the interests of justice every time a new investigation or prosecution is going to be started. However, in all reports on Preliminary Examinations, the Prosecutor states that 'the Office has not identified substantial reasons to believe that the opening of an investigation into the [situation …] would not be in the interests of justice'.[424] This statement lacks transparency on many accounts because it does not explain what issues were considered to reach that conclusion. This sweeping statement, lacking details on what kind of issues were considered in the analysis, contributes in part to the continued controversy around the subject of the interests of justice.

The OTP would use a well-studied contextual analysis to dispel rumours of hidden motives by explaining to the public the issues that were considered, and why an investigation or prosecution and not a truth and reconciliation commission for example is going to benefit them. This is something a Prosecutor who is interested in increasing the transparency of the Office would not find difficult in doing, and it would help in developing more knowledge from commentators on the subject. Otherwise, we will never know for sure whether the Prosecutor is correctly applying Article 53(1)(c) and (2)(c) of the Statute. At the minimum it can serve as a sign of respect to the different consulted stakeholders, by showing to them that this is how the Office appreciated the information they provided. Providing feedback is an important aspect in building trust, since the Prosecutor is required to

> conduct a dialogue with the victims, [communities … and] other actors involved in the situation [… such as local leaders (religious, political, tribal), other states, local and international intergovernmental and nongovernmental organizations] in order to assess the impact for the interests of victims of investigations and prosecutions.[425]

The failure to communicate respectfully can push away some vital national support. Criminal justice systems stand on three legs: law enforcement, judicial process and correction services. The ICC's judicial process leg might be strong but the other two are dependent on state cooperation without which it can collapse.

---

424 This is based on a statement on the situation of Georgia, but this is similar to what is stated on other situations up until 2017 (para. 260 of the Office of the Prosecutor's Report on Preliminary Examination Activities (2015) of 12 November 2015).

425 The ICC OTP Policy Paper on the Interests of Justice (2007), 6.

# CHAPTER 5
# CONCLUDING REMARKS

It is fair to state that the Court's institutional independence is well preserved in the Rome Statute and the Court's staff members are capable of making independent decisions. It is the inbuilt cooperation and interactions with actors of different interests that is problematic. The two competing narratives about the International Criminal Court (ICC) are both to a certain extent intelligibly persuasive. The oddity of this reality becomes more evident when each narrative is taken separately, but when the two are put together, one starts to realise that there are some unsaid truths, inconsistences, exaggerations and misinformation on both sides. These nuances, I argue, demonstrate a possibility of bridging the gap between these two competing arguers if there were goodwill on both sides – to achieve the common good of fighting impunity. Another challenge is that both sides lack a single representative authority and/or a common position on all issues of concern. On the side of supporters, there are some issues that are within the powers of the United Nations Security Council (UNSC), there are those that concern the Assembly of States Parties (ASP), others are at the Office of the Prosecutor (OTP), and there is the Coalition for the ICC that is influencing all actors. On the side of critics, the African states are neither a unified block nor consistent in terms of their rhetoric and conduct. They seem not to have a coherent and shared solution to improve the ICC-Africa relationship, and since the proposed regional criminal court (African solutions to African problems) has not taken off, Africa lacks a viable alternative that would work as a strong stance against impunity.

This could be a good opportunity for the Court to engage with all stakeholders considering their diverse backgrounds and perspectives. It needs to find ways of listening to both critics and supporters. This is possible if the Court is willing to acknowledge that each side of the debate has some legitimate objectives. Whereas the critics of the Court seem to be focused on fighting the existing global power imbalances that have disenfranchised Africa for so long, supporters of the Court are motivated by their belief in developing international norms. The critics' fight against dominance is equally as important as the activism that is aimed at advancing international standards capable of repressing human rights violations is to supporters. Therefore, it is fair to observe that each side's main cause is worthwhile and its proponents are justified in doing whatever is possible in their powers to achieve it. The Court, as an established institution of laws, needs to be aware of this struggle – the struggle between those interested in developing international norms and those interested in resisting domination – and has to decide on how it can navigate between the two without undermining or supporting either cause.

The importance of each side's goal is manifested in the great passion and self-aggrandising that is associated with the nature of their language. Each side believes in its own righteousness and the wickedness of the other. This could be partly blamed on the lack of interactions between the two opposing arguers or simply because of unwillingness to change. The voice of supporters of the Court is not very articulate at the African Union debates, and critics of the Court are not very welcome in different forums advocating for the Court. The Court has been requesting to have a liaison office in Addis Ababa, Ethiopia, at the seat of the African Union, a request that has been denied because some African leaders perceive the Court's attempt to establish such an office in Africa alone as a way of strengthening their feared perpetuation of dominance.[426] The supporters of the Court too are accused of selectivity and intolerance to divergent views in their forums especially through the Coalition of the Court. Certainly, the labelling of some people as 'friends of the Court' denotes an existence of 'enemies of the Court' and others in between.[427] This should be expected, different people ought to have different opinions about different things. However, the problem arises when such labelling of ideas becomes the criteria for selecting participants in different meetings discussing important matters concerning the Court. It undermines the basic values of transparency and limits the possibility of adopting inclusive solutions. This is unfortunate for a court that is purporting to serve humanity, including critics. Perpetuating a single rigid narrative is counterproductive to a project dealing with different societies. In case of limbo, it is the Court's mission of fighting impunity that is likely to suffer. Therefore, it requires both the Court and its supporters to see criticisms as an opportunity to improve it rather than destroying it. As Falsettio notes: 'Differences of opinion lead to discussion, which in turn leads to new definitions for terms we no longer feel fit reality. An immoral act is

---

426 du Plessis, Maluwa and O'Reilly, *Africa and the International Criminal Court* (Chatham House/International Law 2013/01), 11–12; Benson Olugbuo Chinedu. 'The African Union, the United States Security Council and the Politicisation of International Justice in Africa' (2014) 7:3 African Journal of Legal Studies, 372; Mills and Bloomfield, 'African resistance to the International Criminal Court: Halting the advance of the anti-impunity norm' (2018), 113.

427 See e.g. the 'First Annual High Level Meeting of the Group of Friends of the ICC' [22 April 2014, Parliamentarians for Global Action] https://www.youtube.com/watch?v=kiBVlFlOJvw; Sarah Nouwen and Wouter Werner, 'Doing Justice to the Political: The International Criminal Court in Uganda and Sudan' (2011) 21:4 The European Journal of International Law, 941–965.

not a static concept. This is progression and evolution, not destruction and demoralisation.'[428]

The Court and its supporters need to understand that for all states, whether powerful or weak, democratic or despotic, their main objective is the preservation of their national interests. The interpretation of national interests is the unquestionable role to those in leadership – it is done the way they see fit. Therefore, the Court needs to engage them whether they believe in their decisions or not because the idea that the Court can depend on benevolent states blindly supporting it is untenable.

The African states too need to accept that the prosecutor is not simply there taking some instructions from the most powerful. The story about an institution that is still evolving cannot be that of a perfect Court or a total disaster. There are nuances to every perspective that need to be acknowledged. The Court might have different narratives depending on each situation and some narratives might keep changing from time to time depending on circumstances. Whereas it might be true that the Court is careful in its current conduct to avoid upsetting some powerful states, it might not necessarily be interpreted as performing the interests of hegemonic powers all the time. However, stating that the Court is not imperialistic is not the same as saying that it is free from any implicit biases against certain groups of people.

Arguers ought to accept that their descriptions of the Court are mere perspectives that do not exclude other perspectives. There is no understanding that should be seen as more important than others (excluding outright lies on both sides). We might be more inclined to believe one perspective over the other because it is coherent with our own expectations – based on our own biases, affiliations and backgrounds – but that does not mean that the narrative we disagree with is totally inaccurate. Embracing the fact that no one holds the monopoly over truth and knowledge would be a positive step towards a respectful dialogue. The Court cannot claim to exist on a linear story, claiming to be a perfect system. It is operating in realpolitik, where the current world order is built on oblique pillars of state interests. The continued denial of this reality is likely to drive the two sides apart.

However, the conundrum of all this is that the Court seems to have taken a side in this power struggle. This is the downside to finding a lasting solution; the more the Court continues to find comfort in its supporters and the more the gap between supporters and critics continues to widen, the more the legitimacy of the Court will be at stake. All the issues of disagreement are about legitimacy; whether it is about whose role most influenced the creation of the Court (views that were more important in Rome), or whether it is about the

---

428 Falsettio, 'Crossing the Line: Morality, Society, and the Criminal Law' (2009), 185.

Court's current legal and institutional framework and the Prosecutor's powers of selecting situations and cases (prosecutorial decision-making process), all are questions of legitimacy. As d'Aspremont and Brabandere note, the legitimacy of global actors can be assessed from both the origin of their power and how they exercise that power. '[F]ailing to recognize this dual character of legitimacy of actors involved in global and regional governance undermines any endeavour to grasp the contemporary complexity of the latter.'[429] According to Buchanan and Keohane,

> [l]egitimacy has both a normative and a sociological meaning. To say that an institution is legitimate in the normative sense is to assert that it has *the right to rule* [... and] to say that an institution is legitimate in the sociological sense [... is to say that] it is widely *believed* to have the right to rule.[430]

In this understanding, the first meaning is objective, we can assess the Court's origin through the drafting of its Statute, refer to the number of countries that have ratified it and examine whether the rules of procedure are being applied properly, but the second meaning is about the observers' perception, and as such it is subjective.

The question one needs to answer is whether the International Criminal Court needs to be concerned with public perception, if it believes that it is following the law as it is and has some supporters? Certainly, no one is expecting the Court to satisfy everybody at all times. However, even if the Prosecutor does not need to follow perceptions in undertaking the Court's mandate, perceptions might serve as an external judgement on the Court's performance. Accordingly, Kelly and Simmons argue that social pressure is part of international relations.[431] Vasiliev notes that 'legitimacy is as much about perceptions among subjects and constituencies as it is about the actual and objective validity of a given rule, decision, or institution that can be established independently from perceptions'.[432] The fact that there are some people still supporting the Court should not make it ignore those who are critical because they too might have some legitimate concerns as its supporters might be having their own biases. The controversial aspect of legitimacy is that it is a subjective judgement which

---

429 d'Aspremont and de Brabandere, 'The Duality of the Legitimacy of Global Actors in the International Legal Order' (2012), 179.

430 Allen Buchanan and Robert O. Keohane, 'The Legitimacy of Global Governance Institutions' in Rudiger Wolfrum and Volker Roeben (eds.), *Legitimacy in International Law* (Springer, 2008), 25.

431 Judith G. Kelly and Beth A. Simmons, 'Politics by Number: Indicators as Social Pressure in International Relations' (2015) 59:1, 55–70 American Journal of Political Science.

432 Sergey Vasiliev, 'Between International Criminal Justice and Injustice: Theorising Legitimacy' in Nobuo Hayashi and Cecilia M. Bailliet (eds.), *The Legitimacy of International Criminal Tribunals* (Cambridge University Press, 2017), 78.

might depend on the one doing the judging rather than on the conduct that is being judged.[433]

The critics' use of racism, neo-colonialism and imperialism, to appeal to the African emotions, and supporters' use of praising and shaming into compliance undermines a possible respectful dialogue between these two competing arguers. The strategy of praising and shaming into compliance is common among the NGO supporters of the Court. William Pace, the Convenor of the Coalition for the International Criminal Court, responding to a question by Sanji Mmasenono Monageng on what she could do as a former judge of the Court to support it, before responding, first noted that: 'it is the small countries like Botswana, which *have stood up for the Court against dictators and presidents for life*'.[434] In this case Botswana is praised and critics are shamed. What makes this approach very problematic is that it is often used selectively against African leaders. The labelling of critics as dictators conceals the fact that the Court has not attained a democratic popular support around the world, including among countries we consider democratic. So, the idea of describing critics as dictators is diversionary. Whereas the Court can boast of 123 member states, a majority in the world, it still lacks the popular democratic legitimacy among the world's most populous nations. Out of the world's five most populous nations, just one (Brazil) is a state party, China, India, the United States and Indonesia are not parties to the Rome Treaty. In fact as D'Aspremont and Brabandere note '[i]nternational organizations, although created by states, cannot be seen as equivalent to them, especially in terms of democratic legitimacy. (…) since intergovernmental organizations have no direct popular legitimacy of origin'.[435]

Additionally, attacking arguers instead of arguments undermines the possibility of seeing criticisms as probably a result of having different state interests or perspectives. Consequently, contributing to the skewed human rights discourse towards Africa – *aka* Makau Mutua's *Savages, Victims, and Saviors* narrative.[436] According to Persaud and Walker, the ordering of the

> world into various binary opposites such as civilized/uncivilized; modern/backward; rational/superstitious, developed/undeveloped, and so on (…) is readily framed as a

433 John A. Simmons, *Justification and Legitimacy: Essays on Rights and Obligations* (Cambridge University Press, 2001), 122–157; d'Aspremont and de Brabandere, 'The Duality of the Legitimacy of Global Actors in the International Legal Order' (2012); Philip Pettit, 'Legitimacy and Justice in Republican Perspective (2012) 65, 59–82 Current Legal Problems.

434 See the Coalition for the International Criminal Court, 'Rome Statute 20, Interactive Forums/ Session II – Assessing the impact of the RS 20 years out' [14 March 2018] https://www.youtube.com/watch?v=monmXHD38Wo (1.00.00–1.02.19).

435 d'Aspremont and de Brabandere, 'The Duality of the Legitimacy of Global Actors in the International Legal Order' (2012), 193.

436 Makau W. Mutua, 'Savages, Victims, and Saviors: The Metaphor of Human Rights' (2001) 42:1 Harvard International Law Journal, 201–245.

> relation between adult and child, and the processes of colonialism and neocolonialism in which such binary taxonomies have been instantiated have involved both subtle and very unsubtle practices of infantilization.[437]

In psychology, taking the analogy of adult and child relationship, the use of 'praising' and 'shaming' into compliance can be likened to 'operant conditioning', a method of learning that combines rewards and punishments for behaviour change – rewards 'strengthen desired behaviours in children' and punishments 'reduce undesired behaviours'.[438] Bergin and Bergin note that 'punishment suppresses noncompliant behaviours and contingent positive reinforcement, such as praise or candy, strengthens obedience'.[439] This is exactly what supporters of the Court are doing. The praising and shaming approach is a process of enforcing discipline where African leaders who support the Court are praised as 'courageously standing up for humanity' against 'despots or life presidents'. The purpose of enforcing discipline is as Bergin and Bergin note, 'to help children behave in socially pleasing ways so that they will be accepted and liked by others and so that society is not filled with hostile, aggressive people who act on inappropriate impulses (…)'.[440] The use of infantilisation strategies is an expression of power, as Bergin and Bergin further note 'all discipline involves some form of power because there is an inherent imbalance of power between an adult and a child'.[441] In the case of the ICC-Africa debate, the purpose of describing African leaders as illegitimate representatives of African interests is empowering NGOs to speak on behalf of African victims.

Unfortunately, the Court seems not to have understood the danger of using disparaging language in seeking cooperation. Otherwise, it would have adopted an outreach strategy dissociating itself from such sentimental hyperbole used on both sides. Whereas it is not common for officials of the Court to use the concepts of its critics, such as neo-colonialism, as we saw above, when Ocampo was asked about the Court's focus on Africa, he responded that: 'I think it is *neo-colonialism* trying to protect those who commit massive atrocities because they are committed in Africa.'[442] This kind of a response is not appropriate for a Court official, who is expected to respond with facts on matters of policies and

---

437 Randolph B. Persaud and R.B.J. Walker, 'Apertura: Race in International Relations' (2001) 26:4 Alternatives: Global, Local, Political, 374–375.

438 Christi Bergin and David A. Bergin, 'Classroom Discipline That Promotes Self-Control' (1999) 20:2 Journal of Applied Developmental Psychology, 192; Saul McLeod, 'Skinner – Operant Conditioning' (Simply Phycology as updated 2018) https://simplypsychology.org/operant-conditioning.html; Andrew M. Colman (ed.), *Oxford Dictionary of Psychology* (Oxford University Press, 2014).

439 Bergin and Bergin, 'Classroom Discipline That Promotes Self-Control' (1999), 192.

440 ibid.

441 ibid, 194.

442 Al Jazeera English, 'ICC questioned on policy in Africa' [(2011) Moreno Ocampo, 03:48–03:55].

law, and not to appeal to emotions. The use of words like 'dictators' to describe African leaders critical of the Court is common practice.

At some point one has to sympathise with the Court. The Coalition for the International Criminal Court (CICC) has tacitly imposed itself as a *de facto* organ of the Court. The CICC, which is not mentioned anywhere in the Rome Statute,[443] has taken on this position as the rightful creator of the Court. As Haddad notes,

> [s]ince the court became functional and the CICC's raison d'Etre was fulfilled, the CICC did not disband or reorient its campaign to a new cause, but instead incrementally took on additional functions that include a universal ratification and implementation campaign, budgetary assistance, judicial monitoring, and outreach activities.[444]

The term 'non-governmental organisations', which is found twice in the Rome Statute (Article 15(2), on provision of information, and Article 44, on provision of expertise of gratis personnel), has become synonymous with the members of the CICC. This *de facto* relationship has duped the Court into believing that it cannot exist without the Coalition. This is probably true, as Haddad notes: 'After the ICC was established, the CICC defended its vision of the Rome Statute by expanding its mission and helping meet the needs of the fledgling court.'[445] According to deGuzman the OTP 'relies heavily on the input of NGO networks for its investigations'.[446]

However, apart from the arguments mentioned above, what is not often discussed is that this close collaboration might be undermining the Court's independence and affecting its capacity to examine violence objectively because of at least two intrinsic limitations related to the nature of NGOs. First, international NGOs that are considered credible in the eyes of the Court have limited access on the ground – one or two staff members – and they too depend on their local networks, who might be partisan in ongoing conflicts. Second, the mandate of these NGOs is mainly human rights, which is to a certain extent different from international criminal law. This could lead to an expansive interpretation of rules of the Court. Ullrich notes that 'in Kenya and Uganda, my informants felt that both international and local NGOs had fallen

---

443 Leila Ullrich, 'Beyond the 'Global-Local Divide: Local Intermediaries, Victims and the Justice Contestations of the International Criminal Court' (2016) 14, 543–568 Journal of International Criminal Justice, 544–545.

444 Heidi Nichols Haddad, 'After the Norm Cascade: NGO Mission Expansion and the Coalition for the International Criminal Court' (2013) 19, 189 Global Governance, 189.

445 ibid, 189.

446 deGuzman, 'Choosing to Prosecute: Expressive Selection at the International Criminal Court' (2012), 268.

prey to ethnic politics'.[447] She further notes that 'intermediaries may, wittingly or unwittingly, lead the Court to certain groups of victims more than to other groups'.[448] This ought to remind the Court that if it is not careful such similar biases are likely to be introduced in the courtroom. It needs to strengthen its own outreach and investigative capabilities to be able to dissociate itself from this functional dependence and the pejorative language of its supporters.

I am not saying that there is anything wrong with human rights NGOs and others supporting the Court to do so with vigour and devotion. On the contrary, I am arguing that the Court needs to engage with different stakeholders including NGOs, states and other well-wishers. As Bassiouni notes, 'the institution needs friends among its states parties, international civil society and influential world leaders and opinion-makers. Those who believe that justice is an important component of peace must rally to the long march that the ICC has embarked upon'.[449] However, it is the preferential relationship that has been established between the Court and the Coalition for the ICC that is troubling. The current relationship between the Court and the Coalition goes beyond what is provided for in Articles 15(2) and 44 of the Rome Statute.

This inseparable relationship between the Coalition and the Court is in sharp contrast to the absence of a clear communication strategy with African states, its current area of work. The Court is first and foremost a creation of states to address matters of state sovereignty – criminal prosecutions. It should have been logical that even before the opening of the first preliminary examination the Prosecutor should have elaborated a strategic policy on collaboration with states especially focusing on those where the Court is operating. Ciampi in her conclusion notes that

> [t]he real challenge is how to make it in the states' interest to cooperate with the Court in particular, and in the repression of core international crimes, more generally. Political support can hardly be won by legal means. But sound policy choices may help.[450]

Mensa-Bonsu argues that 'the determination of who can be tried by the court, as well as for what crimes, is a political question (…)'.[451] Therefore, as Schabas suggests

> perhaps the medicine for the ailing International Criminal Court is not less politics but more. Once the inevitability of 'politicisation' is acknowledged, it can address

447 Ullrich, 'Beyond the 'Global-Local Divide: Local Intermediaries, Victims and the Justice Contestations of the International Criminal Court' (2016), 550.
448 ibid, 553.
449 Cherif M. Bassiouni, 'The ICC – *Quo Vadis*?' (2006) 4:3 Journal of International Criminal Justice, 427.
450 Ciampi, 'Legal Rules, Policy Choices and Political Realities in the Functioning of the Cooperation Regime of the International Criminal Court' (2016), 48.
451 Mensa-Bonsu, 'The ICC, International Criminal Justice and International Politics' (2015), 38.

> the choices that must be made in a more transparent and therefore more credible manner.[452]

It has been argued that in order for the Court to consider political realities on the ground the Court needs to place its intervention as contributing to resolving governance issues. This is not a suggestion for the Prosecutor to start litigating politics. It is an acknowledgement of what is happening. The decision of sorting situations and cases is political in nature, and in this sense, as Schabas observes, 'it is hard to determine the policy when the Prosecutor denies that one exists and the Pre-Trial Chambers decline to examine if this really is the case. Whatever the agenda may be, it certainly is hidden'.[453] The collaboration policy on broader issues can be creatively developed out of a legal framework that is provided for in the Rome Statute requiring the Prosecutor to communicate with the state concerned considering aspects of complementarity and interests of justice. Greenawalt notes that

> [w]hile the Court is a criminal tribunal charged with the prosecution of individual suspects, it is also empowered, as a necessary incident of its prosecutorial power, with broad administrative policy discretion to evaluate the adequacy of transitional justice policies undertaken by states (…).[454]

This intended collaboration to work would require the Court to acknowledge that all situations of massive violations of human rights cannot be fixed by one single prescription or different uncoordinated measures. The Prosecutor should be open to forthright discussions with other actors on the ground involved in resolving all the issues at stake. In case the Prosecutor is convinced that it is in the best interests of the society concerned to conduct criminal prosecutions over other forms of accountability, the OTP is capable of conducting a convincing thorough analysis of all possible transitional justice mechanisms demonstrating to those actors on the ground that the Court is the best alternative. This is important, even if the Prosecutor might not agree with other actors on the ground, as it would still serve as the best response to criticisms of external influence because observers of what is happening would be availed with a transparent and sound Prosecution analysis. Wolfrum notes that '[a] legitimacy gap can be filled either on the international or on the national level or both. There does not seem to be just one remedy'.[455] May and Fyfe note that 'it is rare that a person who has been

---

452 Schabas, 'The Short Arm of International Criminal Court' (2013), 405.

453 ibid, 404.

454 Alexander K.A. Greenawalt, 'Complementarity in Crisis: Uganda, Alternative Justice, and the International Criminal Court' (2009) 50, 107 Virginia Journal of International Law, 110.

455 Rudiger Wolfrum, 'Legitimacy of International Law from a Legal Perspective: Some Introductory Considerations' in Rudiger Wolfrum and Volker Roeben (eds.), *Legitimacy in International Law* (Springer, 2008), 22.

convicted in any court would agree to having the sentence meted out. But it is crucial for legitimacy that the group from which the convicted person comes assents to these rulings'.[456]

The broader interpretation of principles of complementarity and interests of justice would permit the Prosecutor to consider other alternative forms of accountability. This, however, would also depend on the Prosecutor's decision of when to intervene. The ICC Prosecutor should be cognisant of the meaning of when to intervene. As Fikentscher notes, justice needs to be delivered fast but also not too fast.

> Justice often cannot and should not be rendered at once. Quick justice may be injustice. Lynching is a matter for the mob, not for the Court. [... It is also true that] justice needs to be 'prompt' to make it comprehensible to the parties and the public. Justice done too late is no justice at all.[457]

I have argued that the OTP could start preliminary examinations at any time that there is a reasonable basis to believe that crimes under the jurisdiction of the Court are being committed, and it can go ahead in collecting evidence but the issuance of arrest warrants should wait until the end of conflict/violence, for a number of reasons. First, it would protect the Court from local politics. Second, it would serve as a deterrent to commission of crimes since all belligerents would be put under notice of a possible prosecution. Third, it is practical to arrest suspects after the conflict and the arrest would be based on well-examined evidence beyond the war propaganda. Fourth, it is after the violence that the Prosecution can genuinely examine whether the state concerned is either unwilling or unable to prosecute. It would be disingenuous to determine that the state is either unwilling or unable when it is still undergoing a conflict. During the conflict, prosecution is not a priority, and not being on the national agenda at the moment cannot be interpreted as either unwillingness or inability. Similarly, it would be a narrow interpretation if the Prosecution determined that a state is unwilling/unable when it has examined all mechanisms including prosecution and come to a conclusion that alternative mechanisms of accountability are the most appropriate response for the society to move ahead. As Rawls notes 'one conception of justice is preferable to another when its broader consequences are more desirable'.[458] Similarly, Sellers argues that '[l]egal systems are legitimate when they make the societies they

---

456 Larry May and Shannon Fyfe, 'The Legitimacy of International Criminal Tribunals' in Nobuo Hayashi and Cecilia M. Bailliet (eds.), *The Legitimacy of International Criminal Tribunals* (Cambridge University Press, 2017), 32–33.

457 Wolfgang Fikentscher, *Law and Anthropology* (2nd ed., Beck/Hart, 2016), 439.

458 Rawls, *A Theory of Justice* (1973), 6.

guide more just, and do so better than any available alternative system of legal determination'.[459]

Another related problem is that the ICC's rushed indictments undermine the state in question's opportunity to develop its internal capacities to investigate crimes. In most cases, post-conflict reconstruction efforts involve engaging development partners to rebuild the rule of law. The early involvement of the Court in the situation takes away one of the strongest demands for rebuilding the national judicial sector and other rule of law organs and puts all the attention on the ICC. Even when the state concerned was willing to prosecute the exact same suspects, it would find itself locked in with the Court. This undermines the possibility of creating a sustainable justice system and good governance that is badly needed after a conflict. Cowell argues that 'Article 17 [of the Rome Statute] is an example of the patronising and disempowering features of the Rome Statute, which allows the Court to act in ways that appear to marginalize local concerns'.[460] According to Akhavan: 'The ICC often arrives on the scene as the ambulance and trauma surgeon, while a national system, as next of kin, must nurse the patient back to health at home in a prolonged convalescence.'[461] This is not what the drafters of the Rome Statute envisaged, I argue. The Prosecutor has reversed the complementarity principle. The Court was not expected to arrive as an ambulance; doing so is contrary to the idea that the Court is supposed to intervene when national systems are either unwilling or unable genuinely to investigate and prosecute the alleged crimes. If the Court is willing to remain as truly a court of last resort, it needs to collaborate with (if not, provide enough space and time to) actors on the ground to examine all the critical challenges and mobilise necessary resources to resolve them. The Court should consider itself as part and parcel of transitional justice instead of as a unique justice mechanism overruling all other transitional justice mechanisms.

The argument that the Court intervenes in African situations because national authorities lack capacity to provide justice that meets international standards is wanting. Africa does not lack 'international standards' in criminal justice alone. There is a lack of standards in education, health, infrastructure, food security, and there is still poverty, corruption and many other challenges. This was precisely the main reason to build and strengthen capacities instead of replacing national systems. If the canonical view is that criminals should be taken out of Africa because of inadequacies in the criminal justice system, the next day we would be told that the United Nations Development Programme (UNDP) and/or World Food Programme should start taking the poor and the hungry to

459 Sellers, 'Law, Reason, and Emotion' (2015), 83.

460 Cowell, 'Inherent Imperialism: Understanding the Legal Roots of Anti-imperialist Criticism of the International Criminal Court' (2017), 679.

461 Payam Akhavan, 'Complementarity Conundrums: The ICC Clock in Transitional Times' (2016) 14, 1043–1059 Journal of International Criminal Justice, 1044.

Europe or the USA instead of strengthening local capacities, the World Health Organization (WHO) would start taking the sick to western hospitals instead of supporting local hospitals, the United Nations Educational, Scientific and Cultural Organisation (UNESCO) would take children instead of supporting schools, and Transparency International would take corrupt leaders to its headquarters. Rhetoric aside, my point is that there is a need to strengthen national institutions and this demand is more important in post conflict societies because that is the only sustainable way we can indeed claim that the culture of impunity will be eradicated. This would also save the Court's limited budget from cases that national courts are capable of handling. For instance, if the Court was interested in encouraging national authorities to undertake some of the cases, what reasons justify Uganda's failure to prosecute Dominic Ongwen through its International Crimes Division, if Libya could be allowed to try Mohammed Abdullah Senussi?[462]

Schabas has some unkind words for international criminal law lawyers. He observes that '[b]y comparison [to other professions], criminal justice looks primitive and amateurish. In its defence, it is said that these are "early days". But those who work within it do not seem to have a vision of the future'.[463] I want to be a little more optimistic than that because I don't believe that the situation is completely bleak. There have been some breakthroughs since the creation of military tribunals in Nuremberg and Tokyo, from the creation of the United Nations *ad hoc* tribunals and hybrid courts to the adoption of the Rome Statute in 1998, some positive progress can be observed and more still can be achieved, but only if there is goodwill to genuinely engage all stakeholders. As deGuzman notes, 'efforts to enhance the Court's legitimacy through good process cannot succeed in the absence of goals and priorities that relevant audiences accept as appropriate for the Court'.[464] In the case of the ICC, I have repeatedly argued that the primary audience of the Court should be the affected communities and national authorities that are in charge of dealing with the consequences of the violence. At the moment when there is no global authority capable of enforcing justice that is equitable to all citizens of the world, the Court needs to focus on strengthening its national and local legitimacies. This approach would reduce the suspicion of external interferences. As Nouwen notes,

> [u]nequal application of international criminal law, (...) plays a role in justifying inequality by highlighting the criminality of some and, through its silence, overlooking that of others. [... If it] is exercised only over crimes committed by less

462 The ICC website indicates that the 'case against Abdullah Al-Senussi was declared inadmissible on 11 October 2013', authorising the Libyan authorities to prosecute him, available at https://www.icc-cpi.int/libya/gaddafi.

463 Schabas, 'The Short Arm of International Criminal (2013), 388.

464 deGuzman, 'Choosing to Prosecute: Expressive Selection at the International Criminal Court' (2012), 299.

powerful people, or by the nationals or on the territory of less powerful states, this suggests that international law justifies this different treatment.[465]

To avoid this suspicion, the Court needs to package its message in a respectful language and place its mission into the broader national interests of a post-conflict governance and transitional justice. This suggestion might not necessarily resolve all the current problems, neither would it be a solution to a situation of UNSC referral where the head of a non-state party is wanted, or in the case of a hostile government. However, if decent communication and sound contextual analysis is combined with an outreach strategy that is engaging all other actors on the ground, it would ease some of the tensions.

465 Nouwen, 'Legal Equality on Trial: Sovereigns and Individuals Before the International Criminal Court' (2013), 158.

# BIBLIOGRAPHY

## BOOKS, CHAPTERS AND ARTICLES


Abbott W.K. and Snidal D., 'Why States Act through Formal International Organizations' (1998) 42, 3–32 Journal of Conflict Resolution

Akhavan P., 'Complementarity Conundrums: The ICC Clock in Transitional Times' (2016) 14, 1043–1059 Journal of International Criminal Justice

Almqvist J., 'International Criminal Courts and Tribunals: A Human Rights Appraisal of the Limits to Judicial Independence for International Criminal Justice' (2015) 28, 91–112 Leiden Journal of International Law

Alvarez J.E., *The Impact of International Organizations on International Law* (Brill/Nijhoff, 2017)

Ambos K., 'Confidential Investigations (Article 54(3)(E) ICC Statute) vs. Disclosure Obligations: The Lubanga Case And National Law' (2009) 12:4, 543–568 New Criminal Law Review: An International and Interdisciplinary Journal

Appel B.J., 'In the Shadow of the International Criminal Court: Does the ICC Deter Human Rights Violations?' (2018) 62:1, 3–28 Journal of Conflict Resolution

Austin W.C. and Thieme M., 'Is the International Criminal Court Anti-African?' (2016) 28:3, 342–350 Peace Review

Balint J., Evans J. and McMillan N., 'Rethinking Transitional Justice, Redressing Indigenous Harm: A New Conceptual Approach' (2014) 8, 194–216 The International Journal of Transitional Justice

Bandes S.A., 'Loyalty to One's Convictions: The Prosecutor and Tunnel Vision' (2006) 49, 475 Howard Law Journal

Barkin J.S., *International Organizations: Theories and Institutions* (2nd ed., Palgrave Macmillan, 2013)

Barnett M.N. and Finnemore M., 'The Politics, Power, and Pathologies of International Organizations' (1999) 53:4, 699–732 International Organization

Bassiouni C.M., 'The ICC – *Quo Vadis*?' (2006) 4:3 Journal of International Criminal Justice

Baylis A.E., 'Outsourcing Investigations' (2009) 14 UCLA Journal of International Law and Foreign Affairs (University of Pittsburgh Legal Studies Research Paper No. 2010-20)

Bergin C. and Bergin D.A., 'Classroom Discipline That Promotes Self-Control' (1999) 20:2, 189–206 Journal of Applied Developmental Psychology

Besson S., 'Theorizing the Sources of International Law' in Besson S. and Tasioulas J., *The Philosophy of International Law* (Oxford University Press, 2010)

Bikundo E., 'The International Criminal Court and Africa: Exemplary Justice' (2012) 23:1, 21–41 Law and Critique

Blackledge A., 'Discourse and Power' in Gee J.P. and Handford M. (eds.), *The Routledge Handbook of Discourse Analysis* (Routledge, 2012)

Blasi G., 'Advocacy against the Stereotype: Lessons from Cognitive Social Psychology' (2002) 49, 1241 Los Angeles Law Review

Boehme F., 'Exit, voice and loyalty: state rhetoric about the International Criminal Court' (2018) 22:3, 420–445 The International Journal of Human Rights

Bolton J.R., 'The Risks and Weakness of the International Criminal Court: From America's Perspective' (2001) 64:1, 167–180 Law and Contemporary Problems

Bosco D., *Rough Justice: The International Criminal Court's Battle to Fix the World, One Prosecution at a Time* (Oxford University Press, 2014)

——, 'Discretion and State Influence at the International Criminal Court: The Prosecutor's Preliminary Examinations' (2017) 11:2, 395–414 American Journal of International Law

Branco J., *L'Ordre et le Monde: Critique de la Cour Penale Internationale* (Fayard, 2016)

Brinton A., 'A rhetorical view of the ad hominem' (1985) 63:1, 50–63 Australasian Journal of Philosophy

Brody R., 'Bringing a Dictator to Justice: The Case of Hissène Habré' (2015) 13:2, 209–2017 Journal of International Criminal Justice

Brooks R., 'Friends Don't Let Friends Drive Drunk: The Role of U.S. Allies in Keeping the U.S. Honest' (2017) 48, 923 Georgetown Journal of International Law

Buchanan A. and Keohane R.O., 'The Legitimacy of Global Governance Institutions' in Wolfrum R. and Roeben V. (eds.), *Legitimacy in International Law* (Springer, 2008)

Buckley-Zistel S. and others (eds.), *Transitional Justice Theories* (Routledge, 2014)

Bühlmann M. and Kunz R., 'Confidence in the Judiciary: Comparing the Independence and Legitimacy of Judicial Systems' (2011) 34:2, 317–345 West European Politics

Buisman C., 'Delegating Investigations: Lessons to be Learned from the Lubanga Judgment' (2013) 11:3, 29–82 Northwestern Journal of International Human Rights

Carter E.L., Ellis M.S. and Jalloh C.C., *The International Criminal Court in an Effective Global Justice System* (Edward Elgar Publishing, 2016)

Chaudoin S., 'How Contestation Moderates the Effects of International Institutions: The International Criminal Court and Kenya' (2016) 78:2, 557–571 The Journal of Politics

Chinedu B.O., 'The African Union, the United States Security Council and the Politicisation of International Justice in Africa' (2014) 7:3, 351–379 African Journal of Legal Studies

Ciampi A., 'Legal Rules, Policy Choices and Political Realities in the Functioning of the Cooperation Regime of the International Criminal Court' in Bekou O. and Birkett D.J. (eds.), *Cooperation and the International Criminal Court: Perspectives from Theory and Practice* (Brill/Nijhoff, 2016)

Clark P. and Palmer N.P., 'Challenging Transitional Justice' in Palmer N., Clark P. and Granville D. (eds.), *Critical Perspectives in Transitional Justice* (Intersentia, 2012)

Clarke K.M., 'International Justice and the Politics of Sentimentality' in Clarke K.M., Knottnerus A.S and de Volder E. (eds.), *Africa and ICC: Perceptions of Justice* (Cambridge University Press, 2016)

——, 'Why Africa?' in Steinberg R.H. (ed.), *Contemporary Issues Facing the International Criminal Court* (Brill/Nijhoff, 2016)

Cole J.V.R., 'Africa's Relationship with the International Criminal Court: More Political than Legal' (2013) 14, 670 Melbourne Journal of International Law

Colman A.M. (ed.), *Oxford Dictionary of Psychology* (Oxford University Press, 2014)

Corradetti C. and Rotondi J.V. (eds.), *Theorizing Transitional Justice* (Ashgate, 2015)

Cowan G. and Arsenault A., 'Moving from Monologue to Dialogue to Collaboration: The Three Layers of Public Diplomacy' (2008) 616:1, 10–30 The ANNALS of the American Academy of Political and Social Science

Cowell F., 'Inherent Imperialism: Understanding the Legal Roots of Anti-imperialist Criticism of the International Criminal Court' (2017) 15:4, 667–687 Journal of International Criminal Justice

Cross F.B., 'Thoughts on Goldilocks and Judicial Independence' (2003) 64, 195 Ohio State Law Journal

Danner A.M., 'Enhancing the Legitimacy and Accountability of Prosecutorial Discretion at the International Criminal Court' (2003) 97, 510 The American Journal of International Law

——, 'Enhancing the Legitimacy and Accountability of the Prosecutorial Discretion at the International Criminal Court' in Cassese A. and others (eds.), *International Criminal Law: Critical Concepts in Law* (Routledge, 2015)

d'Aspremont J. and de Brabandere E., 'The Duality of the Legitimacy of Global Actors in the International Legal Order' in Happold M. (ed.), *International Law in a Multipolar World* (Routledge, 2012)

deGuzman M.M., 'Choosing to Prosecute: Expressive Selection at the International Criminal Court' (2012) 33, 265 Michigan Journal of International Law

de Hoon M., 'The Future of the International Criminal Court. On Critique, Legalism and Strengthening the ICC's Legitimacy' (2017) 17, 591–614 International Criminal Law Review

de Souza Dias T., '"Interests of justice": Defining the scope of Prosecutorial discretion in Article 53(1)(c) and (2)(c) of the Rome Statute of the International Criminal Court' (2017) 30:3, 731–751 Leiden Journal of International Law

Dugard J., 'Palestine and the International Criminal Court: Institutional Failure or Bias?' (2013) 11:3, 563–570 Journal of International Criminal Justice

du Plessis M., Maluwa T. and O'Reilly A., *Africa and the International Criminal Court* (Chatham House/International Law, 2013/01)

du Plessis M., Maluwa T., O'Reilly A. and Mettraux G., 'South Africa's Failed Withdrawal from the Rome Statute: Politics, Law, and Judicial Accountability' (2017) 15:2. 361–370 Journal of International Justice

Ent M.R. and Baumeister R.F., 'Obedience, Self-Control, and the Voice of Culture' (2014) 70:3, 574–586 The Society for the Psychological Study of Social Issues

Falsettio B., 'Crossing the Line: Morality, Society, and the Criminal Law' (2009) 5, 182 Cambridge Student Law Review

Fellmeth A. and Horwitz M., (*Argumentum ad hominem.*) *Guide to Latin in International Law* (Oxford University Press, 2009)

Fikentscher W., *Law and Anthropology* (2nd ed., Beck/Hart, 2016)

Flap H., 'The Conflicting Loyalties Theories' (1997) 47:1, 183–215 L'Année sociologique

Follesdal A., 'Kant, Human Rights, and Courts' in Follesdal A. and Maliks R. (eds.), *Kantian Theory and Human Rights* (Routledge, 2013)

Fox J.R., *Dictionary of International and Comparative Law* (3rd ed. Oceana Publications, Inc., 2003)

Fukuyama F., 'What is Governance' (2013) 26:3, 347–368 Governance: An International Journal of Policy, Administration, and Institutions

Funk T.M., *Victims' Rights and Advocacy at the International Criminal Court* (2nd ed., Oxford University Press, 2015)
Garner A.B. (Chief Ed.), *Black's Law Dictionary* (9th ed., Thomson Reuters, 2009)
Gissel E.L., 'Justice Tides: How and When Levels of ICC Involvement Affect Peace Processes' (2015) 9:3, 428–448 International Journal of Transitional Justice
Gready P. and Robins S., 'From Transitional to Transformative Justice: A New Agenda for Practice' (2014) 8, 339–361 The International Journal of Transitional Justice
Greenawalt A.K.A., 'Complementarity in Crisis: Uganda, Alternative Justice, and the International Criminal Court' (2009) 50, 107 Virginia Journal of International Law
Greenwald A.G., Nosek B.A. and Banaji M.R., 'Understanding and using the Implicit Association Test: I. An improved scoring algorithm' (2003) 85:2, 197–216 Journal of Personality and Social Psychology
Groome D., 'No Witness, No Case: An Assessment of the Conduct and Quality of ICC Investigations' (2014) 3:1, 1–29 The Penn State Journal of Law & International Affairs
Gutmann J. and Voigt S., 'The Independence of Prosecutors and Government Accountability' (2017) ILE Working Paper Series, No. 8
Haddad H.N., 'After the Norm Cascade: NGO Mission Expansion and the Coalition for the International Criminal Court' (2013) 19, 189 Global Governance
Hansen T.O., 'Reflections on the ICC Prosecutor's Recent Selection Decisions' (2013) 17, 125–158 Max Planck Yearbook of United Nations Law (Brill)
——, 'The International Criminal Court and the Legitimacy of Exercise' in Andersen P., Eriksen C. and Viskum B. (eds), *Law and Legitimacy* (DJOEF Publishers, 2015)
Hartmann F., *Paix et Châtiment: Les Guerres Secrètes de la Politique et de la Justice Internationales* (Flammarion, 2007)
Heller J.K., 'The Role of the International Prosecutor' in Cesare Romano C., Alter K. and Shany Y. (eds.), *Oxford Handbook of International Adjudication* (Oxford University Press, 2013)
Hillebrecht C., 'The Deterrent Effects of the International Criminal Court: Evidence from Libya' (2016) 42:4, 616–643 International Interactions
Hinman L.M., 'The case for ad hominem arguments' (1982) 60:4, 338–345 Australasian Journal of Philosophy
Holland J. and Aaronson M., 'Dominance through Coercion: Strategic Rhetorical Balancing and the Tactics of Justification in Afghanistan and Libya' (2014) 8:1, 1–20 Journal of Intervention and Statebuilding
Hurd I., 'Legitimacy and Authority in International Politics' (1999) 53:2, 379–408 International Organization
Imoedemhe O.C., *The Complementarity Regime of the International Criminal Court: National Implementation in Africa* (Springer, 2017)
Jackson B.S., *Law, Fact and Narrative Coherence* (Deborah Charles Publications, 1988)
Jalloh C.C., 'The Nature of Crimes in the African Criminal Court' (2017) 15, 799–826 Journal of International Criminal Justice
Jeßberger F. and Geneuss J., 'Litigating Universal Jurisdiction' – Introduction (2015) 13:2, 205–208 Journal of International Criminal Justice
Jolls C. and Sunstein C.R., 'The Law of Implicit Bias' (2006) 94, 969 California Law Review
Jones S., *Criminology* (3rd ed., Oxford University Press, 2009)

Junne G.C.A., 'International Organizations in a Period of Globalization: New (Problems of) Legitimacy' in Coicaud J.M. and Heiskanen V. (eds.), *The Legitimacy of International Organizations* (United Nations University Press, 2001)

Kang E., 'Conflicting Loyalties Theory: A Cross-Cultural Test' (1976) 15:2, 201–210 Ethnology

Kang J. and others, 'Implicit Bias in the Courtroom' (2012) 59, 1124 University of California, Los Angeles, Law Review

Kaul H-P., 'The International Criminal Court of the future' in Schabas W.A. (ed.), *The Cambridge Companion to International Criminal Law* (Cambridge University Press, 2016)

Keller L.M., 'Comparing the "Interests of Justice": What the International Criminal Court Can Learn from New York Law' (2013) 12:1, 1–39 Washington University Global Studies Law Review

Kelly J.G. and Simmons B.A., 'Politics by Number: Indicators as Social Pressure in International Relations' (2015) 59:1, 55–70 American Journal of Political Science

Kendall S., 'Commodifying Global Justice: Economies of Accountability at the International Criminal Court' (2015) 13:1, 113–134 Journal of International Criminal Justice

Kendall S. and Nouwen S., 'Representational Practices at the International Criminal Court: The Gap between Juridified and Abstract Victimhood' (2013) 76, 235–262 Law and Contemporary Problems

Keppler E., 'Managing Setbacks for the International Criminal Court in Africa' (2012) 56:1, 1–14 Journal of African Law

Kiyani A., 'Legitimacy, Legality, and the Possibility of a Pluralist International Criminal Law in Hayashi N. and Bailliet C.M. (eds.), *The Legitimacy of International Criminal Tribunals* (Cambridge University Press, 2017)

Knottnerus S.A. and de Volder E., 'International Criminal Justice and the Early Formation of an African Criminal Court' in Clarke M.K., Knottnerus S.A. and de Volder E., *Africa and the ICC: Perceptions of Justice* (Cambridge University Press, 2016)

Köchler H., 'Justice and Realpolitik: The Predicament of the International Criminal Court' (2017) 16:1, 1–9 Chinese Journal of International Law

Krcmaric D., 'Should I Stay or Should I Go? Leaders, Exile, and the Dilemmas of International Justice' (2018) 62:2, 486–498 American Journal of Political Science

Krisch N., 'International Law in Times of Hegemony: Unequal Power and the Shaping of the International Legal Order' (2005) 16:3, 369–408 The European Journal of International Law

Krzan B., 'International Criminal Court Facing the Peace vs. Justice Dilemma' (2016) 2:2, 81–88 International Comparative Jurisprudence

Kuczyńska H., 'Selection of Defendants Before the ICC: Between the Principle of Opportunism and Legalism' (2014) 34, 187–224 Polish Yearbook of International Law

——, *The Accusation Model Before the International Criminal Court* (Springer, 2015)

Lambourne W., 'Transitional Justice and Peacebuilding after Mass Violence' (2009) 3, 28–48 The International Journal of Transitional Justice

Langvatn S.A. and Squatrito T., 'Conceptualising and Measuring the Legitimacy of International Criminal Tribunals' in Hayashi N. and Bailliet C.M. (eds.), *The Legitimacy of International Criminal Tribunals* (Studies on International Courts and Tribunals, (Cambridge University Press, 2017))

Lee S., *Law and Morals: Warnock, Gillick and Beyond* (Oxford University Press, 1986)
Leipold A.D., 'Objective Tests and Subjective Bias: Some Problems of Discriminatory Intent in the Criminal Law' (1998) 73, 559 Chicago-Kent Law Review
Levi R., Hagan J. and Dezalay S., 'International Courts in Atypical Political Environments: The Interplay of Prosecutorial Strategy, Evidence, and Court Authority in International Criminal Law' (2016) 79, 289 Law and Contemporary Problems
Linde C., 'Narrative in Institutions' in Schiffrin D., Tannen D. and Hamilton H.E. (eds.), *The Handbook of Discourse Analysis* (Blackwell Publishers, 2001)
Lohne K., *Advocates of Humanity: Human Rights NGOs in International Criminal Justice* (A dissertation submitted in partial fulfilment of the requirements for the degree of philosophia doctor (Ph.D.) – Department of Criminology and Sociology of Law Faculty of Law University of Oslo) – (unpublished version)
——, 'Global Civil Society, the ICC, and Legitimacy in International Criminal Justice' in Hayashi N. and Bailliet C.M. (eds.), *The Legitimacy of International Criminal Tribunals* (Cambridge University Press, 2017)
Lovat H., 'Delineating the interests of justice: prosecutorial discretion and the Rome Statute of the International Criminal Court' (2007) 35:2, 275–286 Denver Journal of International Law and Policy
Luban D., 'After the Honeymoon: Reflections on the Current State of International Criminal Justice' (2013) 11, 505–515 Journal of International Criminal Justice
MacCormick N., *Rhetoric and the Rule of Law: A Theory of Legal Reasoning* (Oxford University Press, 2010)
Macdonald A., '"In the interests of justice?" The International Criminal Court, peace talks and the failed quest for war crimes accountability in northern Uganda' (2017) 11:4, 628–648 Journal of Eastern African Studies
Makau M.W., 'Savages, Victims, and Saviors: The Metaphor of Human Rights' (2001) 42:1, 201–245 Harvard International Law Journal
Martin M.W. and Jurgen B., 'Proposed International Criminal Chamber Section of the African Court of Justice and Human Rights: A Legal Analysis' (2012) 37:1, 248–268 South African Yearbook of International Law
May L. and Fyfe S., 'The Legitimacy of International Criminal Tribunals' in Hayashi N. and Bailliet C.M. (eds.), *The Legitimacy of International Criminal Tribunals* (Cambridge University Press, 2017)
McDonald A. and Haveman R., 'Prosecutorial Discretion – Some Thoughts on "Objectifying" the Exercise of Prosecutorial Discretion by the Prosecutor of the ICC: Expert consultation process on general issues relevant to the ICC Office of the Prosecutor' (15 April 2003)
McEvoy K., 'Beyond Legalism: Towards a Thicker Understanding of Transitional Justice' (2007) 34:4, 411–440 Journal of Law and Society
Meierhenrich J., 'The evolution of the office of the prosecutor at the international criminal court: insights from institutional theory' in Minow M., True-Frost C.C. and Whiting A. (eds.), *The First Global Prosecutor: Promise and Constraints. Law, Meaning, and Violence* (University of Michigan Press, 2015)
Mensa-Bonsu J.A.N.H., 'The ICC, International Criminal Justice and International Politics' (2015) XL: 2, 33–53 Africa Development
Meron T., 'Judicial Independence and Impartiality in International Criminal Tribunals' (2005) 99:2, 359–369 The American Journal of International Law

Mills K., 'Bashir Is Dividing Us: Africa and the International Criminal Court' (2012) 34, 404 Human Rights Quarterly

Mills K. and Bloomfield A., 'African resistance to the International Criminal Court: Halting the advance of the anti-impunity norm' (2018) 44:1, 101–127 Review of International Studies

Minow M., True-Frost C.C. and Whiting A., 'The Prosecutor Casts a Shadow: Convener, Collaborator, and Law Enforcer' in Minow M., True-Frost C.C. and Whiting A. (eds.), *The First Global Prosecutor: Promise and Constraints* (University of Michigan, 2015)

Mnookin R.H., 'Rethinking the Tension between Peace and Justice: The International Criminal Prosecutor as Diplomat' in Minow M., True-Frost C.C. and Whiting A. (eds.), *The First Global Prosecutor: Promise and Constraints* (University of Michigan Press, 2015)

Mueller D.S., 'Kenya and the International Criminal Court (ICC): politics, the election and the law' (2014) 8:1, 25–42 Journal of Eastern African Studies

Muleefu A., *Reparation for victims of collateral damage: A normative and theoretical inquiry* (Wolf Legal Publishers, 2014)

Mutua M., 'What Is the Future of Transitional Justice?' (2015) 9, 1–9 International Journal of Transitional Justice

Nathanson S., 'Are Attacks on Civilians Always Wrong?' in Lovell D.W. and Primoratz I. (eds.), *Protecting Civilians during Violent Conflict: Theoretical and Practical Issues for the 21st Century* (Routledge, 2012)

Niang M., 'Africa and the Legitimacy of the ICC in Question' (2017) 17:4, 615–624 International Criminal Law Review

Niezen R., *Public Justice and the Anthropology of Law* (Cambridge University Press, 2010)

Nouwen S., 'Legal Equality on Trial: Sovereigns and Individuals Before the International Criminal Court' (2012) 41, 151–181 Netherlands Yearbook of International Law

Nouwen S. and Werner W., 'Doing Justice to the Political: The International Criminal Court in Uganda and Sudan' (2011) 21:4, 941–965 The European Journal of International Law

Ocampo L.M., 'Prologue: The Prosecutor's Use of Legal Policies' in Minow M., True-Frost C.C. and Whiting A. (eds.), *The First Global Prosecutor: Promise and Constraints* (2015, University of Michigan)

O'Connor C. and Michaels S., 'When Is Dialogue "Dialogic"?' (2007) 50, 275–285 Human Development

Okafor C.O. and Ngwaba U., 'The International Criminal Court as a Transitional Justice' Mechanism in Africa: Some Critical Reflections' (2015) 9, 90–108 International Journal of Transitional Justice

——, 'Between Tunnel Vision and a Sliding Scale: Power, Normativity and Justice in the Praxis of the International Criminal Court' (2017) 31:1, 179–194 Temple International and Comparative Law Journal

Parmentier S., 'Transitional Justice' in Schabas W.A. (ed.), *The Cambridge Companion to International Criminal Law* (Cambridge University Press, 2016)

Perelman C., *The Idea of Justice and the Problem of Argument* (Routledge & Kegan Paul 1977)

Persaud R.B. and Walker R.B.J., 'Apertura: Race in International Relations' (2001) 26:4, 373–376 Alternatives: Global, Local, Political

Pettit P., 'Legitimacy and Justice in Republican Perspective' (2012) 65, 59–82 Current Legal Problems

Posner A.E. and Yoo C.J., 'Judicial Independence in International Tribunals' (2005) 93:1 California Law Review

Poulin A.B., 'Prosecutorial Discretion and Selective Prosecution: Enforcing Protection after United States v. Armstrong' (1997) 34, 1071 American Criminal Law Review

Pues A., 'Towards the "Golden Hour"?: A Critical Exploration of the Length of Preliminary Examinations' (2017) 15:3 Journal of International Criminal Justice (Special Issue: The International Criminal Court's Policies and Strategies)

Rastan R., 'Comment on Victor's Justice & the Visibility of *Ex Ante* Standards' (2010) 43, 569 The John Marshall Law Review

Rawls J., *A Theory of Justice* (Harvard University Press, 1973)

Robertson M., *Stanley Fish on Philosophy, Politics and Law: How Fish Works* (Cambridge University Press, 2014)

Robinson D., 'Serving the Interests of Justice: Amnesties, Truth Commissions and the International Criminal Court' (2003) 14:3, 481–505 European Journal of International Law

——, 'Inescapable Dyads: Why the International Criminal Court Cannot Win' (2015) 28:2, 323–347 Leiden Journal of International Law

Rodman A.K., 'Is Peace in the Interests of Justice? The Case for Broad Prosecutorial Discretion at the International Criminal Court' (2009) 22:1, 99–126 Leiden Journal of International Law

——, 'Justice as a Dialogue Between Law and Politics: Embedding the International Criminal Court within Conflict Management and Peacebuilding' (2014) 1–33 Journal of International Criminal Justice

Rogers D., *Law, Politics and the Limits of Prosecuting Mass Atrocity* (Palgrave Macmillan, 2018)

Rorty R., 'Justice as a Larger Loyalty' (1997) 4:2, 139–151 Ethical Perspectives

Rosenberg T.S., 'International Criminal Court in Cote d'Ivoire: Impartiality at Stake' (2017) 15, 471–490 Journal of International Criminal Justice

Sah S., Robertson C.T. and Baughman S.B., 'Blinding prosecutors to defendants' race: A policy proposal to reduce unconscious bias in the criminal justice system' (2015) 1:2, 69–76 Behavioral Science & Policy

Schabas W.A., 'Victor's Justice: Selecting "Situations" at the International Criminal Court' (2010) 43, 535 The John Marshall Law Review

——, 'The Short Arm of International Criminal Law' in Schabas W.A., McDermott Y. and Hayes N. (eds.), *The Ashgate Research Companion to International Criminal Law: Critical Perspectives* (Ashgate, 2013)

Schein E.H., 'On Dialogue, Culture, and Organizational Learning' (1993) 22:2, 40–51 Organizational Dynamics

Schiff B.N., 'Can the International Criminal Court Contribute to the Responsibility to Protect?' (2016) 30:3, 298–313 International Relations

Schmitt D.P., 'France, Africa, and the ICC: The Neocolonialist Critique and the Crisis of the Institutional Legitimacy' in Clarke M.K., Knottnerus S.A. and de Volder E., *Africa and the ICC: Perceptions of Justice* (Cambridge University Press, 2016)

Schuerch R., *The International Criminal Court at the Mercy of Powerful States: An Assessment of the Neo-Colonialism Claim by African Stakeholders* (T.M.C. Asser Press, 2017)

Sellers M.N.S., 'Law, Reason, and Emotion' in Galuppo M.C. and others (eds.), *Human Rights, Rule of Law and the Contemporary Social Challenges in Complex Societies: Proceedings of the 26th World Congress of the International Association for Philosophy of Law and Social Philosophy in Belo Horizonte, 2013* (Franz Steiner Verlag, 2015)

Seymour L.J.M., 'Rhetoric, Hypocrisy Management, and Legitimacy' in Clarke M.K., Knottnerus S.A. and de Volder E., *Africa and the ICC: Perceptions of Justice* (Cambridge University Press, 2016)

Sharp D.N., 'Emancipating Transitional Justice from the Bonds of the Paradigmatic Transition' (2015) 9, 150–169 International Journal of Transitional Justice

Shuy W.R., 'Discourse Analysis in the Legal Context' in Schiffrin D., Tannen D. and Hamilton H.E. (eds.), *The Handbook of Discourse Analysis* (Blackwell Publishers, 2001)

Siems M.M., 'Legal Originality' (2008) 28:1, 147–164, Oxford Journal of Legal Studies

Simmons J.A., *Justification and Legitimacy: Essays on Rights and Obligations* (Cambridge University Press, 2001)

Smeulers A., Weerdesteijn M. and Hola B., 'The Selection of Situations by the ICC: An Empirically Based Evaluation of the OTP's Performance' (2015) 15, 1–39 International Criminal Law Review

Sperfeldt C., 'The trial against Hissène Habré: networked justice and reparations at the Extraordinary African Chambers' (2017) 21:9, 1243–1260 The International Journal of Human Rights

Stahn C., 'Damned If You Do, Damned If You Don't: Challenges and Critiques of Preliminary Examinations at the ICC' (2017) 15, 413–434 Journal of International Criminal Justice

Stevenson A. and Waite M. (ed.), *Concise Oxford English Dictionary* (12th ed., Oxford University Press, 2011)

Stone C., 'Widening the Impact of the International Criminal Court: The Prosecutor's Preliminary Examinations in the Larger System of International Criminal Justice' in Minow M., True-Frost C.C. and Whiting A. (eds.), *The First Global Prosecutor: Promise and Constraints* (University of Michigan Press, 2015)

Takemura H., 'Prosecutorial Discretion in International Criminal Justice: Between Fragmentation and Unification' in Van den Herik L. and Stahn C. (eds.), *The Diversification and Fragmentation of International Criminal Law* (Brill/Nijhoff, 2012)

Tallgren I., 'The Voice of the International: Who is Speaking?' (2015) 13:1, 135–155 Journal of International Criminal Justice

Teitel R.G., 'Transitional Justice Genealogy' (2003) 16:1, 69–94 Harvard Human Rights Journal

Thakur R., 'International Criminal Justice: At the Vortex of Power, Norms and a Shifting Global Order' in Sampford C. and Thakur R. (eds.), *Institutional Supports for the International Rule of Law* (Routledge, 2015)

Tiemessen A., 'The International Criminal Court and the politics of prosecutions' (2014) 18:4–5 The International Journal of Human Rights

Toledano M., 'Dialogue with the enemy: Lessons for public relations on dialogue facilitation drawn from the Israeli–Palestinian conflict' in Hargie S., Toledano M. and Taylor M., *International Public Relations* (Taylor and Francis, 2016)

True-Frost C.C., 'The International Civil Servant: How the First Prosecutor Engaged the U.N. Security Council' in Minow M., True-Frost C.C. and Whiting A. (eds.), *The First Global Prosecutor: Promise and Constraints* (University of Michigan Press, 2015)

Ullrich L., 'Beyond the 'Global-Local Divide: Local Intermediaries, Victims and the Justice Contestations of the International Criminal Court' (2016) 14, 543–568 Journal of International Criminal Justice

Van Dijk A.T., 'Critical Discourse Analysis' in Schiffrin D., Tannen D. and Hamilton E.H. (eds.), *The Handbook of Discourse Analysis* (Blackwell Publishers, 2001)

——, 'Principles of Critical Discourse Analysis' (2016) 4:2, 249–283 Discourse and Society

Varaki M., 'Introducing a Fairness-Based Theory of Prosecutorial Legitimacy before the International Criminal Court' (2016) 27: 3, 769–788 The European Journal of International Law

——, 'Revisiting the "Interests of Justice" Policy Paper' (2017) 15:3, 455–470 Journal of International Criminal Justice

Vasiliev S., 'Between International Criminal Justice and Injustice: Theorising Legitimacy' in Hayashi N. and Bailliet C.M. (eds.), *The Legitimacy of International Criminal Tribunals* (Cambridge University Press, 2017)

Vilmer J.B.J., 'The African Union and the International Criminal Court: Counteracting the Crisis' (2016) 92: 6, 1319–1342 International Affairs

Vinjamuri L., 'The International Criminal Court and the Paradox of Authority' (2016) 79, 275–288 Law and Contemporary Problems

Voeten E., 'International Judicial Independence' in Dunoff J.L. and Pollack M.A. (eds.), *Interdisciplinary Perspectives on International Law and International Relations: The State of the Art* (Cambridge University Press, 2013)

Voigt S. and Wulf J.A., 'What makes prosecutors independent? Analysing the institutional determinants of prosecutorial independence' (2017) 1–22, 99–120 Journal of Institutional Economics

Walton D.N., 'What is Reasoning? What is an Argument?' (1990) 87:8, 399–419 The Journal of Philosophy

——, 'Argumentation Schemes and Historical Origins of the Circumstantial Ad Hominem Argument' (2004) 18:3, 359–368 Argumentation

Webb P., 'The ICC Prosecutor's Discretion Not to Proceed in the "Interests of Justice"' (2005) 50, 305 Criminal Law Quarterly

Weiner S.A., 'Prudent Politics: The International Criminal Court, International Relations, and Prosecutorial Independence' (2013) 12, 545–562 Washington University Global Studies Law Review

Wells G., 'Semiotic Mediation, Dialogue and Knowledge' (2007) 50, 244–274 Human Development

Whittington K.E., Kelemen R.D. and Caldeira G.A., 'The Study of Law and Politics' in Whittington K.E., Kelemen R.D. and Caldeira G.A. (eds.), *The Oxford Handbook of Law and Politics* (Oxford University Press, 2013)

Winter S.L., 'The Cognitive Dimension of the Agon between Legal Power and Narrative Meaning' (1989) 87:8, 2225–2279 The Michigan Law Review

Wodak R. and Meyer M., 'Critical discourse analysis: history, agenda, theory, and methodology' in Wodak R. and Meyer M. (eds.), *Methods for Critical Discourse Analysis* (2nd rev. ed., Sage, 2009)

Wolfrum R., 'Legitimacy of International Law from a Legal Perspective: Some Introductory Considerations' in Wolfrum R. and Roeben V. (eds.), *Legitimacy in International Law* (Springer, 2008)

——, 'Sources of International Law' in *Oxford Public International Law – Max Planck Encyclopedia of Public International Law* (2011)
Wouters J., Verhoeven S. and Demeyere B., 'The International Criminal Court's Office of the Prosecutor: Navigating between Independence and Accountability?' (2008) 8, 273–318 International Criminal Law Review

## REPORTS

African Union, Assembly, 'Decision on the Meeting of African States Parties to the Rome Statute of the International Criminal Tribunal (ICC) Doc. Assembly/AU/13(XIII)', 3 July 2009, Assembly/AU/Dec.245 (XIII) Rev. 1 ('3 July 2009 AU Decision')
African Union Decision (Assembly/AU/Dec.270(XIV)), 'Decision on the Report of the Second Meeting of States Parties to the Rome Statute on the International Criminal Court (ICC)' – Doc. Assembly/AU/8(XIV) as adopted by the Fourteenth Ordinary Session of the Assembly in Addis Ababa, Ethiopia on 2 February 2010
African Union, 'Decision on the Progress Report of the Commission on the Implementation of Decision Assembly/AU/Dec.270 (XIV) on the second ministerial meeting on the Rome Statute of the International Criminal Court (ICC) Doc. Assembly/AU/10(IX)' (adopted by the Fifteenth Ordinary Session of the Assembly of the Union on 27 July 2010 in Kampala, Uganda) Assembly/AU/Dec.296 (XV)
African Union, 'AU Decision on the Progress Report of the Commission on the Implementation of the Assembly Decisions on the International Criminal Court (ICC) – Doc. EX.CL/710(XX)' (Assembly/AU/Dec.397 (XVIII))
African Union, 'Assembly/AU/Dec.590 (XXVI): Decision on the International Criminal Court' (Doc.EX.CL/952 (XXVIII))
Amnesty International, 'Malabo Protocol: Legal and Institutional Implications of the Merged and Expanded African Court' (22 January 2016, Index number: AFR 01/3063/2016)
Assembly of States Parties: Addendum (ICC-ASP/14/35/Add.2) of 6 November 2015
The Basic Size of the Office of the Prosecutor (17 September 2015) as submitted to the fourteenth session of the Assembly of States Parties (ICC-ASP/14/21)
OTP Report on Preliminary Examination Activities 2015 of 12 November 2015 https://www.icc-cpi.int/iccdocs/otp/otp-pe-rep-2015-eng.pdf
OTP Report on Preliminary Examination Activities 2016 of 14 November 2016 https://www.icc-cpi.int/iccdocs/otp/161114-otp-rep-PE_ENG.pdf
OTP Report on Preliminary Examination Activities 2017 dated 4 December 2017 https://www.icc-cpi.int/itemsDocuments/2017-PE-rep/2017-otp-rep-PE_ENG.pdf
The Report of the Secretary-General of the United Nations on 'The rule of law and transitional justice in conflict and post-conflict societies' (S/2004/616 of 23 August 2004)
United Nations, 'United Nations Diplomatic Conference of Plenipotentiaries on the Establishment of an International Criminal Court' (Rome, 15 June–17 July 1998) Official Records Volume II Summary records of the plenary meetings and of the meetings of the Committee of the Whole (A/CONF.183/13 (Vol.11)) – see the list of delegates circulated under the symbol A/CONF. 183/INF/5 and Corr. 1

## ELECTRONIC SOURCES


AFP News Agency, 'African Union opens talks to discuss ICC withdrawal' [11 October 2013] https://www.youtube.com/watch?v=H-Mqgv2ctYs

Africa Group for Justice and Accountability, 'Panel I — Africa and the ICC: Misperceptions and Realities' [18 October 2016] https://www.youtube.com/watch?v=tKcr6W_N6lk

——, 'PANEL VII: Immunity of Heads of State under International Law' [25 October 2016] https://www.youtube.com/watch?v=VxpGnbZcNNI

——, 'CLOSING REMARKS: Africa Group for Justice and Accountability on conclusions and lessons learnt' [25 October 2016] https://www.youtube.com/watch?v=go1mjEutvFg

Africanews, 'AU urges ICC to respect the immunity of sitting African presidents' [29 January 2016] https://www.youtube.com/watch?v=0rKIEYCXszM

Agence France-Presse 'Burundi becomes first nation to leave international criminal court' [The Guardian, 28 October 2017] https://www.theguardian.com/law/2017/oct/28/burundi-becomes-first-nation-to-leave-international-criminal-court

Akande D., 'The African Union's Response to the ICC's Decisions on Bashir's Immunity: Will the ICJ Get another Immunity Case?' [8 February 2012] http://www.ejiltalk.org/the-african-unions-response-to-the-iccs-decisions-on-bashirs-immunity-will-the-icj-get-another-immunity-case/

Al Hussein Z.R., United Nations High Commissioner for Human Rights, keynote speech at the Assembly of States Parties to the Rome Statute of the International Criminal Court [16 November 2016] https://www.ohchr.org/EN/NewsEvents/Pages/DisplayNews.aspx?NewsID=20873&LangID=E

Al Jazeera, 'ICC debate: Africa vs "Infamous Caucasian Court"?' [28 October 2016] https://www.aljazeera.com/news/2016/10/icc-debate-africa-infamous-caucasian-court-161028142708060.html

Al Jazeera English, 'ICC questioned on policy in Africa' [5 December 2011] https://www.youtube.com/watch?v=fiuMAHes5s8

——, 'Inside Story – Is Africa snubbing the ICC?' [6 September 2013] https://www.youtube.com/watch?v=DfrA98MzoJM

——, 'Kenyan victims concerned as leaders seek ICC immunity' [12 October 2013] https://www.youtube.com/watch?v=UYTXccqEa-I

Al Jazeera: Upfront – Arena: 'Is the ICC biased against African Countries?' [12 March 2016] https://www.youtube.com/watch?v=1XHyJYOYZDk

Annan K., 'State Impunity is back in fashion – we need the international court more than ever' [18 November 2016] https://www.theguardian.com/commentisfree/2016/nov/18/state-impunity-international-criminal-court-african

Assembly of States Parties, Speech of the President of the Assembly of States Parties, Mr. Sidiki Kaba, fifteenth Session of the Assembly of States Parties [16 November 2016] https://asp.icc-cpi.int/iccdocs/asp_docs/ASP15/ASP15-Opening-Statement-PASP-ENG.pdf

BBC News, 'Is this the end for the International Criminal Court?' [24 October 2016] http://www.bbc.com/news/world-africa-37750978

——, 'Bolton Threatens ICC with US Sanctions' [11 September 2018] https://www.bbc.com/news/world-us-canada-45474864

Becker S. and Pieper D., 'The Ocampo Affair: Current ICC Chief Prosecutor Weighed Down by Predecessor' [17 October 2017] http://www.spiegel.de/international/world/international-criminal-court-scandal-widens-a-1173156.html

Biko N., 'Kenya's "victory" at Assembly of States Parties meeting' [The Hague Trials/Kenya, 28 November 2013] https://www.neveragain.co.ke/kenyas-victory-assembly-states-parties-meeting/article

Bolton J., 'The Hague Aims for U.S. Soldiers: A "war crimes" inquiry in Afghanistan shows the danger of the International Criminal Court' [Wall Street Journal, 20 November 2017] https://www.wsj.com/articles/the-hague-tiptoes-toward-u-s-soldiers-1511217136

Bosco D., 'Why is the International Criminal Court picking only on Africa?' [Washington Post, 29 March 2013] https://www.washingtonpost.com/opinions/why-is-the-international-criminal-court-picking-only-on-africa/2013/03/29/cb9bf5da-96f7-11e2-97cd-3d8c1afe4f0f_story.html?utm_term=.1ae3b02d56a6

Branch A., 'The ICC can't live with Africa, but it can't live without it either' [The Conversation, 14 March 2017] http://theconversation.com/the-icc-cant-live-with-africa-but-it-cant-live-without-it-either-74210

Clarke K.M., 'Africa Question: Is the International Criminal Court (ICC) targeting Africa inappropriately?' [Topic for March 2013–January 2014] http://iccforum.com/africa

CNN, 'Bolton: International Criminal Court dead to us' [10 September 2018] https://edition.cnn.com/videos/world/2018/09/10/bolton-us-protect-citizens-international-criminal-court-sot-vpx.cnn

Coalition for the International Criminal Court (CICC), List of State Parties/Senegal http://www.iccnow.org/?mod=country&iduct=152

——, 'Rome Statute 20, Interactive Forums / Session II – Assessing the impact of the RS 20 years out' [14 March 2018] https://www.youtube.com/watch?v=monmXHD38Wo

David K.M., 'Kagame tells why he is against ICC charging Bashir' [Daily Nation, 3 August 2008] https://www.nation.co.ke/news/africa/1066-446426-7ulr1ez/index.html

deGuzman M.M., 'Africa Question: Is the International Criminal Court (ICC) targeting Africa inappropriately?' [Topic for March 2013–January 2014, ICC-FORUM] http://iccforum.com/africa

DW English: Conflict Zone, 'Justice and injustice in Rwanda' [28 October 2015] https://www.youtube.com/watch?v=IsBwbaxsXQ0

Edroos F., 'Rwanda's Paul Kagame accuses ICC of bias against Africa' [Al Jazeera, 29 April 2018] https://www.aljazeera.com/news/2018/04/rwanda-kagame-accuses-icc-bias-africa-180429050656022.html

Escritt T. and Deutsch A., 'ICC Opens Investigation into Israeli-Palestinian Conflict' [Reuters, 16 January 2015] https://www.reuters.com/article/us-icc-palestinians-examination-idUSKBN0KP1PR20150116

Eskowich E., https://www.goodreads.com/author/quotes/7390567.Emily_Eskowich

Euronews: English, 'African Union accuses ICC of race hunt against Africans' [28 May 2013] https://www.youtube.com/watch?v=2rPfBEKAPvA

Evenson E., 'ICC: Challenging Dictators, The Promise of Kampala's International Criminal Court Review Conference' [Human Rights Watch, 27 July 2010] https://www.hrw.org/news/2010/07/27/icc-challenging-dictators

FIDH Press release, 'The Independence of the International Criminal Court must be enhanced' [27 November 2015] https://www.fidh.org/en/issues/international-justice/international-criminal-court-icc/the-independence-of-the-international-criminal-court-must-be-enhanced

——, 'Termination of Ruto and Sang case at the ICC: Witness tampering means impunity prevails over justice again' [5 April 2016] https://www.fidh.org/en/region/Africa/kenya/termination-of-ruto-and-sang-case-at-the-icc-witness-tampering-means

Gevers C., 'SA & the ICC: Justice, or "Just Us"?' [The Con, 18 November 2016] http://www.theconmag.co.za/2016/11/18/sa-the-icc-justice-or-just-us/

Gladstone R. and Simons M., 'Prosecutor's Move in Afghan War Inquiry May Mean Clash With U.S.' [The New York Times, 20 November 2017] https://www.nytimes.com/2017/11/20/world/asia/international-criminal-court-afghanistan-united-states.html

Hamilton J., Presentation delivered at the European Commission for Democracy through Law (VENICE Commission) conference: 'The Independence of Judges and Prosecutors: Perspectives and Challenges' [28 February–3 March 2011] paper entitled 'Prosecutorial Independence and Accountability' and http://www.venice.coe.int/webforms/documents/default.aspx?pdffile=CDL-UDT(2011)008-e

Hammarskjöld D., 'The International Civil Servant in Law and in Fact: Lecture Delivered to Congregation at Oxford University [30 May 1961] http://www.un.org/depts/dhl/dag/docs/internationalcivilservant.pdf

Hazan P., 'ICC scandal: Who is watching the sheriff?' [Justice Info, 18 October 2017] https://www.justiceinfo.net/en/justice-reconciliation/34986-icc-scandal-who-is-watching-the-sheriff.html

HRW, Policy Paper on 'the Meaning of "the Interests of Justice" in Article 53 of the Rome Statute' of 1 June 2005 https://www.hrw.org/news/2005/06/01/meaning-interests-justice-article-53-rome-statute

——, 'African Union: Activists Challenge Attacks on ICC' [5 July 2016] https://www.youtube.com/watch?v=4sbgdFp0Pro

——, 'UN/African Union: Reject ICC Withdrawal/ Security Council Meeting With AU' [22 September 2016] https://www.hrw.org/news/2016/09/22/un/african-union-reject-icc-withdrawal

IBA, Interview with Fatou Bensouda, ICC Chief Prosecutor, (International Bar Association) https://www.ibanet.org/Conferences/141435505.aspx

ICC, Uganda Situation (ICC-02/04) https://www.icc-cpi.int/uganda

——, The 'Statement of the Prosecutor of the International Criminal Court, Mrs Fatou Bensouda, on opening Preliminary Examinations into the situations in the Philippines and in Venezuela' [ICC, 8 February 2018] https://www.icc-cpi.int/Pages/item.aspx?name=180208-otp-stat

——, 'Nigeria and other States renew their support for ICC' [ICC-CPI-20180409-PR1378, 9 April 2018] https://www.icc-cpi.int/Pages/item.aspx?name=pr1378

Kagame P., 'President Kagame speaks out against ICC- Addis Ababa, 26 May 2013' [26 May 2013] https://www.youtube.com/watch?v=aWr5fU58h8c

——, President Paul Kagame addressing the question of Kenya Cases at ICC [President Kagame addresses Print and Broadcast Editors – Amahoro Stadium, 15 June 2013] https://www.youtube.com/watch?v=3e3LQ_3vu9c

Kennedy M., 'Under New Leader, Gambia Cancels Withdrawal from International Criminal Court' [NPR, 12 February 2017] https://www.npr.org/sections/thetwo-way/2017/02/14/515219467/under-new-leader-gambia-cancels-withdrawal-from-international-criminal-court

Kenya Citizen TV, 'Ugandan President Museveni Stirs Fresh ICC Debate' [9 April 2013] https://www.youtube.com/watch?v=3QrL-_X1vGo

Keppler E., 'Gambia Rejoins ICC: South Africa, Burundi Now Outliers on Exit' [HRW, 17 February 2017] https://www.hrw.org/news/2017/02/17/gambia-rejoins-icc

Khelef A.M, 'Fatou Bensouda: Critics "don't understand the ICC"' [DW, 11 April 2017] http://www.dw.com/en/fatou-bensouda-critics-dont-understand-the-icc/a-38372198

Kimani M., 'Pursuit of Justice or Western Plot? International indictments stir angry debate in Africa' [October 2009] http://www.un.org/africarenewal/magazine/october-2009/pursuit-justice-or-western-plot

Kolade H., 'Is the ICC a Western Imperialist Tool Against Africa?' [Swali Africa, 26 December 2016] http://blog.swaliafrica.com/is-the-icc-a-western-imperialist-tool-against-africa/

Krever T., 'Africa in the Dock: On ICC Bias' [30 October 2016] http://criticallegalthinking.com/2016/10/30/africa-in-the-dock-icc-bias/

Labuda I.P, 'The African Union's Collective Withdrawal from the ICC: Does Bad Law make for Good Politics?' [15 February 2017] https://www.ejiltalk.org/the-african-unions-collective-withdrawal-from-the-icc-does-bad-law-make-for-good-politics/

Lingsma T., 'How Ocampogate harms the International Criminal Court' [Grojil-blog, 30 November 2017] https://grojil.org/2017/11/30/how-ocampogate-harms-the-international-criminal-court/

Mahamba F. and Sengenya C., 'Politics and oil: the unseen drivers of violence in Congo's Ituri Province' [IRIN, 4 April 2018] https://www.irinnews.org/analysis/2018/04/04/politics-and-oil-unseen-drivers-violence-congo-s-ituri-province

Maunganidze O. and Louw A., 'An African Advantage: ICC's New Head of Jurisdiction, Complementarity and Cooperation' [Institute for Security Studies, 9 February 2011] https://issafrica.org/iss-today/an-african-advantage-iccs-new-head-of-jurisdiction-complementarity-and-cooperation

Mbaraga R., 'Africa's Push to Withdrawal from ICC blocked, Countries Divided' [The East African, 23 July 2016] http://www.theeastafrican.co.ke/news/Africa-s-push-to-withdraw-from-ICC-blocked--countries-divided/2558-3307472-15hdbkmz/index.html

McLeod S., 'Skinner – Operant Conditioning' [Simply Phycology as updated 2018] https://simplypsychology.org/operant-conditioning.html

Mediapart, 'Retour sur nos enquêtes: les secrets de la justice internationale' [4 October 2017] https://www.youtube.com/watch?v=-FIxo3Ps3Ls

Miles F., '"T.I.A" – this is Africa – so why the ICC?' [29 April 2014] http://works.bepress.com/fletcher_miles/1/

Mills K., 'The International Criminal Court's Africa Problem' [Issue 6, 1 December 2017]

Mkhabela H., 'Africa and ICC Going Forward' [L'Afrique en Questions, No. 31, January 2017] https://www.ifri.org/en/publications/editoriaux-de-lifri/lafrique-questions/africa-and-icc-going-forward

Nantulya P., 'What's next for Africa and the International Criminal Court?' [African Center for Strategic Studies, December 2017] http://africacenter.org/spotlight/whats-next-africa-international-criminal-court-icc/

NBS TV Uganda, 'US Reacts to Museveni Swear In Comment of "ICC is Useless ..."' [13 May 2016] https://www.youtube.com/watch?v=aSrjdgVN8Vw

NYU, School of Law, 'How Best to Assure the Independence of the ICC Prosecutor' https://www.youtube.com/watch?v=zdZbZW7ZD6w

OTP, Statement of the Prosecutor of the International Criminal Court, Fatou Bensouda [24 November 2015] https://www.icc-cpi.int/Pages/item.aspx?name=otp-stat-24-11-2015

Philosophy Talk, 'Loyalty' https://www.philosophytalk.org/blog/loyalty

PressTV Videos, 'Africa Today – ICC vs. African justice' [13 November 2013] https://www.youtube.com/watch?v=mkwfsUsSs8w

Roth K., 'Africa Attacks the International Criminal Court' [The New York Review of Books, 6 February, June 2014 Issue] http://www.nybooks.com/articles/2014/02/06/africa-attacks-international-criminal-court/?printpage=true

SABC Digital News, 'Sitting heads of state should not be tried in the ICC – AU' [12 October 2013] https://www.youtube.com/watch?v=Z3G79RBQotc

Saine P. and Jahateh L., 'Gambia announces plans to stay in International Criminal Court' [Reuters, 13 February 2017] https://www.reuters.com/article/us-gambia-justice-icc-idUSKBN15S2HF

Special Court for Sierra Leone, http://www.rscsl.org/

Statement of the Prosecutor of the International Criminal Court, Fatou Bensouda, on the withdrawal of charges against Mr. Uhuru Muigai Kenyatta [5 December 2014] https://www.icc-cpi.int/Pages/item.aspx?name=otp-statement-05-12-2014-2

Statement of the Prosecutor of the International Criminal Court, Fatou Bensouda, regarding Trial Chamber's decision to vacate charges against Messrs William Samoei Ruto and Joshua Arap Sang without prejudice to their prosecution in the future [6 April 2016] https://www.icc-cpi.int/Pages/item.aspx?name=otp-stat-160406

Sudan Tribune, 'African Union moves aggressively to shield Bashir from prosecution' [29 July 2010] http://www.sudantribune.com/spip.php?article35786

Taku C.A., 'Africa Question: Is the International Criminal Court (ICC) targeting Africa inappropriately?' [Topic for March 2013–January 2014, ICC-FORUM] http://iccforum.com/africa

ThinkingAfrica1, 'The clash between ICC and African Union on justice in Africa?' [13 November 2014] https://www.youtube.com/watch?v=Cbag0ps3DBo

Tigrai Online, 'Ethiopian Prime Minister HaileMariam Desalegn urges African countries to withdraw their membership from ICC' [29 December 2014] http://www.tigraionline.com/articles/ethiopia-rejects-icc.html

TV3 Network Limited Ghana, 'Hot Issues with Fatou Bensouda ICC prosecutor – 19/3/2016' [22 March 2016] https://www.youtube.com/watch?v=cUNFORWlQU4&feature=youtube

TV5MONDE, 'Gbagbo: le livre polémique sur la crise ivoirienne' [16 July 2014] https://www.youtube.com/watch?v=hEGewdYPXiA

——, 'Invité de la semaine du Journal Afrique: Justin Koné Katinan, le porte parole de Laurent Gbagbo' [1 November 2017] https://www.youtube.com/watch?v=ClzaflNfAY4

UChannel, 'What Next for Darfur: Policy Action or the Status Quo?' [3 December 2007] https://www.youtube.com/watch?v=8dpSKYV4yMQ

Vanderbilt University, '2012 VLS Charney Lecture – Reflections from ICC Prosecutor Fatou Bensouda' [28 August 2012] https://www.youtube.com/watch?v=CkuDrnlvKVQ

van Laer T., 'What's Happening in Ituri?' [Guest Blog, Congo Research Group, 5 March 2018] http://congoresearchgroup.org/guest-blog-whats-happening-in-ituri/

Verini J., 'The President and the Prosecutor' [The New York Times Magazine, 22 June 2016] https://mobile.nytimes.com/2016/06/26/magazine/international-criminal-court-moreno-ocampo-the-prosecutor-and-the-president.html

Voice of Nigeria, 'Calls For Africa's Withdrawal From ICC Suffers Set Back At AU Summit' [Sahara Reporters, 29 July 2016] http://saharareporters.com/2016/07/29/calls-africas-withdrawal-icc-suffers-set-back-au-summit

Walker S. and Bowcott O., 'Russia Withdraws Signature from International Criminal Court Statute' [The Guardian, 16 November 2016] https://www.theguardian.com/world/2016/nov/16/russia-withdraws-signature-from-international-criminal-court-statute

Waza Africa, 'Ocampo Exclusive: The first ICC prosecutor talks about the Kenyan trials' [6 February 2014] https://www.youtube.com/watch?v=tHBwQwUzgYo

Whiteley J., 'Compromise with Kony?' a reply by Jack Whiteley to Kenneth Roth [20 March 2014 Issue] http://www.nybooks.com/articles/2014/03/20/compromise-kony/

Wilson A.M., 'Violence Returns to DR Congo's Ituri Province' [Aljazeera, 11 April 2018] https://www.aljazeera.com/indepth/inpictures/violence-returns-dr-congo-ituri-province-180410102912520.html

# INDEX

# ABOUT THE AUTHOR

Dr Alphonse Muleefu is a Senior Lecturer at the School of Law, and Acting Principal of the College of Arts and Social Sciences, University of Rwanda. He is an External Research Fellow at the International Victimology Institute of Tilburg University, the Netherlands. Previously, Dr Muleefu worked with the International Criminal Tribunal for Rwanda (ICTR), International Criminal Court (ICC) and Gacaca Courts. He has provided consultancy services to non-governmental organisations, government institutions and UN agencies. He holds a Bachelor of Laws (LLB) from the National University of Rwanda (as it was then) as well as a Master of Laws (LLM) in Public International and European Law and Doctor of Philosophy (PhD) from Tilburg University. He holds different specialised certificates in international criminal law, international criminal investigations, transitional justice and children's rights. His research interests are in Gacaca Courts and transitional justice in general, international criminal law, laws of war (international humanitarian law) and human rights (victims' rights in particular).

www.ingramcontent.com/pod-product-compliance
Ingram Content Group UK Ltd.
Pitfield, Milton Keynes, MK11 3LW, UK
UKHW051928100926
8556IPUK00022B/1432

9 781780 688572